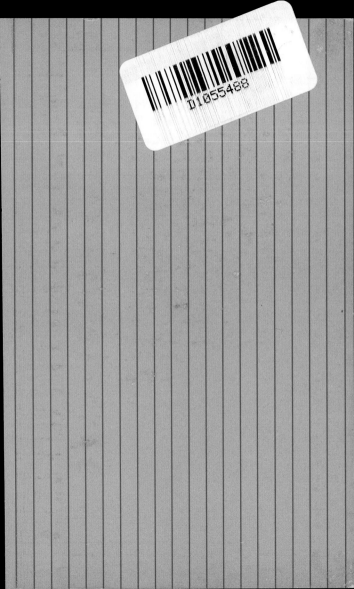

The ONE YEAR®
YEAR®
MINI
Daily
Inspiration

The ONE YEAR® MINI

Daily
Inspiration

Tyndale House Publishers, Inc.
Carol Stream, Illinois

Visit Tyndale's exciting Web site at www.tyndale.com

TYNDALE and Tyndale's quill logo are registered trademarks of Tyndale House Publishers, Inc.

The One Year is a registered trademark of Tyndale House Publishers, Inc.

The One Year Mini Daily Inspiration

Designed by Mark Anthony Lane II

Edited by Susan Taylor

The devotion "Serving God" on January 20 is taken from February 2, "Heart Choice," in *The One Year Mini for Women*, copyright © 2005 by Ronald A. Beers and V. Gilbert Beers.

The devotion "Pursued by God" on February 16 is taken from February 8, "Pursued by God," in *The One Year Mini for Women*, copyright © 2005 by Ronald A. Beers and V. Gilbert Beers.

The devotion "Depression" on February 23 is taken from *Divine Moments for Men*, copyright © 2008 by Ronald A. Beers.

ISBN 978-1-4143-2024-3

Printed in China

15   14   13   12   11   10   09
7   6   5   4   3   2   1

Living Sacrifices

What are the benefits of dedicating my life to God this year?

GOD'S RESPONSE

Dear brothers and sisters, I plead with you to give your bodies to God because of all he has done for you. Let them be a living and holy sacrifice—the kind he will find acceptable. This is truly the way to worship him. Don't copy the behavior and customs of this world, but let God transform you into a new person by changing the way you think. Then you will learn to know God's will for you, which is good and pleasing and perfect. *Romans 12:1-2*

God wants us to offer ourselves as *living* sacrifices—daily laying aside our own desires to obey him, putting all our energy and resources at his disposal, and trusting him to guide us as we follow him. God has good plans for us. He wants to transform us by "changing the way [we] think" so we can live to honor and obey him and receive his best for us. Because we have his Son, Jesus, to make this new kind of life possible, we should joyfully give ourselves as living sacrifices to his service.

GOD'S PROMISE

Commit everything you do to the LORD. Trust him, and he will help you.   PSALM 37:5

Balance

How can I keep my life balanced this year?

GOD'S RESPONSE

"If the Arameans are too strong for me, then come over and help me," Joab told his brother. "And if the Ammonites are too strong for you, I will come and help you. Be courageous! Let us fight bravely for our people and the cities of our God. May the LORD's will be done."   *2 Samuel 10:11-12*

There must be a balance in life between our plans and our faith in God. Joab said, "Let us fight bravely." In other words, they were determined to do all that they could, using their minds to figure out the best strategies, using their strength to fight, and using the other resources God had given them. But Joab also said, "May the Lord's will be done." He knew that when they had done all they could, the outcome was in God's hands. Balance comes as we use our minds and our resources to obey God and, at the same time, trust him for the outcome.

GOD'S PROMISE

How joyful are those who fear the LORD and delight in obeying his commands. . . . They do not fear bad news; they confidently trust the LORD to care for them.   PSALM 112:1, 7

Goals

Why is it important to set goals?

GOD'S RESPONSE

Look straight ahead, and fix your eyes on what lies before you.
Mark out a straight path for your feet; stay on the safe path.
Don't get sidetracked; keep your feet from following evil.

Proverbs 4:25-27

I run with purpose in every step.   *1 Corinthians 9:26*

Let love be your highest goal!   *1 Corinthians 14:1*

The beginning of a new year is a great time to review existing goals and set new ones. Of course, setting goals takes time and thought, and with our busy lives, we may feel as if that's time we can't afford. But goals give us direction. They serve as reminders of what is really important to us, and they help to keep us on track.

You may have many goals for different areas of your life—including those New Year's resolutions you made—but choose to make following God your primary, overarching goal. You do not know what the year ahead will bring, but making following God your number one goal will give you ongoing purpose and keep you from straying away from God, regardless of what the year brings.

GOD'S CHALLENGE

Make it your goal to live a quiet life, minding your own business and working with your hands, just as we instructed you before.

1 THESSALONIANS 4:11

Guidance

When is the time to seek God's guidance?

GOD'S RESPONSE

All of Adonijah's guests jumped up in panic from the banquet table and quickly scattered. Adonijah was afraid of Solomon, so he rushed to the sacred tent and grabbed on to the horns of the altar. Word soon reached Solomon that Adonijah had seized the horns of the altar in fear, and that he was pleading, "Let King Solomon swear today that he will not kill me!"   *1 Kings 1:49-51*

 Sometimes it takes getting caught before someone is willing to give up a scheme. When Adonijah learned that his plans to gain the throne after King David were doomed to fail, he ran in panic to the altar, the place of God's mercy and forgiveness. He went there, however, *after* his treasonous plans had been exposed. If Adonijah had first considered what God wanted, he might have avoided trouble.

Don't wait until you have made a mess of your life to run to God. Make it a point this year to seek God's guidance *before* you act.

GOD'S PROMISE

[Wisdom says,] "They rejected my advice and paid no attention when I corrected them. Therefore, they must eat the bitter fruit of living their own way, choking on their own schemes. For simpletons turn away from me—to death. Fools are destroyed by their own complacency. But all who listen to me will live in peace, untroubled by fear of harm."   PROVERBS 1:30-33

Growth

As a child of God, how can I grow and become more mature this year?

GOD'S RESPONSE

Like newborn babies, you must crave pure spiritual milk so that you will grow into a full experience of salvation. Cry out for this nourishment, now that you have had a taste of the Lord's kindness.

1 Peter 2:2-3

Let us go on . . . and become mature in our understanding.

Hebrews 6:1

When I discovered your words, I devoured them. They are my joy and my heart's delight, for I bear your name, O LORD God of Heaven's Armies. *Jeremiah 15:16*

One characteristic all children share is that they want to grow up to be like their big brothers or sisters or their parents. When we first believe in Christ, we become spiritually newborn babies. If we are healthy, we will yearn to grow to maturity.

The need for milk is a natural instinct for babies, and they express in an unmistakable way their desire for nourishment. Once we see our need for God's Word and begin to find nourishment in Christ, our spiritual appetites will increase, and we will start to mature.

How strong is your appetite for God's Word?

GOD'S PROMISE

Taste and see that the LORD is good. Oh, the joys of those who take refuge in him! PSALM 34:8

Behavior

How can I make sure my behavior is pleasing to God day after day?

GOD'S RESPONSE

May the words of my mouth and the meditation of my heart be pleasing to you, O LORD, my rock and my redeemer.   *Psalm 19:14*

Search me, O God, and know my heart; test me and know my anxious thoughts. Point out anything in me that offends you, and lead me along the path of everlasting life.   *Psalm 139:23-24*

Take control of what I say, O LORD, and guard my lips.
Psalm 141:3

Would you change the way you live if you knew that God would be examining your every word and thought? David asked that God approve his words and thoughts as if they were offerings he had brought to the altar. As you begin each day, determine that God's love will guide what you say and how you think. Then your words and actions will be pleasing gifts to God day after day.

GOD'S CHALLENGE

Whatever you do or say, do it as a representative of the Lord Jesus, giving thanks through him to God the Father.

COLOSSIANS 3:17

Busyness

With all my activities, how can I make sure I stay focused on God?

GOD'S RESPONSE

When all the people had crossed the Jordan, the LORD said to Joshua, "Now choose twelve men, one from each tribe. . . ." So Joshua called together the twelve men he had chosen—one from each of the tribes of Israel. He told them, "Go into the middle of the Jordan, in front of the Ark of the LORD your God. Each of you must pick up one stone and carry it out on your shoulder—twelve stones in all, one for each of the twelve tribes of Israel. We will use these stones to build a memorial." *Joshua 4:1-2, 4-6*

Once the Israelites had safely crossed the river, what would be next—claiming the Promised Land? Not yet. First, God directed them to build a memorial from twelve stones drawn from the river by twelve men, one from each tribe of Israel. This may have seemed like a delay in their mission of conquering the land, but God did not want his people to plunge into their task unprepared. They were to focus on him and remember who was guiding them.

As you are busy with your God-given tasks, set aside quiet moments, times to build your own memorial to God's power. Don't allow your activities to shift your focus away from God.

GOD'S PROMISE

This is what the LORD says: "Stop at the crossroads and look around. Ask for the old, godly way, and walk in it. Travel its path, and you will find rest for your souls." JEREMIAH 6:16

Holy Spirit

How can God guide me if I can't see him or hear him?

GOD'S RESPONSE

One of the twelve disciples, Thomas (nicknamed the Twin), was not with the others when Jesus came. They told him, "We have seen the Lord!" But he replied, "I won't believe it unless I see the nail wounds in his hands, put my fingers into them, and place my hand into the wound in his side."   *John 20:24-25*

[Jesus said,] "When the Father sends the Advocate as my representative—that is, the Holy Spirit—he will teach you everything and will remind you of everything I have told you."

John 14:26

Have you ever wished you could actually see Jesus, touch him, and hear his words aloud? Are there times you wish you could sit down with him to get his advice? Thomas needed Jesus' physical presence in order to believe that Jesus had risen. But God's plan is wiser. He wants to be present with you, and all believers, at all times, so he sent us the Holy Spirit. Even now he is with you in the form of the Holy Spirit. You can talk to him, and you can find his words to you in the pages of the Bible. By his Spirit, Jesus has made himself as real to you as he did to Thomas.

GOD'S PROMISE

"This is my covenant with them," says the LORD. "My Spirit will not leave them, and neither will these words I have given you."

ISAIAH 59:21

Challenges

How can I approach this year's challenges with courage rather than with fear?

GOD'S RESPONSE

After the death of Moses the LORD's servant, the LORD spoke to Joshua. . . . "Moses my servant is dead. Therefore, the time has come for you to lead these people, the Israelites, across the Jordan River into the land I am giving them. I promise you what I promised Moses: 'Wherever you set foot, you will be on land I have given you.' . . . No one will be able to stand against you as long as you live. For I will be with you as I was with Moses. I will not fail you or abandon you." *Joshua 1:1-5*

Joshua's new job consisted of leading more than two million people into a strange, new land and conquering it. What a challenge—even for a man of Joshua's caliber! Without God, every new challenge can be frightening. *With* God, every challenge can be a great adventure.

Just as God was with Joshua, he is with you as you face new challenges. You may not be called to conquer nations, but you will face tough situations, difficult people, and hard temptations. God promises that he will never abandon you or fail to help you. As you depend on God for strength, you can face life's challenges with courage and confidence.

GOD'S PROMISE

Nothing is impossible with God. LUKE 1:37

Help

There are so many things that I need to accomplish this year. How can I find the help I need?

God's Response

After I told him how long I would be gone, the king agreed to my request. I also said to the king, "If it please the king, let me have letters addressed to the governors of the province west of the Euphrates River, instructing them to let me travel safely through their territories on my way to Judah. And please give me a letter addressed to Asaph, the manager of the king's forest, instructing him to give me timber. I will need it to make beams for the gates of the Temple fortress, for the city walls, and for a house for myself." And the king granted these requests, because the gracious hand of God was on me.   *Nehemiah 2:6-8*

After Nehemiah had prayed, he asked the king for permission to go to Judah. As soon as he got a positive answer, he began asking for additional help.

Sometimes when we have needs, we hesitate to ask the right people for help because we are afraid to approach them. Not Nehemiah! He went directly to the person who could help him the most—the king himself! Don't be reluctant to ask for help. Those you ask may be more interested and approachable than you thought. Sometimes God's answers to our prayers come as a result of our asking others.

God's Challenge

Take courage as you fulfill your duties, and may the LORD be with those who do what is right.   2 CHRONICLES 19:11

Change

With so much change going on in my life, how can I keep it all together?

GOD'S RESPONSE

On the day the Tabernacle was set up, the cloud covered it. But from evening until morning the cloud over the Tabernacle looked like a pillar of fire. This was the regular pattern—at night the cloud that covered the Tabernacle had the appearance of fire. Whenever the cloud lifted from over the sacred tent, the people of Israel would break camp and follow it. And wherever the cloud settled, the people of Israel would set up camp. In this way, they traveled and camped at the LORD's command wherever he told them to go.   *Numbers 9:15-18*

Those who travel, move, or face other kinds of change know what it means to be uprooted. Life is full of changes, and few things remain stable. For forty years, the Israelites were moving from one place to the next through the wilderness. They were able to handle ongoing change only because God's presence was always with them in the Tabernacle. The portable Tabernacle signified that God and his people were moving together. As the Israelites experienced, stability does not mean lack of change but, rather, moving with God in every circumstance. His presence is our one constant in any life change.

GOD'S PROMISE

I am the LORD, and I do not change.   MALACHI 3:6

Worship

How can I make the most of my times of worship?

GOD'S RESPONSE

Celebrate the Festival of Trumpets each year on the first day of the appointed month in early autumn. You must call an official day for holy assembly, and you may do no ordinary work. On that day you must present a burnt offering as a pleasing aroma to the LORD. . . . These offerings are given as a special gift to the LORD, a pleasing aroma to him.   *Numbers 29:1-2, 6*

The Festival of Trumpets demonstrated three important principles that we should follow in our worship today: (1) The people gathered together; there is an extra benefit to be gained from worshiping with other believers. (2) The normal daily routine was suspended, and no hard work was done. It takes time to worship, and setting aside the time allows us to adjust our attitudes before we worship and then reflect afterward. (3) The people gave God something of value to them when they sacrificed animals as burnt offerings. We show our commitment to God when we give something of value to him. The best gift, of course, is ourselves.

GOD'S CHALLENGE

Give to the LORD the glory he deserves! Bring your offering and come into his presence. Worship the LORD in all his holy splendor.

1 CHRONICLES 16:29

Work

*I'm intimidated by the work I have ahead of me.
How will God help me when I feel so unprepared?*

GOD'S RESPONSE

Now the LORD says: Be strong, Zerubbabel. Be strong, Joshua son of Jehozadak, the high priest. Be strong, all you people still left in the land. And now get to work, for I am with you, says the LORD of Heaven's Armies. *Haggai 2:4*

The LORD said to Moses, "Why are you crying out to me? Tell the people to get moving!" *Exodus 14:15*

"Get to work, for I am with you" (Haggai 2:4). Judah's people had returned to worshiping God, and God had promised to bless their efforts. But now it was time for them to work. Of course, we must be people of prayer, Bible study, and worship, but we also need to get out and actually do the work God has prepared for us. He wants to change the world through us, his ambassadors. God has given us jobs to do in our churches, at our places of employment, and at home.

So, yes, pray and ask God for his help and for his courage to do the work he has placed before you. Then, realize that the time has come to get to work, because God is with you!

GOD'S PROMISE

Don't be afraid, for I am with you. Don't be discouraged, for I am your God. I will strengthen you and help you. I will hold you up with my victorious right hand.   ISAIAH 41:10

Purpose

How can I live each day with a sense of purpose?

GOD'S RESPONSE

You [God] sweep people away like dreams that disappear. They are like grass that springs up in the morning. In the morning it blooms and flourishes, but by evening it is dry and withered.

Psalm 90:5-6

Teach us to realize the brevity of life, so that we may grow in wisdom.

Psalm 90:12

The realization that life is short should motivate us to use the little time we have wisely and to spend it on activities that will result in eternal good. One way to do this is to ask yourself, *What do I want to see happen in my life before I die? What do I want to accomplish? What small step could I take today that would move me closer to fulfilling that purpose?* Taking time to think about what's really important is a good way to make sure that every day of your life counts.

GOD'S CHALLENGE

I run with purpose in every step.   1 CORINTHIANS 9:26

Help

How is God able to help me when I'm struggling?

GOD'S RESPONSE

This High Priest of ours [Jesus] understands our weaknesses, for he faced all of the same testings we do, yet he did not sin.

Hebrews 4:15

Give all your worries and cares to God, for he cares about you.

1 Peter 5:7

 Because Jesus lived on earth as a fully human man, you can be certain that he completely understands your experiences and your struggles. And because he is fully God, he alone is completely able to carry you through your difficulties and struggles, to fully forgive you when you make mistakes, and to show you unconditional love in the moments of your greatest need. You can tell Jesus all your thoughts, feelings, and doubts. He has been where you are now, and he has the compassion and power to help you through any struggle, no matter how great.

GOD'S PROMISE

Let us come boldly to the throne of our gracious God. There we will receive his mercy, and we will find grace to help us when we need it most.   HEBREWS 4:16

God's Word

Why is daily Bible reading important?

GOD'S RESPONSE

Whenever Moses went into the Tabernacle to speak with the LORD, he heard the voice speaking to him from between the two cherubim above the Ark's cover—the place of atonement—that rests on the Ark of the Covenant.   *Numbers 7:89*

Sometimes God spoke to his people directly to tell them the proper way to live. Imagine hearing the voice of God! Moses must have trembled at the sound. The Bible has recorded some of these conversations to give us insights into God's character, yet we may take those words lightly. How tragic! We should have no less reverence and awe for them than Moses had when he actually heard God speak.

Like Moses, we have the privilege of talking directly to God, but today God speaks to us mainly through the Bible and through the guidance of his Holy Spirit. That's why regular Bible reading and prayer are the keys to finding God's guidance every day of your life.

GOD'S CHALLENGE

My child, listen to what I say, and treasure my commands. Tune your ears to wisdom, and concentrate on understanding. Cry out for insight, and ask for understanding. Search for them as you would for silver; seek them like hidden treasures. Then you will understand what it means to fear the LORD, and you will gain knowledge of God.   PROVERBS 2:1-5

Future

So many things are going wrong in my life. How can I trust God with my future?

GOD'S RESPONSE

For you who fear my name, the Sun of Righteousness will rise with healing in his wings. And you will go free, leaping with joy like calves let out to pasture.   *Malachi 4:2*

The book of Malachi records God's displeasure with his people because of their lack of respect for him, his house, and his decrees. Through the prophet Malachi, God lists the many offenses of the people and the members of the priesthood. But God loves his people, and he promises to honor those who fear him and follow his teachings. Because of God's promises, these last verses of the Old Testament are filled with hope.

Regardless of how life looks now, God controls the future, and everything will be made right. Everyone who loves and serves God can look forward to a joyful celebration, an eternal future in heaven. This hope helps you to trust God with your life in both the present and the future.

GOD'S PROMISE

"I know the plans I have for you," says the LORD. "They are plans for good and not for disaster, to give you a future and a hope."

JEREMIAH 29:11

Waiting

I'm ready to begin my ministry now. Why is God making me wait?

GOD'S RESPONSE

[Jesus said,] "You will receive power when the Holy Spirit comes upon you. And you will be my witnesses, telling people about me everywhere—in Jerusalem, throughout Judea, in Samaria, and to the ends of the earth."   *Acts 1:8*

[Jesus said,] "I will send the Holy Spirit, just as my Father promised. But stay here in the city until the Holy Spirit comes and fills you with power from heaven."   *Luke 24:49*

Jesus told his disciples that they would tell people of all nations about him. But first they had to wait for the Holy Spirit. God has important work for you to do for him, but you must do it by the power of the Holy Spirit, not in your own strength. It's easy to be in a hurry to get on with the job, even if it means running ahead of God. But sometimes, waiting is a part of God's plan for you. Are you waiting and listening for God's complete instructions, or are you running ahead of his plans for you? You need God's timing and power to be truly effective.

GOD'S PROMISE

The LORD is a faithful God. Blessed are those who wait for his help.   ISAIAH 30:18

Abundant Life

What is the key to living a rich and meaningful life?

GOD'S RESPONSE

When the master of ceremonies tasted the water that was now wine, not knowing where it had come from (though, of course, the servants knew), he called the bridegroom over. "A host always serves the best wine first," he said. "Then, when everyone has had a lot to drink, he brings out the less expensive wine. But you have kept the best until now!" This miraculous sign at Cana in Galilee was the first time Jesus revealed his glory.   *John 2:9-11*

You feed them from the abundance of your own house, letting them drink from your river of delights.   *Psalm 36:8*

[Jesus said,] "You haven't done this before. Ask, using my name, and you will receive, and you will have abundant joy."   *John 16:24*

People tend to look everywhere but to God for excitement and meaning. For some reason, they expect God's path to be dull and lifeless.

But just as the wine Jesus made was the best, so life in him is better than any life you could have on your own. Why wait until everything else runs out before you discover the blessings of a relationship with God? Make up your mind that you won't save the best until last.

GOD'S PROMISE

You have given me greater joy than those who have abundant harvests of grain and new wine.   PSALM 4:7

Serving God

How can I serve God today?

GOD'S RESPONSE

Love the LORD your God, walk in all his ways, obey his commands, hold firmly to him, and serve him with all your heart and all your soul. *Joshua 22:5*

[Joshua said,] "Choose today whom you will serve. . . . But as for me and my family, we will serve the LORD." *Joshua 24:15*

 Every day presents new choices. The choice that you can always make—and only you can make—is to honor God and obey his Word. This puts you squarely in the center of his will and makes you available to serve him. It is not complicated, but it is a challenge to put God ahead of everything else. Joshua urged the Israelites to worship and honor God alone and to steer clear of the gods of the people in their new land. Each day offers the choice to serve the Lord.

GOD'S PROMISE

[Jesus said,] "If you give up your life for my sake, you will save it." MATTHEW 16:25

Answered Prayer

Will I know when God answers my prayers?

GOD'S RESPONSE

Peter finally came to his senses. "It's really true!" he said. "The Lord has sent his angel and saved me from Herod. . . ." When he realized this, he went to the home of Mary, the mother of John Mark, where many were gathered for prayer. He knocked at the door in the gate, and a servant girl named Rhoda came to open it. When she recognized Peter's voice, she was so overjoyed that, instead of opening the door, she ran back inside and told everyone, "Peter is standing at the door!" "You're out of your mind!" they said.

Acts 12:11-15

The prayers of the group of believers were being answered while they were praying—but when the answer arrived at the door, they didn't believe it. We should be people of faith who believe that God answers the prayers of those who seek his will. When you pray, believe you'll get an answer. And when the answer comes, don't be surprised—be thankful!

GOD'S CHALLENGE

Jesus said to the disciples, "Have faith in God. I tell you the truth, you can say to this mountain, 'May you be lifted up and thrown into the sea,' and it will happen. . . . I tell you, you can pray for anything, and if you believe that you've received it, it will be yours." MARK 11:22-24

Leadership

Are there any guidelines to help me become a better leader?

GOD'S RESPONSE

Care for the flock that God has entrusted to you. Watch over it willingly, not grudgingly—not for what you will get out of it, but because you are eager to serve God. Don't lord it over the people assigned to your care, but lead them by your own good example.   *1 Peter 5:2-3*

Peter describes several characteristics of good leaders in the church: (1) They realize they are caring for *God's* flock, not their own. (2) They lead out of a genuine desire to serve, not out of a sense of obligation. (3) They are concerned about what they can give, not about what they can get. (4) They lead by example, not by force.

All of us lead others in some way, whether we have an official leadership title or not. Whatever our role, we should be sure that our leadership matches these four biblical characteristics.

GOD'S CHALLENGE

Let your good deeds shine out for all to see, so that everyone will praise your heavenly Father.   MATTHEW 5:16

Grief

Is something wrong with me if I'm still feeling sad long after a great loss?

GOD'S RESPONSE

I will never forget this awful time, as I grieve over my loss. Yet I still dare to hope when I remember this: The faithful love of the LORD never ends! His mercies never cease. Great is his faithfulness; his mercies begin afresh each morning.   *Lamentations 3:20-23*

Our hearts are sick and weary, and our eyes grow dim with tears.
Lamentations 5:17

Are you surprised that Jeremiah is still crying near the end of Lamentations? Even after a stirring declaration of hope (see Lamentations 3:22-27) and a period of thoughtful reflection, Jeremiah's eyes again fill with tears, just as they did in previous chapters and throughout the book of Lamentations. The grief process is not swift, nor is it a steady progression. After a good week, a good month, a good year, or even a good laugh, a theological insight, or a renewal of hope, you may weep again. There is nothing wrong with you; it is all part of the process of grieving and healing. Allow yourself time to grieve, and remember that God is with you and cares about your pain.

GOD'S PROMISE

You keep track of all my sorrows. You have collected all my tears in your bottle. You have recorded each one in your book.

PSALM 56:8

Impossible

What if God asks me to do something that, from a practical perspective, cannot be done?

GOD'S RESPONSE

Jesus soon saw a huge crowd of people coming to look for him. Turning to Philip, he asked, "Where can we buy bread to feed all these people?" He was testing Philip, for he already knew what he was going to do. Philip replied, "Even if we worked for months, we wouldn't have enough money to feed them!" *John 6:5-7*

When Jesus asked Philip where they could buy a great amount of bread, Philip quickly started assessing the cost. But Jesus wanted to teach Philip that financial resources are not the most important ones. We can limit what God does in us by assuming what is and is not possible. Is there some "impossible" task that you believe God wants you to do? Don't let your own estimate of what can or can't be done keep you from taking on the task. God can do the miraculous; trust him to provide the resources.

GOD'S PROMISE

This same God who takes care of me will supply all your needs from his glorious riches, which have been given to us in Christ Jesus.   PHILIPPIANS 4:19

Hope

How can confidence in Christ help me through life's hard times?

GOD'S RESPONSE

All praise to God, the Father of our Lord Jesus Christ. It is by his great mercy that we have been born again, because God raised Jesus Christ from the dead. Now we live with great expectation, and we have a priceless inheritance—an inheritance that is kept in heaven for you, pure and undefiled, beyond the reach of change and decay. *1 Peter 1:3-4*

God loved the world so much that he gave his one and only Son, so that everyone who believes in him will not perish but have eternal life. *John 3:16*

Do you need encouragement? Peter's words offer joy and hope in times of trouble, and he bases his confidence on what God has done for us in Christ Jesus. We can live with the same great expectation Peter had and with the knowledge that we have a "priceless inheritance" of eternal life. No matter what pain or trial we face in this life, it is not our final experience.

GOD'S PROMISE

[Jesus said,] "There is more than enough room in my Father's home. If this were not so, would I have told you that I am going to prepare a place for you? When everything is ready, I will come and get you, so that you will always be with me where I am."

JOHN 14:2-3

Sin

How can I gain a proper perspective about the sin in my life?

GOD'S RESPONSE

At the time of the sacrifice, I stood up from where I had sat in mourning with my clothes torn. I fell to my knees and lifted my hands to the LORD my God. I prayed, "O my God, I am utterly ashamed; I blush to lift up my face to you. For our sins are piled higher than our heads, and our guilt has reached to the heavens. From the days of our ancestors until now, we have been steeped in sin. That is why we and our kings and our priests have been at the mercy of the pagan kings of the land. We have been killed, captured, robbed, and disgraced, just as we are today."

Ezra 9:5-7

After learning about the sins of the people, Ezra fell to his knees in prayer. His heartfelt prayer provides a good perspective on sin. He recognized (1) that sin is serious, (2) that everyone's sin affects others, and (3) that he himself was not sinless.

It is easy to view sin lightly in a world that sees sin as inconsequential, but we should view sin as seriously as Ezra did.

GOD'S PROMISE

If we confess our sins to him, he is faithful and just to forgive us our sins and to cleanse us from all wickedness.   1 JOHN 1:9

God's Laws

What should be my attitude toward God's laws?

GOD'S RESPONSE

The instructions of the LORD are perfect, reviving the soul. The decrees of the LORD are trustworthy, making wise the simple. The commandments of the LORD are right, bringing joy to the heart. The commands of the LORD are clear, giving insight for living. Reverence for the LORD is pure, lasting forever. The laws of the LORD are true; each one is fair. They are more desirable than gold, even the finest gold. They are sweeter than honey, even honey dripping from the comb. They are a warning to your servant, a great reward for those who obey them.   *Psalm 19:7-11*

When we think of laws, we often think of restrictions or rules that keep us from having fun. But in these verses from Psalm 19, we see the opposite: God's laws revive us, make us wise, bring joy to our hearts, give us insight about how to live, alert us to dangers, and serve as their own reward when we know that we have kept them. God's laws are guidelines and lights for our path rather than chains on our hands and feet. They point at danger to warn us and then point at success to guide us.

GOD'S PROMISE

Those who love your instructions have great peace and do not stumble.   PSALM 119:165

Obedience

How can I experience more of God's love and power in my life?

GOD'S RESPONSE

Jonah answered, "I am a Hebrew, and I worship the LORD, the God of heaven, who made the sea and the land." The sailors were terrified when they heard this, for he had already told them he was running away from the LORD. "Oh, why did you do it?" they groaned. And since the storm was getting worse all the time, they asked him, "What should we do to you to stop this storm?" "Throw me into the sea," Jonah said, "and it will become calm again. I know that this terrible storm is all my fault." *Jonah 1:9-12*

You cannot seek God's love and power while you are running from him. Jonah learned that lesson the hard way. He soon realized that no matter where he went, he couldn't get away from God. But before Jonah could return *to* God, he first had to stop going in the opposite direction.

Is there something God has told you to do? If you want more of his love and power, you must be willing to carry out the responsibilities he gives you. You cannot say that you truly believe in God and love him if you don't do what he says.

GOD'S CHALLENGE

We can be sure that we know him if we obey his commandments. If someone claims, "I know God," but doesn't obey God's commandments, that person is a liar and is not living in the truth. But those who obey God's word truly show how completely they love him. That is how we know we are living in him.   1 JOHN 2:3-5

Help

Am I ever beyond the reach of God's care for me?

GOD'S RESPONSE

The official pleaded, "Lord, please come now before my little boy dies." Then Jesus told him, "Go back home. Your son will live!" And the man believed what Jesus said and started home. While the man was on his way, some of his servants met him with the news that his son was alive and well. He asked them when the boy had begun to get better, and they replied, "Yesterday afternoon at one o'clock his fever suddenly disappeared!" Then the father realized that that was the very time Jesus had told him, "Your son will live."   *John 4:49-53*

In today's verses from John 4, the government official's son was in Capernaum, twenty miles away from Cana, where Jesus was. But when Jesus spoke the word, the boy was healed.

Distance is no problem for God because he is everywhere and has mastery over space. You can never put so much space between yourself and Christ that he can't help you. Even if you *feel* far from him, God can come to your rescue when you ask for his help.

GOD'S PROMISE

I can never escape from your Spirit! I can never get away from your presence! If I go up to heaven, you are there; if I go down to the grave, you are there. If I ride the wings of the morning, if I dwell by the farthest oceans, even there your hand will guide me, and your strength will support me.   PSALM 139:7-10

Prayer

What can I use to guide my prayer times?

GOD'S RESPONSE

Praise the LORD. . . . May the LORD our God be with us as he was with our ancestors; may he never leave us or abandon us. May he give us the desire to do his will . . . and to obey all the commands, decrees, and regulations that he gave our ancestors. And may these words that I have prayed in the presence of the LORD be before him constantly, day and night, so that the LORD our God may give justice to me and to his people Israel, according to each day's needs. Then people all over the earth will know that the LORD alone is God and there is no other.   *1 Kings 8:56-60*

 Solomon praised the Lord and prayed for the people. He had five requests: for God's presence, for the desire to do God's will, for the desire to obey God's decrees and commands, for justice, and for people everywhere to know the Lord.

Solomon's requests are just as important today. Do your prayers include requests for more than the fulfillment of your own desires? Follow Solomon's example to gain more depth and compassion in your prayer life.

GOD'S CHALLENGE

Pray for all people. Ask God to help them; intercede on their behalf, and give thanks for them. Pray this way for kings and all who are in authority so that we can live peaceful and quiet lives marked by godliness and dignity.   1 TIMOTHY 2:1-2

Hopelessness

Does the Bible offer an action plan for life's crisis moments?

GOD'S RESPONSE

The king was furious . . . and he ordered that all the wise men of Babylon be executed. And because of the king's decree, men were sent to find and kill Daniel and his friends. . . . Daniel went at once to see the king and requested more time to tell the king what the dream meant. Then Daniel went home and told his friends Hananiah, Mishael, and Azariah what had happened. He urged them to ask the God of heaven to show them his mercy by telling them the secret, so they would not be executed along with the other wise men of Babylon. *Daniel 2:12-13, 16-18*

Imagine going to see the powerful, temperamental king who had just angrily ordered your death! Daniel did not shrink back in fear, however. He confidently believed God would tell him what the king wanted to know. When the king gave Daniel time to find the answer, Daniel found his three friends, and they prayed.

When you find yourself in a tight spot, share your needs with trusted friends who also believe in God's power. Panic confirms your hopelessness; prayer confirms your hope in God. Daniel's trust in God saved not only him but also his three friends and all the other wise men of Babylon. In your crisis moments, what is your natural reaction—to panic or pray?

GOD'S PROMISE

Joyful are those who have the God of Israel as their helper, whose hope is in the LORD their God. PSALM 146:5

The Unknown

How can I enjoy my life and not fear the unknown or the future?

GOD'S RESPONSE

In my search for wisdom and in my observation of people's burdens here on earth, I discovered that there is ceaseless activity, day and night. I realized that no one can discover everything God is doing under the sun. Not even the wisest people discover everything, no matter what they claim.   *Ecclesiastes 8:16-17*

I know the one in whom I trust, and I am sure that he is able to guard what I have entrusted to him until the day of his return.
                                                                                    2 Timothy 1:12

Even if we had access to all the world's wisdom, the wisest of us would know very little. None of us can fully comprehend God and all he has done, and no matter how much we learn, there are always more questions than answers. But thoughts of the unknown should not cast a shadow over our joy, faith, or work, because we know that someone far greater than we are is in control, and we can put our trust in him.

Don't let what you don't know about the future destroy the joy God has for you today.

GOD'S CHALLENGE

Whatever happens, my dear brothers and sisters, rejoice in the Lord.   PHILIPPIANS 3:1

Needs

Has God forgotten about my needs? Why hasn't he provided when I need it most?

GOD'S RESPONSE

One day Ruth the Moabite said to Naomi, "Let me go out into the harvest fields to pick up the stalks of grain left behind by anyone who is kind enough to let me do it." Naomi replied, "All right, my daughter, go ahead." So Ruth went out to gather grain behind the harvesters. And as it happened, she found herself working in a field that belonged to Boaz, the relative of her father-in-law, Elimelech.   *Ruth 2:2-3*

Ruth had voluntarily made her home in a foreign land. Instead of depending on her mother-in-law, Naomi, to provide for her, or waiting for "good fortune" to drop into her lap, she took the initiative. She went to work. She was not afraid to admit her need or work hard to supply it. When Ruth went out to the fields, God provided for her.

If you are waiting for God to provide, consider this: He may be waiting for you to take the first step to demonstrate just how important you feel your need is.

GOD'S PROMISE

Fear the LORD, you his godly people, for those who fear him will have all they need.   PSALM 34:9

Feeling Safe

Why can't I ever seem to feel safe in this world?

GOD'S RESPONSE

I look up to the mountains—does my help come from there? My help comes from the LORD, who made heaven and earth! He will not let you stumble; the one who watches over you will not slumber. Indeed, he who watches over Israel never slumbers or sleeps.

Psalm 121:1-4

God is our refuge and strength, always ready to help in times of trouble.   *Psalm 46:1*

These verses from the book of Psalms express assurance, hope, and confidence in God's protection day and night. You should never trust a lesser power than God himself. Because he is your creator, he watches over you, as he does all of his creation. Nothing can divert his attention or distract him or deter him from caring for you. You can never outgrow your need for God's untiring watch over your life. In him, you are safe.

GOD'S PROMISE

The LORD keeps watch over you as you come and go, both now and forever.   PSALM 121:8

Suffering

Why do people who deny God seem to be happier and wealthier than I am? Why am I suffering when I work so hard to please God?

GOD'S RESPONSE

Look at these wicked people—enjoying a life of ease while their riches multiply. Did I keep my heart pure for nothing? Did I keep myself innocent for no reason? . . . I tried to understand why the wicked prosper. But what a difficult task it is! Then I went into your sanctuary, O God, and I finally understood the destiny of the wicked. . . . Yet I still belong to you; you hold my right hand. You guide me with your counsel, leading me to a glorious destiny. Whom have I in heaven but you? I desire you more than anything on earth.   *Psalm 73:12-13, 16-17, 23-25*

The psalmist asked God a question most people ask at one time or another: Why do evil people prosper while the righteous suffer? It wasn't until the psalmist went into God's sanctuary that he finally began to see things from a long-term perspective: The wicked *don't* really prosper, not in the long run.

God is alive and in control of the world and its events. We cannot see all that God is doing, and we cannot see all that God *will* do. But knowing that we belong to the one who is in charge gives us confidence that God will make everything right in the end.

GOD'S PROMISE

Every word of God proves true. He is a shield to all who come to him for protection.   PROVERBS 30:5

Preparation

Is it really necessary to spend so much time preparing for ministry?

God's Response

In early autumn, when the Israelites had settled in their towns, all the people assembled in Jerusalem with a unified purpose. . . . The people hired masons and carpenters and bought cedar logs. . . . The logs were brought down from the Lebanon mountains and floated along the coast of the Mediterranean Sea to Joppa, for King Cyrus had given permission for this. The construction of the Temple of God began in midspring, during the second year after they arrived in Jerusalem.   _Ezra 3:1, 7-8_

It took seven months just to _prepare_ to rebuild the Temple. The exiles took so much time to make plans and prepare because the project was so important to them.

If you're in the process of preparing for what God has asked you to do, the time spent in preparation may not feel heroic or spiritual, but it is vital to doing any project well.

God's Challenge

Pay careful attention to your own work, for then you will get the satisfaction of a job well done, and you won't need to compare yourself to anyone else.   GALATIANS 6:4

Restoration

I've made a lot of mistakes. Can God really restore my life to the way he intended it to be?

God's Response

Now you have been united with Christ Jesus. Once you were far away from God, but now you have been brought near to him through the blood of Christ.   *Ephesians 2:13*

[Paul said,] "Brothers, listen! We are here to proclaim that through this man Jesus there is forgiveness for your sins. Everyone who believes in him is declared right with God."   *Acts 13:38-39*

God is able to restore and rebuild the lives of all people. No one is so far away from God that he or she cannot be restored. A genuine desire to follow God is all that is required. No matter how far you have strayed or how long it has been since you have worshiped God, he is able to restore you relationship with him and rebuild your life.

God's Promise

This includes you who were once far away from God. You were his enemies, separated from him by your evil thoughts and actions. Yet now he has reconciled you to himself through the death of Christ in his physical body. As a result, he has brought you into his own presence, and you are holy and blameless as you stand before him without a single fault.   COLOSSIANS 1:21-22

God's Care

Sometimes I feel so left out. Does God even notice that I'm here?

GOD'S RESPONSE

[Mary] turned to leave and saw someone standing there. It was Jesus, but she didn't recognize him.

"Dear woman, why are you crying?" Jesus asked her. "Who are you looking for?"

She thought he was the gardener. "Sir," she said, "if you have taken him away, tell me where you have put him, and I will go and get him."

"Mary!" Jesus said. She turned to him and cried out, "Rabboni!" (which is Hebrew for "Teacher"). *John 20:14-16*

[Moses said to the Lord,] "You have told me, 'I know you by name, and I look favorably on you.'" *Exodus 33:12*

Mary didn't recognize Jesus at first. Perhaps her grief had blinded her; she couldn't see him because she didn't expect to see him. Then he spoke her name, and immediately she knew who he was. Imagine the love that flooded her heart when she heard her Savior say her name.

Jesus is always near you, and he knows you by name. If you recognize him as your Lord, he has called you by name. You will never be beyond his notice.

GOD'S PROMISE

[The Lord said,] "Do not be afraid, for I have ransomed you. I have called you by name; you are mine." ISAIAH 43:1

Discouragement

Is it wrong for me to be discouraged when nothing is going my way?

God's Response

Elkanah had two wives, Hannah and Peninnah. Peninnah had children, but Hannah did not. . . . So Peninnah would taunt Hannah and make fun of her because the LORD had kept her from having children. . . . Hannah was in deep anguish, crying bitterly as she prayed to the LORD. And she made this vow: "O LORD of Heaven's Armies, if you will look upon my sorrow and answer my prayer and give me a son, then I will give him back to you."   *1 Samuel 1:2, 6, 10-11*

Hannah had good reason to feel discouraged. She was unable to bear children; she shared her husband with a woman who ridiculed her; her loving husband could not solve her problem; and even the high priest misunderstood her. But instead of retaliating or giving up hope, Hannah continued to pray. She brought her problem honestly to God. Each of us may face times of "barrenness," when nothing "comes to birth" in our work, our service, or our relationships. It is difficult to pray in faith when we feel so powerless, but as Hannah discovered, prayer opens the way for God to work.

God's Promise

Praise the LORD! For he has heard my cry for mercy. The LORD is my strength and shield. I trust him with all my heart. He helps me, and my heart is filled with joy. I burst out in songs of thanksgiving.   PSALM 28:6-7

God's Love

Can I experience God's love every day?

GOD'S RESPONSE

May you have the power to understand, as all God's people should, how wide, how long, how high, and how deep his love is. May you experience the love of Christ, though it is too great to understand fully. Then you will be made complete with all the fullness of life and power that comes from God.   *Ephesians 3:18-19*

God's love is so great, says Paul, that we can never fully understand it. It reaches every corner of our lives. It is *wide*—it covers the breadth of our experience and reaches out to the whole world. God's love is *long*—it continues the length of our lives and for all eternity. It is *high*—it rises to the heights of our celebration and elation. It is *deep*—it reaches to the depths of discouragement, despair, and even death. No matter what each day brings, you can never be lost to God's love.

GOD'S PROMISE

I am convinced that nothing can ever separate us from God's love. Neither death nor life, neither angels nor demons, neither our fears for today nor our worries about tomorrow—not even the powers of hell can separate us from God's love. No power in the sky above or in the earth below—indeed, nothing in all creation will ever be able to separate us from the love of God that is revealed in Christ Jesus our Lord.   ROMANS 8:38-39

Seduction

How can I avoid giving in to the enticement of sin?

GOD'S RESPONSE

Wisdom will save you from the immoral woman, from the seductive words of the promiscuous woman. She has abandoned her husband and ignores the covenant she made before God.
Proverbs 2:16-17

[Jesus said,] "It is what comes from inside that defiles you. For from within, out of a person's heart, come evil thoughts, sexual immorality . . . lustful desires . . . pride, and foolishness."
Mark 7:20-22

Take control of what I say, O LORD, and guard my lips. Don't let me drift toward evil or take part in acts of wickedness. Don't let me share in the delicacies of those who do wrong.   *Psalm 141:3-4*

Two of the most difficult sins to resist are pride and sexual immorality. Both are seductive. Pride says, "I deserve it"; sexual desire says, "I need it." Pride appeals to the empty head; sexual enticement to the empty heart. To overcome these temptations, you need to fill your head with God's wisdom and your heart with love for him. Then ask him for strength to resist these temptations.

GOD'S PROMISE

[God] gives us even more grace to stand against such evil desires. As the Scriptures say, "God opposes the proud but favors the humble." So humble yourselves before God. Resist the devil, and he will flee from you.   JAMES 4:6-7

Confession

My relationship with God feels so robotic. How can I find intimacy with him again?

GOD'S RESPONSE

Do not banish me from your presence, and don't take your Holy Spirit from me. Restore to me the joy of your salvation, and make me willing to obey you.   *Psalm 51:11-12*

If I had not confessed the sin in my heart, the Lord would not have listened.   *Psalm 66:18*

Do you ever feel stagnant in your faith, as if you are only going through the motions? Has sin ever driven a wedge between you and God, making him seem distant? David felt this way because he had sinned with Bathsheba. In his prayer he cried, "Restore to me the joy of your salvation." God wants you to be close to him and to experience his full and rich life. But unconfessed sin makes such intimacy impossible. Confess your sin to God. You may still have to face some earthly consequences, as David did, but God will restore the joy of your relationship with him.

GOD'S PROMISE

The LORD is a friend to those who fear him.   PSALM 25:14

Lust

How can I tell the difference between feelings of real love and lust?

God's Response

Amnon wouldn't listen to [Tamar], and since he was stronger than she was, he raped her. Then suddenly Amnon's love turned to hate, and he hated her even more than he had loved her. "Get out of here!" he snarled at her.   *2 Samuel 13:14-15*

Love is patient and kind. Love is not jealous or boastful or proud or rude. It does not demand its own way. It is not irritable, and it keeps no record of being wronged.   *1 Corinthians 13:4-5*

Love and lust are very different. After Amnon raped his half sister, his "love" turned to hate. Although he had claimed to be in love, he was actually overcome by lust. Love is patient; lust requires immediate satisfaction. Love is kind; lust is harsh. Love does not demand its own way; lust is self-centered. Lust may feel like love at first, but when it is expressed physically, it results in both self-disgust and hatred of the other person. If you just can't wait, what you feel is not true love.

God's Challenge

God's will is for you to be holy, so stay away from all sexual sin. Then each of you will control his own body and live in holiness and honor—not in lustful passion like the pagans who do not know God and his ways.   1 THESSALONIANS 4:3-5

Loving Others

What are some ways that I can show others how much I love them?

GOD'S RESPONSE

[Jesus said,] "This is my commandment: Love each other in the same way I have loved you. There is no greater love than to lay down one's life for one's friends." *John 15:12-13*

Dear friends, since God loved us that much, we surely ought to love each other. *1 John 4:11*

We are to love one another in the same way Jesus loved us, and he loved us enough to give his life for us. Of course, we may not have to die for someone, but there are other ways to practice sacrificial love: listening, helping, encouraging, giving, serving. Think of someone in particular who needs this kind of love today. Give all the love you can in all the ways you can, and then try to give a little more.

GOD'S CHALLENGE

Don't just pretend to love others. Really love them. Hate what is wrong. Hold tightly to what is good. Love each other with genuine affection, and take delight in honoring each other.

ROMANS 12:9-10

Listening

*I'm listening for God, but I can't hear his voice.
Am I doing something wrong?*

God's Response

After the fire there was the sound of a gentle whisper. When Elijah
heard it, he wrapped his face in his cloak and went out and stood
at the entrance of the cave. And a voice said, "What are you doing
here, Elijah?"   *1 Kings 19:12-13*

This is what the Sovereign LORD, the Holy One of Israel, says:
"Only in returning to me and resting in me will you be saved.
In quietness and confidence is your strength."   *Isaiah 30:15*

Elijah knew that the sound of a gentle whisper was God's
voice. He realized that God doesn't always reveal himself in powerful, miraculous ways. To look for God only in something big
(rallies, churches, conferences, highly visible leaders) may be to
miss him, because he is often found gently whispering into the
quietness of a humble heart.

Are you listening for God? Step back from the noise and activity
of your busy life, and listen humbly and quietly for his guidance. It
may come when you least expect it.

God's Promise

I wait quietly before God, for my victory comes from him.

PSALM 62:1

Values

How can I tell if I genuinely value what God values?

GOD'S RESPONSE

Do not love this world nor the things it offers you, for when you love the world, you do not have the love of the Father in you. For the world offers only a craving for physical pleasure, a craving for everything we see, and pride in our achievements and possessions. These are not from the Father, but are from this world.

1 John 2:15-16

Levi invited Jesus and his disciples to his home as dinner guests, along with many tax collectors and other disreputable sinners. (There were many people of this kind among Jesus' followers.) But when the teachers of religious law who were Pharisees saw him eating with tax collectors and other sinners, they asked his disciples, "Why does he eat with such scum?" *Mark 2:15-16*

Like the Pharisees, we can give the impression of avoiding worldly pleasures and still harbor worldly attitudes in our hearts. It is also possible, like Jesus, to love sinners and spend time with them while maintaining a commitment to the values of God's Kingdom. God values self-control, a spirit of generosity, and a commitment to humble service. What values are most important to you? Do your actions reflect the world's values or God's values?

GOD'S PROMISE

Seek the Kingdom of God above all else, and live righteously, and he will give you everything you need. MATTHEW 6:33

Pursued by God

How much does God love me?

GOD'S RESPONSE

[God's] unfailing love toward those who fear him is as great as the height of the heavens above the earth.   *Psalm 103:11*

Surely your goodness and unfailing love will pursue me all the days of my life, and I will live in the house of the LORD forever.

Psalm 23:6

God created you, loves you, and longs to have a relationship with you. He pursues you and draws you to himself with persistent and unfailing love. Ask God to open your spiritual eyes today to see which events, conversations, chance meetings, thoughts, and open doors are God's hand reaching out to show you that he is nearby and at work in your life.

GOD'S PROMISE

Long ago the LORD said to Israel: "I have loved you, my people, with an everlasting love. With unfailing love I have drawn you to myself." JEREMIAH 31:3

Problems

How can I possibly solve my problems when they're so overwhelming?

GOD'S RESPONSE

As [David] was talking with them, Goliath, the Philistine champion from Gath, came out from the Philistine ranks. Then David heard him shout his usual taunt to the army of Israel. As soon as the Israelite army saw him, they began to run away in fright. "Have you seen the giant?" the men asked. . . . David asked the soldiers standing nearby, "What will a man get for killing this Philistine and ending his defiance of Israel? Who is this pagan Philistine anyway, that he is allowed to defy the armies of the living God?"

1 Samuel 17:23-26

[Jesus said to Peter,] "You are seeing things merely from a human point of view, not from God's." *Matthew 16:23*

What a difference perspective can make. Most of the onlookers in Saul's army saw a giant. David, however, saw a mortal man defying an almighty God. He knew he would not be alone when he faced Goliath; God would fight with him. As David looked to God, his perspective broadened. Viewing impossible situations through the lens of God's possibilities and power helps us to put giant problems into perspective. Once we see clearly, we can fight more effectively.

GOD'S PROMISE

All this may seem impossible to you now. . . . But is it impossible for me? says the LORD of Heaven's Armies.   ZECHARIAH 8:6

God's Plans

How can I see God's plans in all of life's circumstances?

God's Response

I create the light and make the darkness. I send good times and bad times. I, the LORD, am the one who does these things.   *Isaiah 45:7*

I want you to know, my dear brothers and sisters, that everything that has happened to me here has helped to spread the Good News. For everyone here, including the whole palace guard, knows that I am in chains because of Christ. And because of my imprisonment, most of the believers here have gained confidence and boldly speak God's message without fear.   *Philippians 1:12-14*

It's easy for us to think that events "just happen" to us, but God may use common occurrences to lead us where he wants us to be. It is important to evaluate all situations as potential "divine appointments" designed to shape our lives.

Think of all the good and bad circumstances you have encountered lately. Are you able to see God's purpose in them? It may be that through those experiences God is building a certain quality into you or leading you to serve him in a new area.

God's Promise

[God] chose us in advance, and he makes everything work out according to his plan.   EPHESIANS 1:11

Honor

Why is it important to make sure I honor God in everything I do?

GOD'S RESPONSE

King Nebuchadnezzar threw himself down before Daniel and worshiped him, and he commanded his people to offer sacrifices and burn sweet incense before him. The king said to Daniel, "Truly, your God is the greatest of gods, the Lord over kings, a revealer of mysteries, for you have been able to reveal this secret." *Daniel 2:46-47*

Whatever I am now, it is all because God poured out his special favor on me—and not without results. For I have worked harder than any of the other apostles; yet it was not I but God who was working through me by his grace. *1 Corinthians 15:10*

 Nebuchadnezzar honored Daniel and Daniel's God. If Daniel himself had taken the credit, the king would have honored only Daniel. But because Daniel gave God the credit, the king honored both of them.

Part of our mission as Christians is to show unbelievers what God is like. We can do that by showing love and compassion, and if we give God credit for our actions, others will want to know more about him. Give thanks to God, and honor him for what he is doing in and through you.

GOD'S CHALLENGE

I have reason to be enthusiastic about all Christ Jesus has done through me in my service to God. Yet I dare not boast about anything except what Christ has done through me. ROMANS 15:17-18

Justice

Is it all right to ask God for justice when I've been wronged?

GOD'S RESPONSE

O LORD, God of Israel, you are just. We come before you in our guilt as nothing but an escaped remnant, though in such a condition none of us can stand in your presence. *Ezra 9:15*

The LORD is compassionate and merciful, slow to get angry and filled with unfailing love. *Psalm 103:8*

Ezra recognized that if God gave the people the justice they deserved, they would receive his judgment. Often we cry out for justice when we feel we are being treated unfairly. In those moments, we forget the reality of our own sin and the judgment we deserve. How fortunate we are that God gives us mercy and grace rather than justice.

The next time you ask God for fair treatment, pause to think what would happen if God gave you what you really deserve. Plead instead for his mercy.

GOD'S PROMISE

Return to the LORD your God, for he is merciful and compassionate, slow to get angry and filled with unfailing love. He is eager to relent and not punish. JOEL 2:13

Prayer

God seems very far away. Should I even keep trying to reach him?

God's Response

O LORD, why do you stand so far away? Why do you hide when I am in trouble? *Psalm 10:1*

I keep praying to you, LORD, hoping this time you will show me favor. In your unfailing love, O God, answer my prayer with your sure salvation. *Psalm 69:13*

Rejoice in our confident hope. Be patient in trouble, and keep on praying. *Romans 12:12*

"Why do you hide when I am in trouble?" To the psalmist, God seemed far away. But even though the writer had honest doubts, he did not stop praying or conclude that God no longer cared. He was not complaining, but he was asking God to please hurry to his aid. It is during the times when we feel most alone or oppressed that we need to keep praying, telling God our troubles, and waiting for him to respond.

God's Promise

[Jesus said,] "I tell you, keep on asking, and you will receive what you ask for. Keep on seeking, and you will find. Keep on knocking, and the door will be opened to you. For everyone who asks, receives. Everyone who seeks, finds. And to everyone who knocks, the door will be opened." LUKE 11:9-10

Love

What does true love look like?

GOD'S RESPONSE

Love is patient and kind. Love is not jealous or boastful or proud or rude. It does not demand its own way. It is not irritable, and it keeps no record of being wronged. It does not rejoice about injustice but rejoices whenever the truth wins out. Love never gives up, never loses faith, is always hopeful, and endures through every circumstance.   *1 Corinthians 13:4-7*

Our society confuses love and lust. Unlike lust, God's kind of love is directed outward toward others, not inward toward ourselves. Because this kind of love is utterly unselfish, expressing it goes against our natural inclinations. It is impossible to have this love unless God helps us set aside our own natural desires so that we can love others without expecting anything in return. The more we become like Christ, the better we can truly love others.

GOD'S PROMISE

If we love each other, God lives in us, and his love is brought to full expression in us.   1 JOHN 4:12

Depression

Does feeling depressed mean something is wrong with my faith?

God's Response

[Jesus said,] "I have told you these things so that you will be filled with my joy. Yes, your joy will overflow!"   *John 15:11*

Those who listen to instruction will prosper; those who trust the Lord will be joyful.   *Proverbs 16:20*

God does not regard depression as sin, nor does he take it lightly. Rather, he responds to those who suffer its darkness with great tenderness, understanding, and compassion. When you are depressed, reading the Bible helps you recognize the lies of Satan, the temptations that will come your way, and how the devil fuels your depression by distracting you from God's promises and power. As these things become clear, your perspective begins to change. Develop the regular habit of seeking God and counting on his Word to be true, and you will discover the encouragement you need.

God's Promise

Even when I walk through the darkest valley, I will not be afraid, for you are close beside me. Your rod and your staff protect and comfort me.   PSALM 23:4

Desires

When do my desires become dangerous?

GOD'S RESPONSE

You were whining, and the LORD heard you when you cried, "Oh, for some meat! We were better off in Egypt!" Now the LORD will give you meat, and you will have to eat it. And it won't be for just a day or two, or for five or ten or even twenty. You will eat it for a whole month until you gag and are sick of it. . . ." But while they were gorging themselves on the meat—while it was still in their mouths—the anger of the LORD blazed against the people, and he struck them with a severe plague.   *Numbers 11:18-20, 33*

Craving or lusting is more than inappropriate sexual desire. It can be a greedy desire for anything—knowledge, possessions, influence over others. In Numbers 11, God punished the Israelites for craving good food! Their desire was not wrong; their sin was that they allowed their desire to turn into greed (they were "gorging themselves"). They felt it was their right to have fine food, and they could think of nothing else.

A desire becomes dangerous when you are so preoccupied with wanting something that it affects your perspective on everything else. At that point you have moved from desire to lust.

GOD'S CHALLENGE

Run from anything that stimulates youthful lusts. Instead, pursue righteous living, faithfulness, love, and peace.   2 TIMOTHY 2:22

God's Care

Does God really understand what I'm going through?

GOD'S RESPONSE

When Jesus saw [Mary] weeping and saw the other people wailing with her, a deep anger welled up within him, and he was deeply troubled. "Where have you put him?" he asked them. They told him, "Lord, come and see." Then Jesus wept. The people who were standing nearby said, "See how much he loved him!" But some said, "This man healed a blind man. Couldn't he have kept Lazarus from dying?" Jesus was still angry as he arrived at the tomb, a cave with a stone rolled across its entrance. *John 11:33-38*

We have a God who cares. In the story of Lazarus, we see many of Jesus' emotions—compassion, indignation, sorrow, even anger. He often expressed deep emotion, and we must never be afraid to reveal our true feelings to him. He understands them, for he has experienced them.

Whether you are hurting, angry, fearful, weary, or feeling any other emotion, share your feelings with your Savior, and don't try to hide those feelings from him. He understands, and he cares.

GOD'S PROMISE

Give all your worries and cares to God, for he cares about you.

1 PETER 5:7

In the Desert

I've fallen on bad times. Where is God leading me?

GOD'S RESPONSE

I will win her back once again. I will lead her into the desert and
speak tenderly to her there. I will return her vineyards to her and
transform the Valley of Trouble into a gateway of hope.

Hosea 2:14-15

Hosea 3–5 tells the story of the prophet and his wife, Gomer,
who was repeatedly unfaithful to him. But Hosea's experience is
also the illustration of a much larger story: God's dealings with
unfaithful Israel. In the verses above, God was promising (1) to
bring the Israelites to the desert, a place free of distractions, so he
could clearly communicate with them and (2) to change what had
been a time of pain and difficulty into a day of hope. God sometimes uses negative experiences in our lives as "desert journeys" to
turn our attention to him alone.

As you face problems and trials, remember that God speaks
tenderly to you in the "desert." Listen for him, and have faith that
through your desert journey, God will bring you to a gateway of
hope.

GOD'S PROMISE

Be truly glad. There is wonderful joy ahead, even though you have
to endure many trials for a little while. 1 PETER 1:6

Hopelessness

My situation is hopeless. What use is there in trusting God?

God's Response

Save me, O God, for the floodwaters are up to my neck. Deeper and deeper I sink into the mire; I can't find a foothold. I am in deep water, and the floods overwhelm me. I am exhausted from crying for help; my throat is parched. My eyes are swollen with weeping, waiting for my God to help me. *Psalm 69:1-3*

Even if my father and mother abandon me, the LORD will hold me close. *Psalm 27:10*

What problems David faced! He was scoffed at, mocked, insulted, humiliated, and made the object of citywide gossip. But still he prayed.

When you are completely beaten down, it can be tempting to turn from God, to give up and quit trusting him. When your situation seems hopeless, determine that, no matter how bad things become, you will continue to pray. God will hear your prayer, he will hold you close to his heart, and in his perfect timing, he will rescue you. Don't turn from your most faithful friend.

God's Promise

The LORD watches over those who fear him, those who rely on his unfailing love. He rescues them from death and keeps them alive in times of famine. We put our hope in the LORD. He is our help and our shield. PSALM 33:18-20

Trusting God

How can I shake the doubts in my heart when I see no reason for my suffering?

God's Response

Job replied to the LORD: ". . . It is I—and I was talking about things I knew nothing about, things far too wonderful for me. You said, 'Listen and I will speak! I have some questions for you, and you must answer them.' I had only heard about you before, but now I have seen you with my own eyes. I take back everything I said, and I sit in dust and ashes to show my repentance." *Job 42:1-6*

Throughout the book of Job, Job's friends had seen his suffering as a consequence of sin in his life. They told him to admit his sin and ask forgiveness, and eventually Job did indeed repent. Ironically, Job's repentance was not the kind his friends had called for. He asked for forgiveness not for committing secret sins but for questioning God's sovereignty and justice. Job repented of his attitude and acknowledged God's great wisdom.

We sin when we angrily ask, "If God is in control, how could he let this happen?" Because we are locked into time and are unable to see beyond today, we cannot know the reasons for everything that happens. Thus, we must often choose between doubt and trust. Will you trust God with your unanswered questions?

God's Promise

He is the Rock; his deeds are perfect. Everything he does is just and fair. He is a faithful God who does no wrong; how just and upright he is! DEUTERONOMY 32:4

God's Nearness

I feel so close to God when I'm at church. How can I experience that closeness throughout the week?

GOD'S RESPONSE

David found favor with God and asked for the privilege of building a permanent Temple for the God of Jacob. But it was Solomon who actually built it. However, the Most High doesn't live in temples made by human hands. *Acts 7:46-48*

Don't you realize that your body is the temple of the Holy Spirit, who lives in you and was given to you by God? *1 Corinthians 6:19*

God's presence is not confined to a house of worship. He lives in the hearts of those who are open to receiving him. The same closeness you feel to God while worshiping him in church can be felt at all times when you allow him to live in you. Ask him to reveal himself to you throughout the week. He will be happy to answer that prayer.

GOD'S PROMISE

Those who obey God's commandments remain in fellowship with him, and he with them. And we know he lives in us because the Spirit he gave us lives in us. 1 JOHN 3:24

The Gift of Life

Sometimes it seems as if I'm alone in the universe. Is there anything special about my life?

GOD'S RESPONSE

The LORD God formed the man from the dust of the ground. He breathed the breath of life into the man's nostrils, and the man became a living person.   *Genesis 2:7*

The Spirit of God has made me, and the breath of the Almighty gives me life.   *Job 33:4*

The body is a lifeless shell until God brings it alive with his "breath of life." When God removes his life-giving breath, our bodies once again return to dust. Therefore, our lives and our worth come from God. Many people boast of their achievements and abilities as if those strengths originated with them. Others feel worthless because their abilities do not stand out. But our worth doesn't come from our achievements; it comes from the God of the universe, who chooses to give us the mysterious and miraculous gift of life.

GOD'S PROMISE

When you give them your breath, life is created, and you renew the face of the earth. May the glory of the LORD continue forever! The LORD takes pleasure in all he has made!   PSALM 104:30-31

Value

Sometimes I feel so worthless. Does God even know I exist?

God's Response

Can a mother forget her nursing child? Can she feel no love for the child she has borne? But even if that were possible, I would not forget you! See, I have written your name on the palms of my hands.   *Isaiah 49:15-16*

God looked over all he had made, and he saw that it was very good!   *Genesis 1:31*

If you sometimes feel worthless or wonder whether God even remembers that you exist, you are not alone! Even his chosen people sometimes felt that he had forgotten them. But God created you, and he can't forget about you any more than a mother can forget her child. You are part of God's creation. He is pleased with the way he made you, and you are precious to him.

Have you ever written something important on your hand so you wouldn't forget it? When you feel worthless, remember that God has written *your* name on the palms of his hands!

God's Promise

What is the price of five sparrows—two copper coins? Yet God does not forget a single one of them. And the very hairs on your head are all numbered. So don't be afraid; you are more valuable to God than a whole flock of sparrows.   LUKE 12:6-7

Sin

Why is sin such a powerful trap?

God's Response

"My people have forgotten how to do right," says the Lord.

Amos 3:10

Beware that in your plenty you do not forget the Lord your God and disobey his commands, regulations, and decrees that I am giving you today.   *Deuteronomy 8:11*

The Scriptures declare that we are all prisoners of sin, so we receive God's promise of freedom only by believing in Jesus Christ.

Galatians 3:22

The people of Israel no longer knew how to do what was right. The more they sinned, the easier it became to continue sinning, and the harder it was to remember what God wanted.

The same is true for us. The longer we wait to deal with sin, the greater the hold it has on us. Eventually, we forget what it means to do right. If you are on the verge of "forgetting," talk to God about your sin, seek his forgiveness, and when you are tempted to sin, ask him to remind you of what he wants you to do and to give you the strength and freedom to do it.

God's Promise

If you look carefully into the perfect law that sets you free, and if you do what it says and don't forget what you heard, then God will bless you for doing it.   JAMES 1:25

Weaknesses

I'm afraid that by revealing my sins to God I'll upset him. Does he really understand my weaknesses?

GOD'S RESPONSE

If we claim we have no sin, we are only fooling ourselves and not living in the truth. But if we confess our sins to him, he is faithful and just to forgive us our sins and to cleanse us from all wickedness.   *1 John 1:8-9*

The LORD supports the humble, but he brings the wicked down into the dust.   *Psalm 147:6*

It takes humility and honesty to recognize our weaknesses, and most of us would rather pretend that we are strong. But we don't need to fear revealing our sins to God—he knows them already. He will not push us away, no matter what we've done. Instead, he will draw us to himself so that we might be supported by his strength. Where do you pretend to be strong?

GOD'S PROMISE

Let the wicked change their ways and banish the very thought of doing wrong. Let them turn to the LORD that he may have mercy on them. Yes, turn to our God, for he will forgive generously.

ISAIAH 55:7

Tomorrow

I know I can trust God for my eternal future, but what about the future that will be here tomorrow?

GOD'S RESPONSE

You saw me before I was born. Every day of my life was recorded in your book. Every moment was laid out before a single day had passed.   *Psalm 139:16*

God has plans for your life—plans he made before you were born. He has already laid out all of your days. He knows what tomorrow holds, and next week, and next year—and the next ten years. And he promises to go through every tomorrow with you, so you can anticipate each new day with peace and hope.

The future and even the next twenty-four hours may look uncertain to you. But God is with you every moment, and perhaps tomorrow you will see his plan for you more clearly than ever before.

GOD'S PROMISE

We know that God causes everything to work together for the good of those who love God and are called according to his purpose for them.   ROMANS 8:28

God's Image

In what ways am I made in God's image?

GOD'S RESPONSE

God said, "Let us make human beings in our image, to be like us. They will reign over the fish in the sea, the birds in the sky, the livestock, all the wild animals on the earth, and the small animals that scurry along the ground." So God created human beings in his own image. In the image of God he created them; male and female he created them.   *Genesis 1:26-27*

Obviously, God did not create us exactly like himself, because God is spirit. Instead, we are reflections of God's glory. Some feel that our ability to reason, our creativity, our speech, or our self-determination is the image of God. More likely, it is our entire being that reflects his image. We will never be totally like God because he is our infinite Creator. But we do have the ability to reflect his character in love, patience, forgiveness, kindness, and faithfulness.

GOD'S CHALLENGE

Don't lie to each other, for you have stripped off your old sinful nature and all its wicked deeds. Put on your new nature, and be renewed as you learn to know your Creator and become like him.   COLOSSIANS 3:9-10

Advice

Why should I be open to advice from others?

GOD'S RESPONSE

How I hated discipline! If only I had not ignored all the warnings!
Oh, why didn't I listen to my teachers? Why didn't I pay attention
to my instructors?   *Proverbs 5:12-13*

Fools think their own way is right, but the wise listen to others.

Proverbs 12:15

Plans go wrong for lack of advice; many advisers bring success.

Proverbs 15:22

At the end of your life, it will be too late to ask for advice.
The best time to learn the dangers of making wrong choices is
long before you encounter those choices. Resisting temptation is
easier if you have already made the right decision before you are
tempted. This is where listening to the good advice of others comes
in. Listen to good advice while you can. Prepare for temptation by
deciding now how you will act when you face it. Don't wait to see
what happens. Be prepared ahead of time!

GOD'S CHALLENGE

Get all the advice and instruction you can, so you will be wise the
rest of your life.   PROVERBS 19:20

Invitation

How does Jesus invite me to experience him?

GOD'S RESPONSE

Jesus called out to [Peter and Andrew], "Come, follow me, and I
will show you how to fish for people!" And they left their nets at
once and followed him.   *Matthew 4:19-20*

The invitation and promise of Jesus are clear, but they remain
only opportunities until you take Jesus up on his invitation. If Peter
and Andrew had merely listened to Jesus and then said, "That's a
very interesting invitation; maybe we can talk about it again after
fishing season," they would not have become Jesus' disciples. Jesus'
invitation requires a decision: to follow him or to remain where
you are. Acceptance of his invitation leads to action—the disciples
left their nets and the life they knew and followed Jesus. God is
constantly extending invitations to you to experience life with him.
Does your RSVP say, "Accepted with gratitude!"?

GOD'S PROMISE

God will do this, for he is faithful to do what he says, and he has
invited you into partnership with his Son, Jesus Christ our Lord.

1 CORINTHIANS 1:9

Guidance

Why is it important to seek God's guidance when I'm making decisions?

GOD'S RESPONSE

[Mary] was engaged to be married to Joseph. But before the marriage took place, while she was still a virgin, she became pregnant through the power of the Holy Spirit. Joseph, her fiancé, was a good man and did not want to disgrace her publicly, so he decided to break the engagement quietly. As he considered this, an angel of the Lord appeared to him in a dream. "Joseph, son of David," the angel said, "do not be afraid to take Mary as your wife. For the child within her was conceived by the Holy Spirit." *Matthew 1:18-20*

Perhaps Joseph thought he had only two options: either divorce Mary quietly or see her stoned, according to God's law regarding sexual immorality. But God gave him a third option, one that had not occurred to Joseph: go ahead with the marriage.

God often shows you that there are more options available than you might think of on your own. Although Joseph seemed to be doing the right thing by breaking the engagement, only God's guidance helped him to make the best decision.

GOD'S PROMISE

My child, listen to what I say, and treasure my commands. . . . Then you will understand what is right, just, and fair, and you will find the right way to go.   PROVERBS 2:1, 9

Forgiveness

Do my sins exclude me from serving God?

GOD'S RESPONSE

Peter stepped forward with the eleven other apostles and shouted to the crowd, "Listen carefully, all of you, fellow Jews and residents of Jerusalem! Make no mistake about this. These people are not drunk, as some of you are assuming. Nine o'clock in the morning is much too early for that. No, what you see was predicted long ago by the prophet Joel."   *Acts 2:14-16*

Peter continued preaching for a long time, strongly urging all his listeners, "Save yourselves from this crooked generation!"   *Acts 2:40*

Peter had been an impulsive leader during Jesus' earthly ministry, and his bravado had become his downfall, even to the point of denying that he knew Jesus. But Christ forgave Peter and restored him. This restored Peter was bold but humble. His confidence came from the Holy Spirit, who made him a powerful and dynamic speaker.

Have you ever felt as if you've made such serious mistakes that God could never forgive you and use you? No matter what sins you have committed, God can forgive you and make you useful for his Kingdom. Ask him to forgive you and to restore you so that you can serve him effectively.

GOD'S PROMISE

There is no condemnation for those who belong to Christ Jesus.

ROMANS 8:1

Direction

Sometimes I feel so lost. Where does God want me to go next?

God's Response

Whether the cloud stayed above the Tabernacle for two days, a month, or a year, the people of Israel stayed in camp and did not move on. But as soon as it lifted, they broke camp and moved on. So they camped or traveled at the LORD's command, and they did whatever the LORD told them through Moses.   *Numbers 9:22-23*

The Israelites traveled and camped as God guided them. When you follow God's direction, you know you are where God wants you, whether you are moving or staying where you are. You are physically somewhere right now. Instead of praying, "God, what do you want me to do next?" ask, "God, what do you want me to do while I'm right here?" Direction from God is not just for your next big move. He has a purpose in placing you where you are right now. Begin to understand God's purpose for your life by discovering what he wants you to do right now! When he wants you to move, he'll make it clear.

God's Promise

You saw me before I was born. Every day of my life was recorded in your book. Every moment was laid out before a single day had passed.   PSALM 139:16

Making Choices

How can I learn to make better choices?

God's Response

The Lord God placed the man in the Garden of Eden to tend and watch over it. But the Lord God warned him, "You may freely eat the fruit of every tree in the garden—except the tree of the knowledge of good and evil. If you eat its fruit, you are sure to die."   *Genesis 2:15-17*

God gave Adam responsibility for the Garden and told him not to eat from the tree of the knowledge of good and evil. Rather than physically prevent Adam from eating, God gave him a choice and, thus, the possibility of choosing wrongly.

God still gives us choices, and we, too, often choose wrongly. These wrong choices may cause us pain, but they can help us grow and learn to make better choices in the future. Living with the consequences of our choices teaches us to think carefully and choose wisely.

God's Promise

Who are those who fear the Lord? He will show them the path they should choose.   PSALM 25:12

Happiness

Can God make me happy?

GOD'S RESPONSE

They do not cry out to me with sincere hearts. Instead, they sit on their couches and wail. They cut themselves, begging foreign gods for grain and new wine, and they turn away from me. I trained them and made them strong, yet now they plot evil against me. They look everywhere except to the Most High.   *Hosea 7:14-16*

Be merciful to me, O Lord, for I am calling on you constantly. Give me happiness, O Lord, for I give myself to you.   *Psalm 86:3-4*

 People tend to look everywhere except to God for happiness and fulfillment. They spend their days pursuing possessions, recreation, and relationships. In reality, only God can truly satisfy the deep longings of the soul. In the verses from Psalm 86, David seeks God for all that he needs. He knows that God is the source of every good and lasting gift, and he looks to God, even asking for happiness.

The happiness the world offers doesn't last. So before you look there for what makes you happy, look first to heaven, to the Most High God. He will meet your spiritual needs and fill you with joy and gladness. Where do you search for happiness?

GOD'S PROMISE

May all who search for you be filled with joy and gladness in you. May those who love your salvation repeatedly shout, "The LORD is great!"   PSALM 40:16

Volunteer

Does my church really need me or my acts of service?

GOD'S RESPONSE

I assembled the exiles at the Ahava Canal, and we camped there for three days while I went over the lists of the people and the priests who had arrived. I found that not one Levite had volunteered to come along.   *Ezra 8:15*

Just as our bodies have many parts and each part has a special function, so it is with Christ's body. We are many parts of one body, and we all belong to each other. In his grace, God has given us different gifts for doing certain things well.   *Romans 12:4-6*

Ezra's progress back to Jerusalem was halted while he waited to recruit Levites. God had called these men to a special service, yet none had been willing to volunteer when their services were needed. God has gifted each of us with specific abilities so that we can make a contribution to his Kingdom work. Don't wait to be recruited; rather, look for opportunities to volunteer. Don't withhold the gift he's given you.

GOD'S PROMISE

God has given each of you a gift from his great variety of spiritual gifts. Use them well to serve one another. . . . Then everything you do will bring glory to God through Jesus Christ.

1 PETER 4:10-11

Refreshment

I'm feeling tired in my spiritual walk. How can I be refreshed?

God's Response

Repent of your sins and turn to God, so that your sins may be wiped away. Then times of refreshment will come from the presence of the Lord.   *Acts 3:19-20*

Wash me clean from my guilt. Purify me from my sin. . . . Create in me a clean heart, O God. Renew a loyal spirit within me. . . . Restore to me the joy of your salvation, and make me willing to obey you.   *Psalm 51:2, 10, 12*

God promises that when we turn from sins, he not only will cleanse us of our sins but will also give us spiritual refreshment. Turning away from sin may seem painful, because it is hard to break old habits. But God will give you a better way. Hosea declared, "Oh, that we might know the Lord! Let us press on to know him. He will respond to us as surely as the arrival of dawn or the coming of rains in early spring" (Hosea 6:3).

Do you feel a need to be refreshed? Talk to God about that need, and he will help you.

God's Promise

"Come now, let's settle this," says the Lord. "Though your sins are like scarlet, I will make them as white as snow. Though they are red like crimson, I will make them as white as wool."

ISAIAH 1:18

Joy

What is joy?

GOD'S RESPONSE

Let the godly rejoice. Let them be glad in God's presence. Let them be filled with joy.   *Psalm 68:3*

Our hearts ache, but we always have joy. We are poor, but we give spiritual riches to others. We own nothing, and yet we have everything.   *2 Corinthians 6:10*

Joy is the celebration of walking in God's presence. It is an inner happiness that lasts despite the circumstances around you because it is based on a relationship with Jesus Christ. If you are a believer, this gives you absolute confidence that God is real, personal, and involved in your life, that evil will one day be defeated forever, and that heaven is a reality. When you have that perspective, you grow in your realization that your happy or sad feelings may go up and down, but the joy God gives runs so deep that nothing can take it away.

GOD'S PROMISE

Those who have been ransomed by the LORD will return. They will enter Jerusalem singing, crowned with everlasting joy. Sorrow and mourning will disappear, and they will be filled with joy and gladness.   ISAIAH 51:11

Amazement

How can I recapture that feeling of amazement I first had about God?

GOD'S RESPONSE

You are the God of great wonders! You demonstrate your awesome power among the nations.   *Psalm 77:14*

The heavens proclaim the glory of God. The skies display his craftsmanship. Day after day they continue to speak; night after night they make him known.   *Psalm 19:1-2*

Pay attention—to the stories of others and to the world around you. God is doing amazing work everywhere. Don't forget the quiet miracles that take place each day: the birth of a baby, a beautiful sunset, close friends, joy in the midst of overwhelming circumstances. Being in awe of God over these small miracles prepares your heart to experience even more amazing things from God. Listen to how God has amazed others, and add those amazing events to your own list. The more you look for God's work, the more amazed you will be.

GOD'S PROMISE

He has given me a new song to sing, a hymn of praise to our God. Many will see what he has done and be amazed. They will put their trust in the LORD.   PSALM 40:3

Transformation

How does God's Word give power to the Christian life?

GOD'S RESPONSE

The rain and snow come down from the heavens and stay on the ground to water the earth. They cause the grain to grow, producing seed for the farmer and bread for the hungry. It is the same with my word. I send it out, and it always produces fruit. It will accomplish all I want it to, and it will prosper everywhere I send it. *Isaiah 55:10-11*

This same Good News that came to you is going out all over the world. It is bearing fruit everywhere by changing lives, just as it changed your lives from the day you first heard and understood the truth about God's wonderful grace. *Colossians 1:6*

I am not ashamed of this Good News about Christ. It is the power of God at work, saving everyone who believes. *Romans 1:16*

God's Word is not just for our information; it's for our *transformation*! Becoming a Christian means beginning a whole new relationship with God, not just turning over a new leaf or making up our minds to try to do what is right. New believers have changed purposes, directions, attitudes, and behaviors. They are no longer seeking to serve themselves; they are seeking to bear fruit for God.

How is the Good News transforming you?

GOD'S CHALLENGE

Get rid of all the filth and evil in your lives, and humbly accept the word God has planted in your hearts, for it has the power to save your souls. JAMES 1:21

New Life

Can I ever truly change and become a new person?

GOD'S RESPONSE

To all who believed him and accepted him, he gave the right to become children of God. They are reborn—not with a physical birth resulting from human passion or plan, but a birth that comes from God.   *John 1:12-13*

Humans can reproduce only human life, but the Holy Spirit gives birth to spiritual life.   *John 3:6*

[Christ] died for everyone so that those who receive his new life will no longer live for themselves. Instead, they will live for Christ, who died and was raised for them.   *2 Corinthians 5:15*

All who welcome Jesus Christ as Lord of their lives are reborn spiritually and have received new life from God. Through faith in Christ, you are changed from the inside out. God rearranges your attitudes, your desires, and your motives. Being born physically places you in your parents' family. Being born of God makes you spiritually alive and makes you a member of God's family. Have you asked God to make you a new person? This fresh start is available to all who believe in Christ.

GOD'S PROMISE

You have been born again, but not to a life that will quickly end. Your new life will last forever because it comes from the eternal, living word of God.   1 PETER 1:23

Fresh Start

*I'm ready to leave my sinful life behind me. Will
God really give me a fresh start?*

GOD'S RESPONSE

David replied, "I fasted and wept while the child was alive, for I
said, 'Perhaps the LORD will be gracious to me and let the child
live.' But why should I fast when he is dead? Can I bring him
back again? I will go to him one day, but he cannot return to me."
Then David comforted Bathsheba, his wife, and slept with her. She
became pregnant and gave birth to a son, and David named him
Solomon. The LORD loved the child and sent word through Nathan
the prophet that they should name him Jedidiah (which means
"beloved of the LORD").   *2 Samuel 12:22-25*

David's sin with Bathsheba was great, but David did not continue to dwell on his sin indefinitely. He confessed his wrongdoing
to God. God forgave him and opened the door to David's restora-
tion. Even *Jedidiah*, the name God gave Solomon, means "beloved
of the LORD" and served as a reminder of God's grace to David.

When we return to God, accept his forgiveness, and change our
ways, he gives us a fresh start. To feel forgiven as David did, turn to
God and admit your sins to him. Then move ahead with a new and
fresh approach to life, doing your best to obey God.

GOD'S PROMISE

I—yes, I alone—will blot out your sins for my own sake and will
never think of them again.   ISAIAH 43:25

Living Water

Is there really such a thing as spiritual hunger or thirst?

GOD'S RESPONSE

Jesus replied, "If you only knew the gift God has for you and who you are speaking to, you would ask me, and I would give you living water." *John 4:10*

As the deer longs for streams of water, so I long for you, O God. I thirst for God, the living God. When can I go and stand before him?
Psalm 42:1-2

What did Jesus mean by "living water"? In the Old Testament, many verses speak of thirsting after God as one thirsts for water. God is called the fountain of life and the fountain of living water. When Jesus said in John 4 that he would give living water that could forever quench a person's thirst for God, Jesus was claiming to be the Messiah. Only the Messiah could give this gift that satisfies the soul's deepest desire. Do you look to Jesus to quench the desires and longings within your own soul? He is the source of those desires, and he offers you the peace of his presence in this life and the gift of eternal life forever.

GOD'S PROMISE

[Jesus said,] "Those who drink the water I give will never be thirsty again. It becomes a fresh, bubbling spring within them, giving them eternal life." JOHN 4:14

Joy

What is the secret to lasting joy?

GOD'S RESPONSE

You will show me the way of life, granting me the joy of your presence and the pleasures of living with you forever.   *Psalm 16:11*

You satisfy me more than the richest feast. I will praise you with songs of joy.   *Psalm 63:5*

David's heart was glad—he had found the secret to joy. True joy is far deeper than happiness. Happiness is temporary because it is based on external circumstances: When things are going well, we feel happy. But joy is lasting because it is the fruit of God's presence with us. We can experience great joy in spite of our deepest troubles. As we contemplate this each day, we will find contentment. And as we think about the future God has for us and experience his presence with us, we will experience joy.

Don't base your feelings on fleeting circumstances but on the constant presence of God.

GOD'S CHALLENGE

Sing praises to God and to his name! Sing loud praises to him who rides the clouds. His name is the LORD—rejoice in his presence!

PSALM 68:4

Let Jesus In

I have these nagging thoughts about God. Could he be seeking me out?

GOD'S RESPONSE

The Lord isn't really being slow about his promise, as some people think. No, he is being patient for your sake. He does not want anyone to be destroyed, but wants everyone to repent. . . . And remember, our Lord's patience gives people time to be saved.

2 Peter 3:9, 15

[Jesus said,] "Look! I stand at the door and knock. If you hear my voice and open the door, I will come in, and we will share a meal together as friends." *Revelation 3:20*

Jesus knocks at the doors of our hearts because he wants to save us and have fellowship with us. He is patient and persistent in getting through to us—not breaking and entering but knocking. He allows us to decide whether or not to answer his knock and open the door to him.

Are you intentionally keeping his life-changing presence and power on the other side of the door?

GOD'S PROMISE

The LORD must wait for you to come to him so he can show you his love and compassion. For the LORD is a faithful God. Blessed are those who wait for his help.   ISAIAH 30:18

Tragedy

How should I respond when tragedy strikes?

GOD'S RESPONSE

I asked them about the Jews who had returned there from captivity and about how things were going in Jerusalem. They said to me, "Things are not going well for those who returned to the province of Judah. They are in great trouble and disgrace. The wall of Jerusalem has been torn down, and the gates have been destroyed by fire." When I heard this, I sat down and wept. In fact, for days I mourned, fasted, and prayed to the God of heaven. . . . "The people you rescued by your great power and strong hand are your servants. O Lord, please hear my prayers! . . . Please grant me success today by making the king favorable to me. Put it into his heart to be kind to me." *Nehemiah 1:2-4, 10-11*

Nehemiah was deeply grieved about the condition of Jerusalem, but he didn't just brood about it. After his initial grief, he still mourned, prayed, and poured out his heart to God, and he looked for ways to improve the situation. Nehemiah put all his resources of knowledge, experience, and organization into determining what to do.

When you receive tragic news, the first thing to do is pray. Then seek ways to move beyond grief to specific action that helps those who need it.

GOD'S PROMISE

Day by day the LORD takes care of the innocent, and they will receive an inheritance that lasts forever. They will not be disgraced in hard times; even in famine they will have more than enough.

PSALM 37:18-19

Character

Does having godly character really affect anyone else but me?

GOD'S RESPONSE

When the time came, we set sail for Italy. Paul and several other prisoners were placed in the custody of a Roman officer named Julius, a captain of the Imperial Regiment. . . . The next day when we docked at Sidon, Julius was very kind to Paul and let him go ashore to visit with friends so they could provide for his needs.   *Acts 27:1, 3*

The soldiers wanted to kill the prisoners to make sure they didn't swim ashore and escape. But the commanding officer wanted to spare Paul, so he didn't let them carry out their plan.   *Acts 27:42-43*

Julius, a hardened Roman army officer, was assigned to guard Paul. Obviously he had to remain close to his prisoner at all times. Through this contact, Julius developed respect for Paul. He gave Paul a certain amount of freedom (see Acts 27:3) and later spared his life (see Acts 27:43).

How does your character look, up close and personal? Is it the kind of character that inspires trust and respect in others?

GOD'S PROMISE

Never let loyalty and kindness leave you! Tie them around your neck as a reminder. Write them deep within your heart. Then you will find favor with both God and people, and you will earn a good reputation.   PROVERBS 3:3-4

Wisdom

What is wisdom?

GOD'S RESPONSE

How wonderful to be wise, to analyze and interpret things. Wisdom lights up a person's face, softening its harshness.

Ecclesiastes 8:1

Fear of the LORD is the foundation of wisdom. Knowledge of the Holy One results in good judgment.   *Proverbs 9:10*

Fear of the LORD is the foundation of true knowledge, but fools despise wisdom and discipline.   *Proverbs 1:7*

Wisdom is the ability to see life from God's perspective and then to know the best course of action to take. Most people would agree that wisdom is a valuable asset, but how can we acquire it? Proverbs 9:10 teaches that the fear (respect and honor) of the Lord is the beginning, or foundation, of wisdom. Wisdom comes as a result of knowing and trusting God; it is not merely the way to find God. Knowing God will lead to understanding and then to sharing that wisdom and understanding with others.

GOD'S CHALLENGE

Let the message about Christ, in all its richness, fill your lives. Teach and counsel each other with all the wisdom he gives.

COLOSSIANS 3:16

Running Away

Is there someplace I can go to escape my problems?

GOD'S RESPONSE

Balaam replied to Balak, "Didn't I tell you that I can do only what the LORD tells me?" Then King Balak said to Balaam, "Come, I will take you to one more place. Perhaps it will please God to let you curse them from there." *Numbers 23:26-27*

King Balak took Balaam to several places to try to entice him to curse the Israelites. He thought a change of scenery might help change Balaam's mind. But changing locations didn't change God's will in Balaam's case, and it won't change God's will for us.

Trying to escape our problems only makes solving them more difficult. We must learn to deal with the source of our problems. Problems that have their roots inside us aren't eliminated by a change of scenery. In fact, a change of location or job may only distract us from the need for a change of heart.

GOD'S CHALLENGE

Be careful that you do not refuse to listen to the One who is speaking. For if the people of Israel did not escape when they refused to listen to Moses, the earthly messenger, we will certainly not escape if we reject the One who speaks to us from heaven! HEBREWS 12:25

Prayer

What assurance do I have that God can hear my prayers?

GOD'S RESPONSE

You can be sure of this: The LORD set apart the godly for himself. The LORD will answer when I call to him.   *Psalm 4:3*

The LORD hears his people when they call to him for help. He rescues them from all their troubles.   *Psalm 34:17*

David knew that God would hear him when he called and that God would answer him too. We can be confident that God listens to our prayers and answers them. We may sometimes think that God will not hear us because we have fallen short of his high standards for holy living. But if we have trusted Christ for salvation, God has forgiven us, and he will listen to us.

When you feel as if your prayers are bouncing off the ceiling, remember that as a believer you have been set apart by God and that he loves you. And although his answers may not be what you expect, he does hear and answer every time you call to him. The next time you're not sure that God is hearing your prayers, try looking at your problems in the light of God's power instead of looking at God in the shadow of your problems.

GOD'S PROMISE

The eyes of the Lord watch over those who do right, and his ears are open to their prayers.   1 PETER 3:12

Obedience

Does it matter when I respond to God's commands, as long as I do so?

GOD'S RESPONSE

The LORD gave this message to Jonah son of Amittai: "Get up and go to the great city of Nineveh. Announce my judgment against it because I have seen how wicked its people are." But Jonah got up and went in the opposite direction to get away from the LORD.

Jonah 1:1-3

If you rebel against the LORD's commands and refuse to listen to him, then his hand will be as heavy upon you as it was upon your ancestors. *1 Samuel 12:15*

Jonah knew that God had a specific job for him. He just didn't want to do it. So Jonah decided to go as far in the opposite direction from Nineveh as he could. The consequences of that decision were dramatic.

When God gives us directions through his Word, we may run from them out of fear or stubbornness, claiming that God is asking too much. It may have been fear or anger at God's request that made Jonah run. But running got him into worse trouble. And in the end, Jonah still had to do what God had asked in the first place. Obeying God from the start prevents many problems later on.

GOD'S CHALLENGE

Put all your rebellion behind you, and find yourselves a new heart and a new spirit. . . . Turn back and live! EZEKIEL 18:31-32

Worship

What does true worship look like?

GOD'S RESPONSE

God is Spirit, so those who worship him must worship in spirit and in truth.   *John 4:24*

[The wise men] entered the house and saw the child with his mother, Mary, and they bowed down and worshiped him. Then they opened their treasure chests and gave him gifts of gold, frankincense, and myrrh.   *Matthew 2:11*

These people honor me with their lips, but their hearts are far from me. Their worship is a farce, for they teach man-made ideas as commands from God.   *Matthew 15:8-9*

Asking what true worship looks like is sort of like asking what true love looks like. Like love, worship is an issue of the heart, not just of the mind. Worship may involve music, prayers, and religious symbols, but if your heart is not engaged in what you are doing, your worship will be empty.

Jesus confronted the religious leaders who made a public show of worship but inwardly had hearts that were far from God. In contrast, the wise men bowed in humility before Jesus and worshiped him. Worship may look different for different people, but when people worship with their hearts and minds fully engaged, they are worshiping "in spirit and in truth."

GOD'S PROMISE

Joyful are those who obey his laws and search for him with all their hearts.   PSALM 119:2

Stress

How can I cope with stressful situations in life?

God's Response

Rescue me from my enemies, O God. Protect me from those who have come to destroy me. . . . But as for me, I will sing about your power. Each morning I will sing with joy about your unfailing love. For you have been my refuge, a place of safety when I am in distress.   *Psalm 59:1, 16*

Throughout this psalm, David describes in grim detail the behavior of his enemies. He conveys his own feelings of dread with the desperation and despair that he sees in the lives of those who want to harm him. What a delight, then, in these final verses, to read about God's role in David's life as a refuge, a place of safety, and a source of unfailing love. David had learned to turn negative circumstances into reminders of God's faithful presence.

What stresses in your life might be transformed today if you were to make them a starting point for praising God?

God's Promise

Let all the godly pray to you while there is still time, that they may not drown in the floodwaters of judgment. For you are my hiding place; you protect me from trouble. You surround me with songs of victory.   PSALM 32:6-7

Vows

If I make a vow in prayer, will God be more likely to give me what I ask?

God's Response

[Hannah] made this vow: "O LORD of Heaven's Armies, if you will look upon my sorrow and answer my prayer and give me a son, then I will give him back to you. He will be yours for his entire lifetime." . . . Sir, do you remember me?" Hannah asked. "I am the woman who stood here several years ago praying to the LORD. I asked the LORD to give me this boy, and he has granted my request. Now I am giving him to the LORD, and he will belong to the LORD his whole life." And they worshiped the LORD there.   *1 Samuel 1:10-11, 26-28*

Be careful what you promise God. Hannah was so desperate for a child that she promised to give back to God the son she had asked for. God heard Hannah's pleas and gave her a son, and to Hannah's credit, she kept her promise, even though it must have been very painful.

Although you are not in a position to bargain with God, he may still choose to answer a prayer that has a vow attached. When you pray, ask yourself, *Will I follow through on any vows I make to God if he grants my request?* God keeps his promises, and he expects you to keep yours.

God's Challenge

When you make a promise to God, don't delay in following through. . . . It is better to say nothing than to make a promise and not keep it. ECCLESIASTES 5:4-5

Money

Why does the Bible have so many warnings against seeking material wealth?

GOD'S RESPONSE

They will throw their money in the streets, tossing it out like worthless trash. Their silver and gold won't save them on that day of the LORD's anger. It will neither satisfy nor feed them, for their greed can only trip them up.   *Ezekiel 7:19*

The love of money is the root of all kinds of evil. And some people, craving money, have wandered from the true faith and pierced themselves with many sorrows.   *1 Timothy 6:10*

God's people had allowed their love of money to lead them into sin (see Ezekiel 7:19). Money has a strange power over people. In 1 Timothy, Paul said that "the love of money is the root of all kinds of evil." It is ironic that we use money—a gift from God—to buy things that separate us from him. It is tragic that we spend so much seeking to satisfy ourselves and we spend so little to honor God, the source of true satisfaction.

What ways could you use your financial resources to bring yourself and others closer to God?

GOD'S PROMISE

A person is a fool to store up earthly wealth but not have a rich relationship with God.   LUKE 12:21

Challenges

Why does God allow us to struggle with the things that challenge us?

GOD'S RESPONSE

As soon as I pray, you answer me; you encourage me by giving me strength.   *Psalm 138:3*

God arms me with strength, and he makes my way perfect. He makes me as surefooted as a deer, enabling me to stand on mountain heights. He trains my hands for battle; he strengthens my arm to draw a bronze bow.   *Psalm 18:32-34*

Have you ever watched babies learning to walk? They fall and get back up many times before they can toddle around with confidence. It's the same way with you as God's child. God promises to give you strength to meet challenges, but he doesn't promise to eliminate them. Challenges stretch your character, test your faith, and help you to mature and grow stronger. If God gave you no rough roads to walk, no mountains to climb, and no battles to fight, you would never grow.

He does not leave you alone with your challenges, however. Just as good parents hold their babies' hands, walk beside them, and help them up when they fall, God stands beside you, teaches you, and strengthens you as you face each new challenge.

GOD'S PROMISE

The LORD himself watches over you! The LORD stands beside you as your protective shade.   PSALM 121:5

Messiah

Why do I have trouble understanding who Jesus is?

GOD'S RESPONSE

[Jesus said,] "When I am lifted up from the earth, I will draw everyone to myself." He said this to indicate how he was going to die. The crowd responded, "We understood from Scripture that the Messiah would live forever. How can you say the Son of Man will die? Just who is this Son of Man, anyway?" *John 12:32-34*

The crowd could not believe what Jesus was saying about the Messiah. They were waving palm branches and cheering for a Messiah who would set up a political, earthly kingdom that would never end. From their reading of the Scriptures, they thought the Messiah would never die, even though other passages indicated that he would. Jesus' words did not mesh with their concept of the Messiah. First he had to suffer and die—then he would set up his eternal Kingdom.

What kind of Messiah, or Savior, are you seeking? Are you trying to force Jesus into your own mold? As you read the Bible, ask the Holy Spirit to help you discover what kind of Messiah Jesus really is.

GOD'S PROMISE

[God] has rescued us from the kingdom of darkness and transferred us into the Kingdom of his dear Son, who purchased our freedom and forgave our sins. COLOSSIANS 1:13-14

Laziness

How can I stay motivated when Christ's return seems so far away?

God's Response

Since everything around us is going to be destroyed like this, what holy and godly lives you should live, looking forward to the day of God and hurrying it along. We are looking forward to the new heavens and new earth he has promised, a world filled with God's righteousness. And so, dear friends, while you are waiting for these things to happen, make every effort to be found living peaceful lives that are pure and blameless in his sight. And remember, our Lord's patience gives people time to be saved. *2 Peter 3:11-15*

When we're waiting for something that takes a long time, it's easy to begin to "slack off" and not wait as actively as we did at first. But Christ does not want us to become lazy and complacent just because he has not yet returned. Instead, we should live in eager expectation of his coming.

What would you like to be doing when Christ returns? That is how you should be living each day.

God's Challenge

Dear brothers and sisters, be patient as you wait for the Lord's return. Consider the farmers who patiently wait for the rains in the fall and in the spring. They eagerly look for the valuable harvest to ripen. You, too, must be patient. Take courage, for the coming of the Lord is near. JAMES 5:7-8

Answers

Why doesn't God allow me to see the reasons why things happen to me?

GOD'S RESPONSE

There once was a man named Job who lived in the land of Uz. He was blameless—a man of complete integrity. He feared God and stayed away from evil. *Job 1:1*

[Job] said, "I came naked from my mother's womb, and I will be naked when I leave. The LORD gave me what I had, and the LORD has taken it away. Praise the name of the LORD!" In all of this, Job did not sin by blaming God. *Job 1:21-22*

As you read the book of Job, you have information that the characters of the story do not. Job had lost virtually everything through no fault of his own. As he struggled to understand why all this had happened to him, it became clear that he was not meant to know the reasons. He would have to face life without answers and explanations. As a result, Job learned to trust God even when he didn't understand God's ways.

You must learn to live as Job did—one day at a time and without answers to all of life's questions. It is in that way that you, like Job, will learn to trust God no matter what.

GOD'S CHALLENGE

The LORD directs our steps, so why try to understand everything along the way? PROVERBS 20:24

Eternity

Why are we never satisfied in this life?

GOD'S RESPONSE

[God] has planted eternity in the human heart.   *Ecclesiastes 3:11*

I heard a loud shout from the throne, saying, "Look, God's home is now among his people! He will live with them, and they will be his people. God himself will be with them. He will wipe every tear from their eyes, and there will be no more death or sorrow or crying or pain. All these things are gone forever."   *Revelation 21:3-4*

God has "planted eternity in the human heart" (Ecclesiastes 3:11). This means that we can never be completely satisfied with earthly pleasures and pursuits. Because we are created in God's image, nothing but the eternal God can truly satisfy us. He has built into us a restless yearning for the kind of world that can be found only in the perfect home Jesus has prepared for us. He has given us a glimpse of the perfection of his creation. When you see injustice and pain in this world, does your heart long for the perfection of heaven? Let this longing motivate you to do God's work to further his Kingdom here on earth.

GOD'S PROMISE

This world is not our permanent home; we are looking forward to a home yet to come.   HEBREWS 13:14

Jesus Christ

Does it matter what I believe about Jesus?

GOD'S RESPONSE

[Jesus] has come from above and is greater than anyone else. We are of the earth, and we speak of earthly things, but he has come from heaven and is greater than anyone else. He testifies about what he has seen and heard.　*John 3:31-33*

Christ is the visible image of the invisible God.　*Colossians 1:15*

The Word became human and made his home among us. He was full of unfailing love and faithfulness. And we have seen his glory, the glory of the Father's one and only Son.　*John 1:14*

 Your whole spiritual life depends on your answer to one question: Who is Jesus Christ? If you accept Jesus as only a prophet or a teacher, you have to reject his teaching, for he claimed to be God himself. The heartbeat of John's Gospel is the dynamic truth that Jesus Christ is God's Son, the Messiah, the Savior, who has always existed and will live forever. Jesus came from heaven and spoke of what he had seen there. That's why what he said is trustworthy. His words are the very words of God.

This same Jesus has called you to believe him and to live with him eternally. When you know who Jesus really is, it becomes easier to believe what he said.

GOD'S PROMISE

To all who believed him and accepted him, he gave the right to become children of God.　JOHN 1:12

Jesus' Name

Is there really power in Jesus' name?

GOD'S RESPONSE

[Peter said,] "Through faith in the name of Jesus, this man was healed—and you know how crippled he was before. Faith in Jesus' name has healed him before your very eyes."   *Acts 3:16*

Jesus called his twelve disciples together and gave them authority to cast out evil spirits and to heal every kind of disease and illness.
Matthew 10:1

Jesus, not the apostles, received the glory for the healing of the lame man. In those days a man's name represented his character; it stood for his authority and power. When Peter used Jesus' name in Acts 3:16, he showed those around him who had given him the authority and power to heal. The apostles did not emphasize what *they* could do but what God could do *through* them.

Jesus' name is not to be used as if it were magic—it must be used in faith. When we pray in Jesus' name, we must remember that it is Christ himself, not merely the sound of his name, who gives our prayers their power.

GOD'S PROMISE

LORD, there is no one like you! For you are great, and your name is full of power.   JEREMIAH 10:6

Resurrection

How will others respond when I tell them that Jesus rose from the dead?

GOD'S RESPONSE

[Mary] ran and found Simon Peter and the other disciple, the one whom Jesus loved. She said, "They have taken the Lord's body out of the tomb, and we don't know where they have put him!" . . . Simon Peter arrived and went inside. He also noticed the linen wrappings lying there, while the cloth that had covered Jesus' head was folded up and lying apart from the other wrappings. . . . Mary Magdalene found the disciples and told them, "I have seen the Lord!"   *John 20:2, 6-7, 18*

 People who hear about the Resurrection for the first time may need a while before they can believe this amazing story. At first, they may think the story is a fabrication, impossible to believe. Like Peter, they may check out the facts and still be puzzled about what happened. Only when they encounter Jesus personally are they able to accept the fact of the Resurrection. Then, as they commit themselves to the risen Lord and devote their lives to him, they begin to accept the reality of his living presence with them.

Be patient with those who have just heard of the Resurrection. It may take time for them to move from initial belief to a life of commitment.

GOD'S PROMISE

My old self has been crucified with Christ. It is no longer I who live, but Christ lives in me. So I live in this earthly body by trusting in the Son of God, who loved me and gave himself for me.

GALATIANS 2:20

My Redeemer Lives

How can I have faith in a God who allows so much tragedy in my life?

GOD'S RESPONSE

As for me, I know that my Redeemer lives, and he will stand upon the earth at last. And after my body has decayed, yet in my body I will see God! I will see him for myself. Yes, I will see him with my own eyes. I am overwhelmed at the thought!   *Job 19:25-27*

At the heart of the book of Job stands his ringing affirmation of confidence: "I know that my Redeemer lives." What tremendous faith Job had, especially in light of the fact that he was unaware of Satan's role in his sufferings. Job thought that *God* had brought all the disasters upon him! Faced with tragedy and even death, Job still expected to see God—and he expected to do so in his body. Although Job struggled with the idea that God was presently against him, he firmly believed that in the end, God would be on his side.

When trouble strikes, can you claim with confidence, "My Redeemer lives"?

GOD'S PROMISE

Our hope is in the living God, who is the Savior of all people and particularly of all believers.   1 TIMOTHY 4:10

Worship

Does it really matter where I worship?

God's Response

The Lord has rejected his own altar; he despises his own sanctuary. He has given Jerusalem's palaces to her enemies. They shout in the Lord's Temple as though it were a day of celebration.

Lamentations 2:7

[God says,] "I hate all your show and pretense—the hypocrisy of your religious festivals and solemn assemblies. . . . Instead, I want to see a mighty flood of justice, an endless river of righteous living."

Amos 5:21, 24

Our place of worship is not as important to God as our pattern of worship. A church building may be beautiful, but if its people don't sincerely follow God, the church will decay from within. The people of Judah, despite their beautiful Temple, had rejected in their daily lives what they proclaimed in their worship rituals. Thus, their worship had turned into a mocking lie.

When you worship, are you merely mouthing words you don't really mean? Do you pray for help you don't really believe will come? Do you profess a love for God you don't really feel? Earnestly seek God, and catch a fresh vision of his love and care. Then worship him wholeheartedly—wherever you are.

God's Challenge

Let all that I am praise the Lord; with my whole heart, I will praise his holy name.   PSALM 103:1

God's Word

How can I be sure my faith won't collapse one day?

GOD'S RESPONSE

I saw the Lord standing beside a wall that had been built using a plumb line. He was using a plumb line to see if it was still straight. And the LORD said to me, "Amos, what do you see?" I answered, "A plumb line." And the Lord replied, "I will test my people with this plumb line. I will no longer ignore all their sins."   *Amos 7:7-8*

My child, listen to me and do as I say, and you will have a long, good life. I will teach you wisdom's ways and lead you in straight paths. . . . Take hold of my instructions; don't let them go. Guard them, for they are the key to life.   *Proverbs 4:10-11, 13*

A plumb line is a device that uses gravity to determine vertical straightness. A wall that is not straight will eventually collapse. God wants people to be right with him; he wants us to deal with the sin that makes us crooked. God's Word is the plumb line that helps us become aware of our sin and gives us wisdom for walking in "straight paths."

How do you measure up to God's Word, his plumb line for your life?

GOD'S PROMISE

All Scripture is inspired by God. . . . It corrects us when we are wrong and teaches us to do what is right.   2 TIMOTHY 3:16

The Way

Isn't it a little narrow-minded to say that Jesus is the only way to God?

God's Response

John saw Jesus coming toward him and said, "Look! The Lamb of God who takes away the sin of the world!" *John 1:29*

[Jesus said,] "I am the way, the truth, and the life. No one can come to the Father except through me." *John 14:6*

Some people may argue that to say Jesus is the only way is narrow and unloving. But we aren't claiming it as our own idea. We're only repeating what we find in the Bible. *Jesus* said he is the way to God the Father. So is this really narrow? Not really. It is actually wide enough for the whole world to come to the Father, if the world chooses to accept Jesus' statement as the truth. Instead of worrying about whether this belief sounds narrow-minded, we should be thankful that Jesus has provided *a sure way* to God—a way that is open and available to everyone.

God's Promise

All of us can come to the Father through the same Holy Spirit because of what Christ has done for us. EPHESIANS 2:18

Character

What is the key to becoming a person of strong character?

God's Response

The righteous keep moving forward, and those with clean hands become stronger and stronger.   *Job 17:9*

If you are wise and understand God's ways, prove it by living an honorable life, doing good works with the humility that comes from wisdom.   *James 3:13*

Endurance develops strength of character, and character strengthens our confident hope of salvation.   *Romans 5:4*

 God is not pleased with spurts of religiosity. Building strong character takes a lifetime of consistent obedience. Heroic spiritual lives are built one obedient act at a time, act upon act, day upon day. Like the bricks in a building, each instance of obedience may seem small at the time, but as those "bricks" pile up, a great wall of strong spiritual character—and a great defense against temptation—will result.

If you want your life to be evidenced by strong character, strive for consistent obedience each day.

God's Challenge

I will keep on obeying your instructions forever and ever.

PSALM 119:44

Eternal Perspective

How does knowing about heaven affect how I live today?

GOD'S RESPONSE

When people live to be very old, let them rejoice in every day of life. But let them also remember there will be many dark days.
Ecclesiastes 11:7-8

Teach us to realize the brevity of life, so that we may grow in wisdom.   *Psalm 90:12*

Solomon is no dreary pessimist in Ecclesiastes 11:7-8. He encourages us to rejoice in every day but to remember that eternity is far longer than a person's life span. Psalm 90:12 teaches us to remember that life is short and therefore, we ought to make the most of the time we have so that we may use it to become wise. Those who are wise do not think only about the moment and its impact; they consider their actions in light of eternity.

Consider the impact your decisions will have ten years from now and into eternity. Your earthly life may be short, but you will live with God forever.

GOD'S PROMISE

Our present troubles are small and won't last very long. Yet they produce for us a glory that vastly outweighs them and will last forever! So we don't look at the troubles we can see now; rather, we fix our gaze on things that cannot be seen. For the things we see now will soon be gone, but the things we cannot see will last forever.   2 CORINTHIANS 4:17-18

Readiness

How can I follow God with a sense of urgency?

GOD'S RESPONSE

You know quite well that the day of the Lord's return will come unexpectedly, like a thief in the night.   *1 Thessalonians 5:2*

You, too, must keep watch! For you don't know what day your Lord is coming.   *Matthew 24:42*

[Jesus said,] "Look, I will come as unexpectedly as a thief! Blessed are all who are watching for me, who keep their clothing ready so they will not have to walk around naked and ashamed."

Revelation 16:15

Christ will return unexpectedly—only the Father knows when—and he wants us to be ready when he comes back. We can prepare ourselves by standing firm against temptation and by committing ourselves to living according to God's moral guidelines.

In what ways does your life show either your readiness or your lack of preparation for Christ's return?

GOD'S PROMISE

Don't be so surprised! Indeed, the time is coming when all the dead in their graves will hear the voice of God's Son, and they will rise again. Those who have done good will rise to experience eternal life, and those who have continued in evil will rise to experience judgment.   JOHN 5:28-29

Trust

God has helped me in the past. Why am I having trouble trusting him this time?

GOD'S RESPONSE

I am the LORD your God, who brought you out of the land of Egypt.   *Leviticus 26:13*

[Joshua and Caleb said,] "Do not rebel against the LORD, and don't be afraid of the people of the land. They are only helpless prey to us! They have no protection, but the LORD is with us! Don't be afraid of them!"   *Numbers 14:7-9*

With great miracles, God had led the Israelites out of Egypt, through the Red Sea, and up to the very edge of the Promised Land. He had protected them, fed them, and fulfilled every promise. Yet when it came time to actually enter the land, which had been the goal since leaving Egypt, the people wouldn't go. After witnessing so many miracles, why did they stop trusting God? They were afraid.

We sometimes have the same problem. Maybe we trust God to handle our "small" problems but doubt his ability or willingness to help us with the big ones. God has brought you this far, and he won't let you go. Remembering all he has done for you in the past will help you to keep trusting him in the future.

GOD'S PROMISE

I hold you by your right hand—I, the LORD your God. And I say to you, "Don't be afraid. I am here to help you."   ISAIAH 41:13

Meaning

Why don't the events of my life always make sense?

GOD'S RESPONSE

[Jesus'] disciples didn't understand at the time that [his Triumphal Entry] was a fulfillment of prophecy. But after Jesus entered into his glory, they remembered what had happened and realized that these things had been written about him. *John 12:16*

After Jesus' resurrection, the disciples began to understand for the first time the meaning of many of the prophecies about Jesus that they had missed before. Now Jesus' words and actions took on new meaning and made more sense. In retrospect, the disciples saw how Jesus had led them into a deeper and better understanding of his truth.

Stop and think about the events in your life that have led up to where you are now. How has God directed you to this point? As you grow older, you will look back and see God's involvement more clearly than you do now. You will discover new meaning in the events of your life as you realize how God has led you every step of the way.

GOD'S PROMISE

I will be your God throughout your lifetime—until your hair is white with age. I made you, and I will care for you. I will carry you along and save you.   ISAIAH 46:4

Belief

What does it mean to "believe" in Jesus?

GOD'S RESPONSE

Through Christ you have come to trust in God. And you have placed your faith and hope in God because he raised Christ from the dead and gave him great glory.   *1 Peter 1:21*

Faith is the confidence that what we hope for will actually happen; it gives us assurance about things we cannot see.   *Hebrews 11:1*

 To "believe" is more than agreeing intellectually that Jesus is God. It means to put your trust and confidence in his ability to save you. It is to put Christ in charge of your present plans and your eternal destiny. Believing is both trusting his words as reliable and relying on him for the power to change. If you have never trusted Christ, let this promise of everlasting life be yours—and believe.

GOD'S PROMISE

All glory to God, who is able to keep you from falling away and will bring you with great joy into his glorious presence without a single fault. All glory to him who alone is God, our Savior through Jesus Christ our Lord. All glory, majesty, power, and authority are his before all time, and in the present, and beyond all time! Amen.   JUDE 1:24-25

Stewardship

What does it mean to be a good steward?

GOD'S RESPONSE

I said to these priests, "You and these treasures have been set apart as holy to the LORD." *Ezra 8:28*

Honor the LORD with your wealth and with the best part of everything you produce. Then he will fill your barns with grain, and your vats will overflow with good wine. *Proverbs 3:9-10*

Every object used in the service of the Temple was dedicated to God; each was considered a holy treasure, set apart for God's service, and therefore required utmost care. Being a good steward means that you take special care of whatever God has entrusted to you. It means having the perspective that what God has given you still belongs to him, not to you. It has come *from* him and is meant for his use.

What has God entrusted to you?

GOD'S PROMISE

If you will obey me and keep my covenant, you will be my own special treasure from among all the peoples on earth; for all the earth belongs to me. EXODUS 19:5

Testing

How can I be sure to pass the tests that come from God?

God's Response

The LORD examines both the righteous and the wicked.

Psalm 11:5

I have refined you, but not as silver is refined. Rather, I have refined you in the furnace of suffering.   *Isaiah 48:10*

[God said,] "I will bring that group through the fire and make them pure. I will refine them like silver and purify them like gold. They will call on my name, and I will answer them. I will say, 'These are my people,' and they will say, 'The LORD is our God.'"

Zechariah 13:9

God does not preserve believers from difficult circumstances, but he does examine (or test) both the righteous and the wicked. For those who are righteous, God's tests become a refining fire, melting away the impurities in the heart to produce character that is godly and pure.

Don't ignore or defy the tests and challenges that come your way. Use them as opportunities for you to grow in character and purity and become more like Christ.

God's Promise

God blesses those who patiently endure testing and temptation. Afterward they will receive the crown of life that God has promised to those who love him.   JAMES 1:12

Spiritual Nourishment

How can I nourish my spiritual life?

GOD'S RESPONSE

"But sir, you don't have a rope or a bucket," [the Samaritan woman] said, "and this well is very deep. Where would you get this living water? And besides, do you think you're greater than our ancestor Jacob, who gave us this well? How can you offer better water than he and his sons and his animals enjoyed?" Jesus replied, "Anyone who drinks this water will soon become thirsty again. But those who drink the water I give will never be thirsty again. It becomes a fresh, bubbling spring within them, giving them eternal life." "Please, sir," the woman said, "give me this water! Then I'll never be thirsty again, and I won't have to come here to get water." *John 4:11-15*

Many spiritual needs parallel physical needs. Just as our bodies hunger and thirst, so do our souls. Our souls need spiritual food and water. The woman at the well confused the two kinds of water, perhaps because no one had ever talked with her about spiritual hunger and thirst before. We would not think of depriving our bodies of food and water when we are hungry and thirsty. Why, then, would we deprive our souls? The living Word, Jesus Christ, and the written Word, the Bible, can refresh our hungry and thirsty souls.

GOD'S PROMISE

Jesus replied, "I am the bread of life. Whoever comes to me will never be hungry again. Whoever believes in me will never be thirsty." JOHN 6:35

Failure

How can my failures be opportunities for growth?

GOD'S RESPONSE

A man named Achan had stolen some of these dedicated things, so the LORD was very angry with the Israelites. . . . Joshua sent some men to make a search. They ran to the tent and found the stolen goods hidden there. . . . Then Joshua and all the Israelites took Achan, the silver, the robe, the bar of gold, his sons, daughters, cattle, donkeys, sheep, goats, tent, and everything he had, and they brought them to the valley of Achor. . . . And all the Israelites stoned Achan and his family and burned their bodies. . . . Then the LORD said to Joshua, "Do not be afraid or discouraged. Take all your fighting men and attack Ai, for I have given you the king of Ai, his people, his town, and his land." *Joshua 7:1, 22-26; 8:1*

 From what happened when Achan sinned, Joshua learned important lessons that you can follow: Confess your sins when God reveals them to you, and when you fail, refocus on God's grace and deal with the problem so you can move on. God wants the cycle of sin, repentance, and forgiveness to strengthen you; the lessons you learn from your failures should make you better able to handle the same situation the next time. You can tell what kind of a person you will be by what you do on your second and third attempts.

GOD'S PROMISE

No discipline is enjoyable while it is happening—it's painful! But afterward there will be a peaceful harvest of right living for those who are trained in this way. HEBREWS 12:11

Adversity

What is the value of adversity in our lives?

GOD'S RESPONSE

Better to spend your time at funerals than at parties. After all, everyone dies—so the living should take this to heart. Sorrow is better than laughter, for sadness has a refining influence on us. A wise person thinks a lot about death, while a fool thinks only about having a good time. *Ecclesiastes 7:2-4*

By means of their suffering, [God] rescues those who suffer. For he gets their attention through adversity. *Job 36:15*

Although God wants us to enjoy what he has given us while we have the opportunity, we must also realize that adversity can strike at any time. Adversity reminds us that life is short, teaches us to live wisely, and refines our characters. We often learn more about God from difficult times than from easy times.

Do you try to avoid sorrow and suffering at all costs? The Holy Spirit can help you to see your struggles as great opportunities to learn from God.

GOD'S PROMISE

Though the Lord gave you adversity for food and suffering for drink, he will still be with you to teach you. You will see your teacher with your own eyes. ISAIAH 30:20

Appearances

I always feel as if people judge who I am by my image. How does God evaluate who I am?

GOD'S RESPONSE

The LORD said to Samuel, "Don't judge by his appearance or height, for I have rejected him. The LORD doesn't see things the way you see them. People judge by outward appearance, but the LORD looks at the heart." *1 Samuel 16:7*

As for me, it matters very little how I might be evaluated by you or by any human authority. I don't even trust my own judgment on this point. My conscience is clear, but that doesn't prove I'm right. It is the Lord himself who will examine me and decide.
1 Corinthians 4:3-4

The LORD's light penetrates the human spirit, exposing every hidden motive. *Proverbs 20:27*

God judges by faith and character, by what he sees on the inside, not by appearances. And because only God can see what's on the inside, only he can accurately judge people. Most people spend hours each week maintaining their outward appearance; they should spend even more time developing their inner character.

Everyone can see your face, but only God knows what your heart really looks like. What steps are you taking to improve what God sees in your heart?

GOD'S CHALLENGE

May the words of my mouth and the meditation of my heart be pleasing to you, O LORD, my rock and my redeemer. PSALM 19:14

Loneliness

Am I alone in my stand for God?

GOD'S RESPONSE

Elijah replied, "I have zealously served the LORD God Almighty. But the people of Israel have broken their covenant with you, torn down your altars, and killed every one of your prophets. I am the only one left, and now they are trying to kill me, too."

1 Kings 19:10

Elijah thought he was the only person left who was still true to God. Lonely and discouraged, he forgot that others had remained faithful during the nation's wickedness. When you are tempted to think that you are the only one remaining faithful to a task, don't feel sorry for yourself. Self-pity will dilute the good you are doing. You may feel alone right now, but be assured that even if you don't know who they are, others are faithfully obeying God and fulfilling his call for their lives.

GOD'S CHALLENGE

Since we are surrounded by such a huge crowd of witnesses to the life of faith, let us strip off every weight that slows us down, especially the sin that so easily trips us up. And let us run with endurance the race God has set before us.   HEBREWS 12:1

Belonging

What are some of the privileges of belonging to God?

GOD'S RESPONSE

Those who die in the LORD will live; their bodies will rise again!
Isaiah 26:19

Now that you belong to Christ, you are the true children of
Abraham. You are his heirs, and God's promise to Abraham
belongs to you.   *Galatians 3:29*

All praise to God, the Father of our Lord Jesus Christ, who has
blessed us with every spiritual blessing in the heavenly realms
because we are united with Christ.   *Ephesians 1:3*

Belonging to God carries so many privileges. It means you
are no longer enslaved to sin; you can overcome it. Belonging to
God means you can be certain that you will rise from the dead,
live eternally with God, and receive all that God has promised
his people in the Bible. Here on earth you can experience peace
of heart, comfort, Christian friendships, and the fulfillment that
comes from knowing you are doing what God has created you
to do. The privileges of belonging to God are countless, and the
more you give yourself to him, the more you will discover and
experience them.

GOD'S PROMISE

The eternal God is your refuge, and his everlasting arms are
under you.   DEUTERONOMY 33:27

Values

What is a good way to measure how much I value Jesus?

God's Response

I was circumcised when I was eight days old. I am a pure-blooded citizen of Israel and a member of the tribe of Benjamin—a real Hebrew if there ever was one! I was a member of the Pharisees, who demand the strictest obedience to the Jewish law. I was so zealous that I harshly persecuted the church. And as for righteousness, I obeyed the law without fault. I once thought these things were valuable, but now I consider them worthless because of what Christ has done. Yes, everything else is worthless when compared with the infinite value of knowing Christ Jesus my Lord. *Philippians 3:5-8*

 After Paul had considered everything he had accomplished in his life, he said that it was all "worthless" when compared with the "infinite value" of knowing Christ. This is a profound statement about values: A person's relationship with Christ is more important than anything else.

Knowing Christ should be your ultimate goal. Consider your values. Do you place anything above your relationship with Christ? If your priorities are wrong, what steps will you take to reorder them?

God's Challenge

When you discipline us for our sins, you consume like a moth what is precious to us. Each of us is but a breath. . . . Whom have I in heaven but you? I desire you more than anything on earth. PSALMS 39:11; 73:25

Troubles

If I obey God, will he keep troubles from coming into my life?

GOD'S RESPONSE

The LORD asked Satan, "Have you noticed my servant Job? He is the finest man in all the earth. He is blameless—a man of complete integrity. He fears God and stays away from evil." Satan replied to the LORD, "Yes, but Job has good reason to fear God. . . . Reach out and take away everything he has, and he will surely curse you to your face!" "All right, you may test him," the LORD said to Satan. "Do whatever you want with everything he possesses, but don't harm him physically." So Satan left the LORD's presence.

Job 1:8-9, 11-12

Job was a model of trust in God and obedience toward him, yet God permitted Satan to attack him in an especially harsh manner. Although God loves us, our faith and obedience do not shelter us from life's calamities. Setbacks, tragedies, and sorrows strike Christians and non-Christians alike. But in our troubles, God expects us to express our faith to the world.

How do you respond to your troubles? Do you ask God, "Why me?" or do you say, "Use me!"

GOD'S PROMISE

No one is abandoned by the Lord forever. Though he brings grief, he also shows compassion because of the greatness of his unfailing love. For he does not enjoy hurting people or causing them sorrow. LAMENTATIONS 3:31-33

Enthusiasm

What can cause me to lose my enthusiasm for following God?

GOD'S RESPONSE

I have this complaint against you. You don't love me or each other as you did at first! Look how far you have fallen! Turn back to me and do the works you did at first. *Revelation 2:4-5*

Supplement your faith with a generous provision of moral excellence, and moral excellence with knowledge, and knowledge with self-control, and self-control with patient endurance, and patient endurance with godliness, and godliness with brotherly affection, and brotherly affection with love for everyone. . . . Those who fail to develop in this way are shortsighted or blind, forgetting that they have been cleansed from their old sins. *2 Peter 1:5-7, 9*

Just as when a man and woman fall in love, new believers also rejoice at their newfound relationship with Jesus. But unless you are purposeful about keeping that relationship alive, over time you will lose your enthusiasm for it. To keep your love for God intense and untarnished, you need to spend time with him and learn about him. Do you love God with the same fervor as when you were a new Christian?

GOD'S CHALLENGE

Think back on those early days when you first learned about Christ. Remember how you remained faithful even though it meant terrible suffering. . . . So do not throw away this confident trust in the Lord. Remember the great reward it brings you! HEBREWS 10:32, 35

Purpose

I don't understand why God has put me where I am. Will I ever understand his reasons?

GOD'S RESPONSE

The king loved Esther more than any of the other young women. He was so delighted with her that he set the royal crown on her head and declared her queen instead of Vashti.   *Esther 2:17*

O LORD, you have examined my heart and know everything about me. . . . You go before me and follow me. You place your hand of blessing on my head. Such knowledge is too wonderful for me, too great for me to understand!   *Psalm 139:1, 5-6*

God placed Esther on the throne even before the Jews faced the possibility of complete destruction so that when that trouble came, he would already have her in the position to help. No human effort can thwart God's plans. If you are changing jobs, position, or location and can't see God's purpose in your situation, remind yourself that God is in control. You may not understand the reason for the change, but God knows what he is doing. He may be placing you in a position today so that you can help when a need arises in the future.

GOD'S PROMISE

Do not be afraid or discouraged, for the LORD will personally go ahead of you. He will be with you; he will neither fail you nor abandon you.   DEUTERONOMY 31:8

Sacrifice

What kind of giving shows a life sacrificed for God?

GOD'S RESPONSE

"Sir, do you remember me?" Hannah asked. "I am the woman who stood here several years ago praying to the LORD. I asked the LORD to give me this boy, and he has granted my request. Now I am giving him to the LORD, and he will belong to the LORD his whole life." *1 Samuel 1:26-28*

[David said,] "O our God, we thank you and praise your glorious name! But who am I, and who are my people, that we could give anything to you? Everything we have has come from you, and we give you only what you first gave us!" *1 Chronicles 29:13-14*

 In order to keep her promise to God, Hannah gave up what she wanted most—her young son—and presented him to Eli to serve in the house of the Lord. In dedicating her son to God's service, Hannah was giving sacrificially. Do your gifts cost you little (a couple of hours on Sunday mornings, a comfortable tithe), or are they gifts of sacrifice? Are you presenting only tokens to God, or are you presenting him your entire life?

GOD'S PROMISE

Everyone who has given up houses or brothers or sisters or father or mother or children or property, for my sake, will receive a hundred times as much in return and will inherit eternal life.

MATTHEW 19:29

Celebration

I know God is to be revered, but can God be honored through fun and celebration?

God's Response

These are the LORD's appointed festivals. Celebrate them each year as official days for holy assembly by presenting special gifts to the LORD—burnt offerings, grain offerings, sacrifices, and liquid offerings—each on its proper day.   *Leviticus 23:37*

This festival will be a happy time of celebrating. . . . For seven days you must celebrate this festival to honor the LORD your God at the place he chooses, for it is he who blesses you with bountiful harvests and gives you success in all your work. This festival will be a time of great joy for all.   *Deuteronomy 16:14-15*

Honoring God involves both celebration and confession. But in the Old Testament, Israel's national holidays seem to have tipped the balance heavily in favor of celebration—the Bible lists five joyous occasions but two solemn ones. The God of the Bible encourages joy! He does not intend for our faith to consist only of meditation and introspection. He also wants us to celebrate. Serious reflection and immediate confession of sin are essential, of course. But we should balance these by celebrating who God is and what he has done for his people.

God's Challenge

Come, everyone! Clap your hands! Shout to God with joyful praise! For the LORD Most High is awesome. He is the great King of all the earth.   PSALM 47:1-2

Seeds

I just try to do whatever makes me happy, so why is my life such a mess sometimes?

GOD'S RESPONSE

Don't be misled—you cannot mock the justice of God. You will always harvest what you plant. Those who live only to satisfy their own sinful nature will harvest decay and death from that sinful nature. But those who live to please the Spirit will harvest everlasting life from the Spirit.   *Galatians 6:7-8*

The tongue can bring death or life; those who love to talk will reap the consequences.   *Proverbs 18:21*

It would certainly be a surprise if you planted corn, and pumpkins came up. It's a natural law that you reap what you sow. Every action has consequences. If you plant seeds of gossip, you will lose the trust of your friends. If you plant seeds only to please your own desires, you'll reap a crop of sorrow, confusion, and possibly even disastrous outcomes. If you plant seeds to please God, you'll reap joy and confidence in all circumstances and in the end, everlasting life. What kind of seeds are you sowing?

GOD'S CHALLENGE

I said, "Plant the good seeds of righteousness, and you will harvest a crop of love. Plow up the hard ground of your hearts, for now is the time to seek the LORD, that he may come and shower righteousness upon you."   HOSEA 10:12

Wisdom

Can I be wise?

GOD'S RESPONSE

The LORD appeared to Solomon in a dream, and God said, "What do you want? Ask, and I will give it to you!" Solomon replied, ". . . Give me an understanding heart so that I can govern your people well and know the difference between right and wrong. For who by himself is able to govern this great people of yours?"   *1 Kings 3:5-9*

If you need wisdom, ask our generous God, and he will give it to you. He will not rebuke you for asking.   *James 1:5*

When given the opportunity to ask God for anything he wanted, Solomon asked God for wisdom—"an understanding heart"—in order to lead God's people well and to make right decisions.

You can ask God for this same wisdom. Notice that Solomon asked for understanding to carry out his job; he did not ask God to do the job for him. Don't ask God to do for you what he wants to do through you. Instead, ask him to give you the wisdom to know what he wants you to do and the courage to follow through with it.

GOD'S PROMISE

Fear of the LORD is the foundation of true wisdom. All who obey his commandments will grow in wisdom.   PSALM 111:10

Adversity

How can I be sure I'll hold on to my faith in times of adversity?

GOD'S RESPONSE

Satan replied to the LORD, "Yes, but Job has good reason to fear God. You have always put a wall of protection around him and his home and his property. You have made him prosper in everything he does. Look how rich he is! But reach out and take away everything he has, and he will surely curse you to your face!" *Job 1:9-11*

Satan accurately analyzed why many people trust God: They are fair-weather believers, following God only when everything is going well or for what they can get. Adversity destroys this super-ficial faith. But adversity strengthens real faith because it causes believers to sink the roots of their faith deeper into God and his truth in order to withstand the storm.

How deep does your faith go? Put the roots of your faith deep down into God and his Word so that when adversity comes, you can withstand the storm you will have to face.

GOD'S CHALLENGE

Just as you accepted Christ Jesus as your Lord, you must continue to follow him. Let your roots grow down into him, and let your lives be built on him. Then your faith will grow strong in the truth you were taught, and you will overflow with thankfulness.

COLOSSIANS 2:6-7

Blessings

It feels as if my troubles will never end. Is there any hope of God's blessing?

GOD'S RESPONSE

Boaz took Ruth into his home, and she became his wife. When he slept with her, the LORD enabled her to become pregnant, and she gave birth to a son. Then the women of the town said to Naomi, "Praise the LORD, who has now provided a redeemer for your family! May this child be famous in Israel. May he restore your youth and care for you in your old age. For he is the son of your daughter-in-law who loves you and has been better to you than seven sons!" *Ruth 4:13-15*

Naomi had suffered great tragedy—first the death of her husband and then the deaths of her two grown sons. So great was her sorrow that she told people to call her "Mara," which means bitter. Throughout her tough times, however, Naomi continued to trust the God of her people, and in time, God brought great blessing out of her tragedy, blessing even greater than having "seven sons," or an abundance of heirs.

From your sorrow and calamity, God can bring great blessing. Don't turn your back on him when tragedy strikes. Instead of asking, "How could God allow this to happen to me?" ponder how you can remain faithful in the situation. God can redeem even your hardest times and bring great blessing from great sorrow.

GOD'S PROMISE

Blessed are those who trust in the LORD and have made the LORD their hope and confidence. **JEREMIAH 17:7**

Family

How should I prioritize my responsibilities with work, service, and family?

GOD'S RESPONSE

Standing near the cross were Jesus' mother, and his mother's sister, Mary (the wife of Clopas), and Mary Magdalene. When Jesus saw his mother standing there beside the disciple he loved, he said to her, "Dear woman, here is your son." And he said to this disciple, "Here is your mother." And from then on this disciple took her into his home.   *John 19:25-27*

Those who won't care for their relatives, especially those in their own household, have denied the true faith.   *1 Timothy 5:8*

Children are a gift from the LORD; they are a reward from him.
Psalm 127:3

Even when Jesus was dying on the cross, he was concerned about his family. He delegated the responsibility for caring for his mother, Mary, to John.

Your family members are gifts from God, and he wants you to value and care for them. Neither Christian work nor key responsibilities in any other job or position excuse you from caring for your family. What can you do today to show your love to your family?

GOD'S CHALLENGE

Share your food with the hungry, and give shelter to the homeless. Give clothes to those who need them, and do not hide from relatives who need your help. ISAIAH 58:7-8

Vision

When God shows me an opportunity for his work in the world, how can I get others to catch the vision?

GOD'S RESPONSE

I said to them, "You know very well what trouble we are in. Jerusalem lies in ruins, and its gates have been destroyed by fire. Let us rebuild the wall of Jerusalem and end this disgrace!" Then I told them about how the gracious hand of God had been on me, and about my conversation with the king.   *Nehemiah 2:17-18*

Spiritual revival often begins with one person's vision. Nehemiah had a vision for rebuilding Jerusalem's walls. He shared it with enthusiasm and inspired Jerusalem's leaders to join him.

It's easy to underestimate people and not challenge them with your dreams for God's work in the world. But when God plants an idea in your mind to accomplish something for him, share that idea with others and trust the Holy Spirit to impress them with similar thoughts. Don't regard yourself as the only one through whom God is working. Often God uses one person to express the vision and others to turn it into reality. When you encourage and inspire others, you put teamwork into action to accomplish God's goals.

GOD'S PROMISE

It's not important who does the planting, or who does the watering. What's important is that God makes the seed grow. The one who plants and the one who waters work together with the same purpose. And both will be rewarded for their own hard work.

1 CORINTHIANS 3:7-8

The Body of Christ

Does my church really need me?

GOD'S RESPONSE

Eliashib the high priest and the other priests started to rebuild at the Sheep Gate. . . . People from the town of Jericho worked next to them, and beyond them was Zaccur son of Imri. . . . The Fish Gate was built by the sons of Hassenaah. . . . Meremoth son of Uriah and grandson of Hakkoz repaired the next section of wall. Beside him were Meshullam son of Berekiah and grandson of Meshezabel, and then Zadok son of Baana. *Nehemiah 3:1-4*

All of you together are Christ's body, and each of you is a part of it.
1 Corinthians 12:27

All the citizens of Jerusalem did their part in rebuilding the city wall (see Nehemiah 3). Similarly, the work of the church requires every member's effort in order for the body of Christ to function effectively. The body needs you! Find a place to serve God, and start contributing whatever time, talent, and resources God has given you. Are you doing your part?

GOD'S CHALLENGE

If your gift is serving others, serve them well. If you are a teacher, teach well. If your gift is to encourage others, be encouraging. If it is giving, give generously. If God has given you leadership ability, take the responsibility seriously. And if you have a gift for showing kindness to others, do it gladly. ROMANS 12:7-8

Neighbors

How am I to love my neighbors?

GOD'S RESPONSE

Love your neighbor as yourself.   *Matthew 22:39*

"The Samaritan soothed [the man's] wounds with olive oil and wine and bandaged them. Then he put the man on his own donkey and took him to an inn, where he took care of him. The next day he handed the innkeeper two silver coins, telling him, 'Take care of this man. If his bill runs higher than this, I'll pay you the next time I'm here.'

"Now which of these three would you say was a neighbor to the man who was attacked by bandits?" Jesus asked.

The man replied, "The one who showed him mercy."

Then Jesus said, "Yes, now go and do the same."

Luke 10:34-37

Why did Jesus say to love your neighbor as yourself? Because he knows that our first instinct is to take care of ourselves. If we can train ourselves to care for others the way we care for ourselves, then we will have truly made our neighbors a priority. And caring for others is what love is all about. Every time you show love to your neighbors, God is touching hearts—theirs and yours.

GOD'S CHALLENGE

It is good when you obey the royal law as found in the Scriptures: "Love your neighbor as yourself." JAMES 2:8

Testimony

***What are the ways in which my life can be a
testimony for Jesus?***

GOD'S RESPONSE

The members of the council were amazed when they saw the
boldness of Peter and John, for they could see that they were
ordinary men with no special training in the Scriptures. They also
recognized them as men who had been with Jesus.   *Acts 4:13*

Those who obey God's word truly show how completely they love
him. That is how we know we are living in him. Those who say
they live in God should live their lives as Jesus did.   *1 John 2:5-6*

Knowing that Peter and John were ordinary men, the council
was amazed at what being with Jesus had done for them. No longer
were they backward, fearful disciples. Now, through the Holy
Spirit, they were courageous and able to boldly share the truth of
Jesus with others.

A changed life convinces people of Christ's power. One of your
clearest testimonies is the difference others see in your life and
attitudes since you believed in Christ.

GOD'S CHALLENGE

Be careful to live properly among your unbelieving neighbors.
Then even if they accuse you of doing wrong, they will see your
honorable behavior, and they will give honor to God when he
judges the world.   1 PETER 2:12

Love

How can I grow in my love for others?

GOD'S RESPONSE

Dear brothers and sisters, we can't help but thank God for you, because your faith is flourishing and your love for one another is growing.   *2 Thessalonians 1:3*

Dear friends, let us continue to love one another, for love comes from God. Anyone who loves is a child of God and knows God. But anyone who does not love does not know God, for God is love.   *1 John 4:7-8*

What is the key to a growing love for other people? A vital faith in God. When your faith in God flourishes, you develop an increasing ability to love others. Why? Because God is love. When the love of God flows into you, the love of God must flow out of you. A strong and loving upward connection with the Lord builds a strong and loving outward love connection with others.

GOD'S PROMISE

This hope will not lead to disappointment. For we know how dearly God loves us, because he has given us the Holy Spirit to fill our hearts with his love.   ROMANS 5:5

Making a Difference

How can I make a difference in the lives of those around me?

GOD'S RESPONSE

O people, the LORD has told you what is good, and this is what he requires of you: to do what is right, to love mercy, and to walk humbly with your God. *Micah 6:8*

In an age in which religion was making little difference in people's lives, the prophet Micah said that what God required of his people was to do what was right, to show mercy to others, and to walk humbly with God.

The same requirements hold for us today. In a world that is unjust, we must act justly and do what is right. In a world of tough breaks, we must be merciful. In a world of pride and self-sufficiency, we must walk humbly with God. Only when we live according to God's way will we begin to make a difference in our homes, our society, and our world.

GOD'S PROMISE

God blesses those who are humble, for they will inherit the whole earth. God blesses those who hunger and thirst for justice, for they will be satisfied. God blesses those who are merciful, for they will be shown mercy. MATTHEW 5:5-7

Spiritual Gifts

How can I use my spiritual gifts more effectively?

GOD'S RESPONSE

In his grace, God has given us different gifts for doing certain things well. So if God has given you the ability to prophesy, speak out with as much faith as God has given you. If your gift is serving others, serve them well. If you are a teacher, teach well. If your gift is to encourage others, be encouraging. If it is giving, give generously. If God has given you leadership ability, take the responsibility seriously. And if you have a gift for showing kindness to others, do it gladly.   *Romans 12:6-8*

God's gifts differ in nature, power, and effectiveness according to his wisdom and graciousness, not according to our faith. God will give us the spiritual power necessary and appropriate to carry out each responsibility. Although we can work diligently to sharpen our ministry skills, we cannot, by our own effort or willpower, drum up more "spiritual giftedness" and thus become more effective teachers or servants. These are God's gifts to his people, and he gives faith and power as he wills. Our role is to be faithful and to seek ways to serve others with the gifts Christ has given us.

GOD'S PROMISE

God has given each of you a gift from his great variety of spiritual gifts. Use them well to serve one another. . . . Do it with all the strength and energy that God supplies. Then everything you do will bring glory to God through Jesus Christ.   1 PETER 4:10-11

Light

How can I be a light to those around me who don't know God?

GOD'S RESPONSE

Jesus asked them, "Would anyone light a lamp and then put it under a basket or under a bed? Of course not! A lamp is placed on a stand, where its light will shine." *Mark 4:21*

What is the purpose of a lamp? To illuminate the darkness and help you see. If a lamp doesn't provide light, it is useless. Complacency, resentment, stubbornness of heart, or disobedience could keep God's light from shining through you to others. Does your life show other people how to see God more clearly and live for him? If not, ask yourself whether there are some "baskets" in your life that have hidden your light. In what ways can you set up "stands" for the light of God's love to shine out from you?

GOD'S CHALLENGE

Once you were full of darkness, but now you have light from the Lord. So live as people of light! For this light within you produces only what is good and right and true. EPHESIANS 5:8-9

Appearances

How can I "look good" on the inside?

GOD'S RESPONSE

[Kish's] son Saul was the most handsome man in Israel—head and shoulders taller than anyone else in the land.   *1 Samuel 9:2*

[Jesus said,] "You are like whitewashed tombs—beautiful on the outside but filled on the inside with dead people's bones and all sorts of impurity. Outwardly you look like righteous people, but inwardly your hearts are filled with hypocrisy and lawlessness."

Matthew 23:27-28

Saul was tall, handsome, strong, rich, and powerful, but all of those qualities were not enough to make him someone we should emulate. He was tall physically, but he was small in God's eyes. He was handsome, but his sin made him ugly. He was strong, but his lack of faith made him weak. He was rich, but he was spiritually bankrupt. He could give orders to many, but he couldn't command their respect or allegiance. Saul looked good on the outside, but he was decaying on the inside. A right relationship with God and a strong character are much more important than a good-looking exterior.

GOD'S CHALLENGE

Don't be concerned about the outward beauty of fancy hairstyles, expensive jewelry, or beautiful clothes. You should clothe yourselves instead with the beauty that comes from within, the unfading beauty of a gentle and quiet spirit, which is so precious to God.

1 PETER 3:3-4

Character

What is one of the marks of a person of strong character?

GOD'S RESPONSE

Better to be patient than powerful; better to have self-control than to conquer a city.   *Proverbs 16:32*

Avoiding a fight is a mark of honor; only fools insist on quarreling.
Proverbs 20:3

Sensible people control their temper; they earn respect by overlooking wrongs.   *Proverbs 19:11*

A person who is truly confident of his or her physical strength does not need to parade it. A truly brave person does not look for chances to prove it. A resourceful person can find a way out of a fight. A sensible person chooses to avoid retaliating. Foolish people find it impossible to avoid conflict. Men and women of character can. What kind of person are you?

GOD'S PROMISE

Don't repay evil for evil. Don't retaliate with insults when people insult you. Instead, pay them back with a blessing. That is what God has called you to do, and he will bless you for it.

1 PETER 3:9

Standing for God

Will God come to my rescue when I stand up for him?

GOD'S RESPONSE

Daniel was determined not to defile himself by eating the food
and wine given to them by the king. He asked the chief of staff
for permission not to eat these unacceptable foods. Now God had
given the chief of staff both respect and affection for Daniel.

Daniel 1:8-9

God moved with an unseen hand to change the heart of this
Babylonian chief of staff. Daniel's moral conviction made a strong
impact on the king's representative.

God promises to be with his people in times of trial and temptation. He was with Daniel and his friends in their determination
not to eat of the king's rich foods. And his active intervention may
come for you just when you take a stand for him. Stand strong for
God, and trust him to protect you in ways you may not be able to
see right now.

GOD'S PROMISE

When you go through deep waters, I will be with you. When you
go through rivers of difficulty, you will not drown. When you walk
through the fire of oppression, you will not be burned up; the
flames will not consume you.   ISAIAH 43:2

Talking about It

Where can I find the confidence to talk to others about God?

GOD'S RESPONSE

The high priest and his officials, who were Sadducees, were filled with jealousy. They arrested the apostles and put them in the public jail. But an angel of the Lord came at night, opened the gates of the jail, and brought them out. Then he told them, "Go to the Temple and give the people this message of life!" So at daybreak the apostles entered the Temple, as they were told, and immediately began teaching.   *Acts 5:17-21*

Suppose someone threatened to kill you if you didn't stop talking about God. You might think seriously about keeping quiet. But after being threatened by powerful religious leaders, arrested, jailed, and miraculously released, the apostles went right back to preaching the Good News. This was nothing less than the evidence of God's power working through them! When you are convinced of the truth of Christ's resurrection and have experienced the presence and power of his Holy Spirit, you also will have confidence to speak out for Christ.

GOD'S PROMISE

I pray that God, the source of hope, will fill you completely with joy and peace because you trust in him. Then you will overflow with confident hope through the power of the Holy Spirit.

ROMANS 15:13

Boldness

When I stand boldly for God, what outcomes can I expect?

GOD'S RESPONSE

[The astrologers] said to King Nebuchadnezzar, "Long live the king! You issued a decree requiring all the people to bow down and worship the gold statue. . . . That decree also states that those who refuse to obey must be thrown into a blazing furnace. But there are some Jews—Shadrach, Meshach, and Abednego—whom you have put in charge of the province of Babylon. They pay no attention to you, Your Majesty. They refuse to serve your gods and do not worship the gold statue you have set up." *Daniel 3:9-12*

Why didn't Shadrach, Meshach, and Abednego just bow to the statue of the king and then tell God they didn't mean it? Because they had determined never to worship another god, and they boldly stood by their commitment. As a result, they were led away to be executed. These men did not know whether or not God would deliver them, but they *did* know they would not worship an idol. Are you ready to take a stand for God no matter what? When you do, you will stand out. The consequences may be painful, and your action may not always have a happy ending in this life. But you can be prepared to say, "If God rescues me, or if he doesn't, I will serve only him."

GOD'S CHALLENGE

Fear the LORD and serve him wholeheartedly. . . . Serve the LORD alone. But if you refuse to serve the LORD, then choose today whom you will serve. . . . But as for me and my family, we will serve the LORD. JOSHUA 24:14-15

Church

Can I help make my church more attractive to unbelievers?

GOD'S RESPONSE

The apostles performed many miraculous signs and wonders.
. . . [The believers] worshiped together at the Temple each day,
met in homes for the Lord's Supper, and shared their meals with
great joy and generosity—all the while praising God and enjoying
the goodwill of all the people. And each day the Lord added to
their fellowship those who were being saved.   *Acts 2:43, 46-47*

What makes Christianity attractive? It is easy to be drawn to a
church because of its programs, good speakers, size, beautiful facilities, or opportunities for fellowship. In the New Testament, people
were attracted to the early church by expressions of God's power
at work: the character of the leaders and the generosity, sincerity,
honesty, and unity of the members.

God wants to add believers to his church, but newer and better
programs or larger and fancier facilities are not the answer. It is the
power and love of Jesus radiating out of his people that is attractive
to others.

GOD'S CHALLENGE

Because of God's grace to me, I have laid the foundation like an
expert builder. Now others are building on it. But whoever is building on this foundation must be very careful. For no one can lay any
foundation other than the one we already have—Jesus Christ.

1 CORINTHIANS 3:10-11

Making Peace

What does it look like to live in peace with others?

GOD'S RESPONSE

The Scriptures say, "If you want to enjoy life and see many happy days, keep your tongue from speaking evil and your lips from telling lies. Turn away from evil and do good. Search for peace, and work to maintain it." *1 Peter 3:10-11*

Encourage each other. Live in harmony and peace. Then the God of love and peace will be with you. *2 Corinthians 13:11*

Work at living in peace with everyone, and work at living a holy life, for those who are not holy will not see the Lord.

Hebrews 12:14

Too often we see peace as merely the absence of conflict, and we may think of peacemaking as a somewhat passive role. But an effective peacemaker actively pursues peace by building good relationships, knowing that peace is a by-product of commitment. The peacemaker anticipates problems and deals with them before they occur. When conflicts arise, a peacemaker brings them into the open and deals with them before they grow unmanageable. Making peace can be harder than waging war, but it can result in harmony and happiness.

GOD'S PROMISE

Look at those who are honest and good, for a wonderful future awaits those who love peace. PSALM 37:37

Patience

Why does it sometimes seem as if God is indifferent to the evil in the world? Why doesn't he do something?

GOD'S RESPONSE

This vision is for a future time. It describes the end, and it will be fulfilled. If it seems slow in coming, wait patiently, for it will surely take place. It will not be delayed.   *Habakkuk 2:3*

Be still in the presence of the LORD, and wait patiently for him to act. Don't worry about evil people who prosper or fret about their wicked schemes.   *Psalm 37:7*

Evil and injustice often seem to have the upper hand in the world. Like the prophet Habakkuk, Christians may feel angry and discouraged as they see what is going on around them. When Habakkuk complained to God about the situation, God answered him the same way he would answer us: "If it seems slow in coming, wait patiently, for it will surely take place." It isn't easy to be patient, but it helps to remember that God hates sin far more than we do. Punishment of sin will certainly come. When we don't understand why God allows events to occur as they do, we need to remember God's words to Habakkuk: "Wait patiently."

GOD'S PROMISE

Sin will be rampant everywhere, and the love of many will grow cold. But the one who endures to the end will be saved.

MATTHEW 24:12-13

Caring for Others

How should I care for others? What should be my motive?

GOD'S RESPONSE

I myself, as well as my brothers and my workers, have been lending the people money and grain, but now let us stop this business of charging interest.　*Nehemiah 5:10*

There were no needy people among them, because those who owned land or houses would sell them and bring the money to the apostles to give to those in need.　*Acts 4:34-35*

If one part suffers, all the parts suffer with it, and if one part is honored, all the parts are glad.　*1 Corinthians 12:26*

 Nehemiah told the Israelites to stop charging interest on the loans they made to the needy. God never intended that people profit from others' misfortune. In contrast to the values of this world, God says that caring for one another is more important than personal gain. When a Christian brother or sister suffers, we all suffer. God wants us to help needy believers, not exploit them for our own monetary gain. The Jerusalem church was praised for working together to eliminate poverty. Make it a practice to help those in need.

GOD'S PROMISE

Whoever gives to the poor will lack nothing, but those who close their eyes to poverty will be cursed.　PROVERBS 28:27

Religion

I'm a religious person, but am I missing the point?

God's Response

[Jesus said,] "You search the Scriptures because you think they give you eternal life. But the Scriptures point to me! Yet you refuse to come to me to receive this life." *John 5:39-40*

The people in Jerusalem and their leaders did not recognize Jesus as the one the prophets had spoken about. Instead, they condemned him, and in doing this they fulfilled the prophets' words that are read every Sabbath. *Acts 13:27*

The religious leaders knew the teachings of their Scriptures, but they failed to recognize the Messiah to whom the Scriptures pointed. They knew the rules but missed the Savior. Entrenched in their own religious system, they refused to acknowledge the Son of God, even when he stood before them.

Are there places in your spiritual walk where you ignore Christ? Do you serve in your church but forget for whom you work? Do you worship on Sunday mornings but forget the one you're praising? Are your prayers personal conversations with God or empty words and requests? Don't become so involved in "religion" that you miss Christ.

God's Challenge

True circumcision is not merely obeying the letter of the law; rather, it is a change of heart produced by God's Spirit. And a person with a changed heart seeks praise from God, not from people. ROMANS 2:23, 29

Adaptability

How can I learn to adapt when life changes so quickly?

GOD'S RESPONSE

It was by faith that Abraham obeyed when God called him to leave home and go to another land that God would give him as his inheritance. He went without knowing where he was going.

Hebrews 11:8

The ability to adapt goes hand in hand with trusting God. When you trust that he loves you and has the best plans for your life, you can learn to adapt willingly and quickly when the road of life encounters sharp turns. You don't need to know all the details of God's plan in order to adapt to it. Full knowledge of all the details is not necessary for obedience. Sometimes, adapting to God's way means moving forward in faith and obedience and acknowledging that when he knows the way, you don't have to.

GOD'S PROMISE

For those who are righteous, the way is not steep and rough. You are a God who does what is right, and you smooth out the path ahead of them.   ISAIAH 26:7

Conscience

How can I keep my conscience clear?

GOD'S RESPONSE

[Job declared,] "I vow by the living God, who has taken away my rights, by the Almighty who has embittered my soul—As long as I live, while I have breath from God, my lips will speak no evil, and my tongue will speak no lies. I will never concede that you are right; I will defend my integrity until I die. I will maintain my innocence without wavering. My conscience is clear for as long as I live." *Job 27:2-6*

How important Job's record became as he was being accused. In spite of the accusations of his friends, Job was able to declare that his conscience was clear. Only God's forgiveness and the determination to live right before God can give a clear conscience.

Like Job, we can't claim sinless lives, but we can claim forgiven lives. When we confess our sins to God, he forgives us. Then we can live with clear consciences.

GOD'S PROMISE

Just think how much more the blood of Christ will purify our consciences from sinful deeds so that we can worship the living God. For by the power of the eternal Spirit, Christ offered himself to God as a perfect sacrifice for our sins. . . . For Christ died to set them free from the penalty of the sins they had committed.

HEBREWS 9:14-15

Friendship

What is the mark of genuine friendship?

GOD'S RESPONSE

A friend is always loyal, and a brother is born to help in time of need.   *Proverbs 17:17*

There are "friends" who destroy each other, but a real friend sticks closer than a brother.   *Proverbs 18:24*

Many will say they are loyal friends, but who can find one who is truly reliable?   *Proverbs 20:6*

There is a vast difference between knowing someone well and being a true friend. The greatest evidence of genuine friendship is loyalty—being available to help in times of distress or personal struggle. Too many people are fair-weather friends. They stick around when the friendship helps them and things are going smoothly and then leave when the relationship hits a bump or when they're not getting anything out of it themselves. Think of your friends and assess your loyalty to them. What kind of friend are you?

GOD'S PROMISE

Love never gives up, never loses faith, is always hopeful, and endures through every circumstance.   1 CORINTHIANS 13:7

Commitment

How can I remain focused in my commitment to God?

GOD'S RESPONSE

Fear God and obey his commands, for this is everyone's duty.

Ecclesiastes 12:13

Now, Israel, what does the LORD your God require of you? He requires only that you fear the LORD your God, and live in a way that pleases him, and love him and serve him with all your heart and soul.   *Deuteronomy 10:12*

 In the conclusion to the book of Ecclesiastes, Solomon presents his antidotes for the two main ailments of the human condition. Those who struggle with a lack of purpose and direction in life need to fear God and live in a way that pleases him. It is more than a coincidence that Moses gave these same instructions to the people of Israel as they prepared to enter the Promised Land. Fearing God puts your relationship with him in proper perspective. Living in a way that pleases him (obeying his commands) demonstrates the importance you place on your relationship with him. If you do these things, your life will maintain purpose and direction.

GOD'S PROMISE

This is the message I proclaim—that the day is coming when God, through Christ Jesus, will judge everyone's secret life.

ROMANS 2:16

First Step

I know what God wants me to do, but how do I find the courage to take that next step?

GOD'S RESPONSE

The people left their camp to cross the Jordan, and the priests who were carrying the Ark of the Covenant went ahead of them. It was the harvest season, and the Jordan was overflowing its banks. But as soon as the feet of the priests who were carrying the Ark touched the water at the river's edge, the water above that point began backing up. . . . And the water below that point flowed on to the Dead Sea until the riverbed was dry. Then all the people crossed over near the town of Jericho.   *Joshua 3:14-16*

The Israelites were eager to enter the Promised Land, conquer the people living there, and live peacefully. But first they had to cross the flood-level waters of the Jordan River. God gave them specific instructions: In order to cross, the priests had to step into the water. What if the priests had been afraid to take that first step?

Often God provides no solution to your problems until you trust him and move ahead with what you know you should do. What are the rivers, or obstacles, in your life? In obedience to God, take that first step into the water.

GOD'S PROMISE

When you go through deep waters, I will be with you. When you go through rivers of difficulty, you will not drown. When you walk through the fire of oppression, you will not be burned up; the flames will not consume you. For I am the LORD, your God, the Holy One of Israel, your Savior.   ISAIAH 43:2

Regrets

How do I deal with regrets about my past?

GOD'S RESPONSE

[God] has removed our sins as far from us as the east is from the west.   *Psalm 103:12*

Now, once for all time, [Christ] has appeared at the end of the age to remove sin by his own death as a sacrifice.   *Hebrews 9:26*

Have you ever tried to drive far enough west that you would end up going east? It's not possible. East and west never meet. This is a powerful picture of God's forgiveness: When he forgives your sin, he separates it from you and chooses never to bring it to mind again.

Because God forgives and forgets, you don't need to wallow in feelings of regret for things that happened in the past. If you tend to dredge up the ugly moments, remind yourself that God has wiped your record clean. When you're still feeling tied to the memories of past sins, ask God to release you with his forgiveness!

GOD'S PROMISE

I will forgive their wickedness, and I will never again remember their sins.   HEBREWS 8:12

Worth

How does knowing God affect my sense of self-worth?

GOD'S RESPONSE

Man is made in God's image and reflects God's glory.
1 Corinthians 11:7

Put on your new nature, created to be like God—truly righteous and holy.   *Ephesians 4:24*

Be honest in your evaluation of yourselves, measuring yourselves by the faith God has given us.   *Romans 12:3*

Knowing that you are made in God's image and thus share many of his characteristics provides a solid basis for self-worth. Human worth is not based on possessions, achievements, physical attractiveness, or public acclaim. Instead, it is based on being made in God's image. Likewise, criticizing or degrading yourself is criticizing what God has made and the abilities he has given you. Remembering you are made in the image of God but that you owe everything you are to him keeps your self-worth in a healthy balance.

GOD'S CHALLENGE

Imitate God, therefore, in everything you do, because you are his dear children. Live a life filled with love, following the example of Christ.   EPHESIANS 5:1-2

Value

How should I treat those whom our society devalues?

God's Response

A man with leprosy came and knelt in front of Jesus, begging to be healed. "If you are willing, you can heal me and make me clean," he said. Moved with compassion, Jesus reached out and touched him. "I am willing," he said. "Be healed!"   *Mark 1:40-41*

The real value of a person is on the inside, not on the outside. Although someone's body may be diseased or deformed, that person is no less valuable to God. No person is too disgusting for God's loving touch. In a sense, we are all diseased, deformed by the ugliness of sin. But in sending his Son, Jesus, our heavenly Father has touched us, healing us and proving his unconditional love for us. When you feel ugly or feel repulsed by someone else, stop and picture God reaching out and touching that person—and you!

God's Challenge

Accept each other just as Christ has accepted you so that God will be given glory.   ROMANS 15:7

Miracles

Can God really do miraculous things in my life?

GOD'S RESPONSE

Who can list the glorious miracles of the LORD? Who can ever praise him enough?   *Psalm 106:2*

[The God of Daniel] rescues and saves his people; he performs miraculous signs and wonders in the heavens and on earth.

Daniel 6:27

How precious are your thoughts about me, O God. They cannot be numbered!   *Psalm 139:17*

If you ever stopped to list all the mighty acts in the Bible, you would be astounded. They cover every aspect of life. The more you think about what God has done, the more you can appreciate the miracles he has done for you—your birth, personal development, salvation, specific guidance, healing, protection, loving friends and family—the list goes on and on. If you think you have never seen a miracle, look closer. You will see God's power and loving intervention on your behalf. God still performs great miracles!

GOD'S PROMISE

May all who search for you be filled with joy and gladness in you. May those who love your salvation repeatedly shout, "The LORD is great!"   PSALM 40:16

God's No

When God says no to my prayers, is he rejecting me?

GOD'S RESPONSE

David said, "I am living in a beautiful cedar palace, but the Ark of God is out there in a tent!" . . . That same night the LORD said to Nathan, "Go and tell my servant David, 'This is what the LORD has declared: Are you the one to build a house for me to live in? . . . When you die and are buried with your ancestors, I will raise up one of your descendants, your own offspring, and I will make his kingdom strong. He is the one who will build a house—a temple—for my name. And I will secure his royal throne forever. Your house and your kingdom will continue before me for all time, and your throne will be secure forever.'" *2 Samuel 7:2, 4-5, 12-13, 16*

David's desire to build a beautiful house for God was good, but God said no. Was God rejecting David? No, in fact, God was planning to do something even greater in David's life than allowing him the prestige of building the Temple. Although God turned down David's request, he promised to continue the house of David forever. David's earthly dynasty ended four centuries later, but Jesus Christ, a direct descendant of David, was the ultimate fulfillment of this promise. Have you prayed with good intentions, only to have God say no? This is God's way of directing you to a greater purpose in your life. Accepting God's no requires as much faith as carrying out his yes.

GOD'S PROMISE

The LORD will not reject his people; he will not abandon his special possession. PSALM 94:14

Coincidence

Is God really in control, or are the events of my life just coincidence?

God's Response

The king had trouble sleeping, so he ordered an attendant to bring the book of the history of his reign so it could be read to him. In those records he discovered an account of how Mordecai had exposed the plot of Bigthana and Teresh, two of the eunuchs who guarded the door to the king's private quarters. They had plotted to assassinate King Xerxes.   *Esther 6:1-2*

One night, unable to sleep, King Xerxes decided to review the history of his reign, and his servants read to him about Mordecai's good deed. This might seem merely coincidental, but God is always at work. He had placed Esther in the palace so that in time, she would be able to play a part in God's plan to save his people from a plot to destroy them.

God works quietly and patiently throughout your life as well. The events that have come together are not mere coincidence. You may not see the connection right now, but they are the result of God's sovereign control over the course of your life.

God's Challenge

[Mordecai told Esther,] "If you keep quiet at a time like this, deliverance and relief for the Jews will arise from some other place, but you and your relatives will die. Who knows if perhaps you were made queen for just such a time as this?"   ESTHER 4:14

Disagreement

How can I witness to someone who disagrees with my beliefs?

GOD'S RESPONSE

John's disciples came to him and said, "Rabbi, the man you met on the other side of the Jordan River, the one you identified as the Messiah, is also baptizing people. And everybody is going to him instead of coming to us." John replied, "No one can receive anything unless God gives it from heaven. You yourselves know how plainly I told you, 'I am not the Messiah. I am only here to prepare the way for him.'" *John 3:26-28*

Some people look for points of disagreement so they can sow seeds of discord, discontent, and doubt. John the Baptist ended this theological argument by focusing on his devotion to Christ. It is divisive to try to force others to believe your way. You can't do it anyway, because only God can change hearts and give people the faith to believe in him. Instead, live in such a way that others will take notice and ask questions about what "makes you tick." Then, when God gives you the opportunity, you can tell them what Christ has done for you. No one can argue with that.

GOD'S CHALLENGE

A servant of the Lord must not quarrel but must be kind to everyone, be able to teach, and be patient with difficult people. Gently instruct those who oppose the truth. Perhaps God will change those people's hearts, and they will learn the truth.

2 TIMOTHY 2:24-25

Assumptions

Is it safe to assume that someone's suffering is a consequence of sin?

GOD'S RESPONSE

Eliphaz the Temanite replied to Job: ". . . Stop and think! Do the innocent die? When have the upright been destroyed? My experience shows that those who plant trouble and cultivate evil will harvest the same." *Job 4:1, 7-8*

[Eliphaz concluded,] "We have studied life and found all this to be true. Listen to my counsel, and apply it to yourself." *Job 5:27*

Part of what Eliphaz said is true, and part is false. It is true that those who promote sin and trouble eventually will be punished. It is false that all suffering is brought about by personal sin. Some suffering may be the result of someone else's sin, or it may be a testing from God. Some suffering is simply the result of living in a fallen world. Eliphaz's comments are an example of what we should try to avoid—making false assumptions about others based on our own experiences.

GOD'S PROMISE

Don't make judgments about anyone ahead of time—before the Lord returns. For he will bring our darkest secrets to light and will reveal our private motives. Then God will give to each one whatever praise is due. 1 CORINTHIANS 4:5

Sin

Will a onetime sinful action really hurt me in the long run?

God's Response

Solomon built such shrines for all his foreign wives to use for burning incense and sacrificing to their gods. The LORD was very angry with Solomon, for his heart had turned away from the LORD, the God of Israel, who had appeared to him twice. He had warned Solomon specifically about worshiping other gods, but Solomon did not listen to the LORD's command.   *1 Kings 11:8-10*

 Solomon didn't turn away from God all at once or even in a brief moment. His spiritual coldness started with a minor departure from God's laws. Over the years, that "little" sin grew until it resulted in Solomon's downfall. A little sin can be the first step in turning away from God.

It is not the sins you don't know about but the sins you know about and yet excuse that cause the greatest trouble. Never let any sin go unchallenged. Is such a sin spreading in your life like a deadly cancer? Don't excuse it. Confess it to God, and ask him for strength to resist further temptation.

God's Challenge

Be careful then, dear brothers and sisters. Make sure that your own hearts are not evil and unbelieving, turning you away from the living God. You must warn each other every day, while it is still "today," so that none of you will be deceived by sin and hardened against God.   HEBREWS 3:12-13

Motives

Does God know when I mean to do the right or wrong thing?

God's Response

End the evil of those who are wicked, and defend the righteous. For you look deep within the mind and heart, O righteous God.

Psalm 7:9

If you plan to do evil, you will be lost; if you plan to do good, you will receive unfailing love and faithfulness. *Proverbs 14:22*

 God looks "deep within the mind and heart." Nothing is hidden from him—and this can be either terrifying or comforting. Your thoughts are an open book to him. Because he knows even your motives, you have no place to hide, no way to pretend you can get away with sin. But that very knowledge also gives you great comfort. You don't have to impress God or maintain a false front of respectability. He knows when your motives are good and right, even if the end result doesn't turn out as you hoped.

God's Promise

I, the LORD, search all hearts and examine secret motives. I give all people their due rewards, according to what their actions deserve. JEREMIAH 17:10

June 13

Trials

I'm a Christian, so why do I experience so many trials?

GOD'S RESPONSE

There is wonderful joy ahead, even though you have to endure many trials for a little while. These trials will show that your faith is genuine. . . . When your faith remains strong through many trials, it will bring you much praise and glory and honor on the day when Jesus Christ is revealed to the whole world.   *1 Peter 1:6-7*

When your faith is tested, your endurance has a chance to grow. So let it grow, for when your endurance is fully developed, you will be perfect and complete, needing nothing.   *James 1:3-4*

When Peter speaks of trials in 1 Peter 1:6-7, he is not talking about natural disasters or general difficulties but rather about how the unbelieving world responds to people of faith. All believers face trials when they let their light shine into the darkness. You must accept these trials as part of the refining process that burns away impurities in your faith and makes you more and more like Christ. Trials teach you patience and help you to grow in endurance and maturity.

GOD'S PROMISE

In his kindness God called you to share in his eternal glory by means of Christ Jesus. So after you have suffered a little while, he will restore, support, and strengthen you, and he will place you on a firm foundation.   **1 PETER 5:10**

Witnessing

What is the approach of an effective witness for Christ?

GOD'S RESPONSE

[Jesus said,] "You will receive power when the Holy Spirit comes upon you. And you will be my witnesses, telling people about me everywhere—in Jerusalem, throughout Judea, in Samaria, and to the ends of the earth."   *Acts 1:8*

When we brought you the Good News, it was not only with words but also with power, for the Holy Spirit gave you full assurance that what we said was true.   *1 Thessalonians 1:5*

It was also written that this message would be proclaimed in the authority of [Jesus'] name to all the nations, beginning in Jerusalem: "There is forgiveness of sins for all who repent."   *Luke 24:47*

Jesus promised his disciples that they would receive power to witness when they had received the Holy Spirit. Notice the progression: (1) They would receive the Holy Spirit, (2) he would give them power, and (3) they would witness with extraordinary results. Often we try to reverse the order and witness by our own power and authority. Effective witnessing is not showing what you can do for God. It is showing and telling what God has done for you.

GOD'S CHALLENGE

Has the LORD redeemed you? Then speak out! Tell others he has redeemed you from your enemies.   PSALM 107:2

June 15

Unity

How can I be unified with someone I don't agree with or can't even understand?

GOD'S RESPONSE

Some of the believers who went to Antioch from Cyprus and Cyrene began preaching to the Gentiles about the Lord Jesus. The power of the Lord was with them, and a large number of these Gentiles believed and turned to the Lord. . . . (It was at Antioch that the believers were first called Christians.)   *Acts 11:20-21, 26*

The young church at Antioch was a curious mixture of Jews (who spoke Greek or Aramaic) and Gentiles. It is significant that this is the first place where the believers were called Christians (or "Christ-ones"), because all they had in common was Christ—not their race, not their culture, not even their language. Christ's love crosses all boundaries and unites all people.

GOD'S PROMISE

You are all children of God through faith in Christ Jesus. And all who have been united with Christ in baptism have put on Christ, like putting on new clothes. There is no longer Jew or Gentile, slave or free, male and female. For you are all one in Christ Jesus.   GALATIANS 3:26-28

Mercy

How does God's mercy affect my daily life?

GOD'S RESPONSE

The LORD is compassionate and merciful, slow to get angry and filled with unfailing love.   *Psalm 103:8*

Sin is no longer your master, for you no longer live under the requirements of the law. Instead, you live under the freedom of God's grace.   *Romans 6:14*

Let us come boldly to the throne of our gracious God. There we will receive his mercy, and we will find grace to help us when we need it most.   *Hebrews 4:16*

Mercy is another word for not getting what we deserve. Although all people deserve God's judgment, in his greatest act of mercy, he offers salvation and eternal life even though we often ignore him, neglect him, and rebel against him. Because of God's mercy, he forgives us and sets us free from the power of sin so that we can choose each day to fight our sinful nature.

God's mercy changes your life when you understand what it feels like to be loved even if you have not loved in return. This should cause you to love others in the same way that God loves you. To whom can you be an example of God's mercy today?

GOD'S PROMISE

I promise this very day that I will repay two blessings for each of your troubles.   ZECHARIAH 9:12

Remember

What should I reflect on when thinking of God?

GOD'S RESPONSE

Stand here quietly before the LORD as I remind you of all the great things the LORD has done for you and your ancestors.

1 Samuel 12:7

Be sure to fear the LORD and faithfully serve him. Think of all the wonderful things he has done for you.   *1 Samuel 12:24*

I said, "This is my fate; the Most High has turned his hand against me." But then I recall all you have done, O LORD; I remember your wonderful deeds of long ago. They are constantly in my thoughts. I cannot stop thinking about your mighty works.   *Psalm 77:10-12*

Consider all the great things God has done for you. Taking time for reflection allows you to focus your attention upon God's character and goodness and strengthens your faith. It is easy to become so focused on progress and the future that you fail to take time to recall all that God has already done. Remembering how God has worked in the past will allow you to move ahead with gratitude and increased faith.

GOD'S PROMISE

How amazing are the deeds of the LORD! All who delight in him should ponder them. Everything he does reveals his glory and majesty. His righteousness never fails. He causes us to remember his wonderful works. How gracious and merciful is our LORD!

PSALM 111:2-3

Oneness

What does it mean when the Bible talks about a husband and wife being "united into one"?

GOD'S RESPONSE

The Scriptures say, "A man leaves his father and mother and is joined to his wife, and the two are united into one."

Ephesians 5:31

The union of husband and wife merges two people in such a close way that little can affect one without also affecting the other. Oneness in marriage does not mean that one partner loses his or her personality in the personality of the other. Instead, it means that husbands and wives share such intimacy that they care for their spouses in the same way that they care for themselves. They learn to anticipate each other's needs, empathize with each other, and support each other in becoming all that they can be.

GOD'S CHALLENGE

We must not just please ourselves. We should help others do what is right and build them up in the Lord.   ROMANS 15:1-2

Discipline

Why is God punishing me? Doesn't he love me?

GOD'S RESPONSE

Joyful are those you discipline, LORD, those you teach with your instructions.   *Psalm 94:12*

[God said,] "My child, don't make light of the LORD's discipline, and don't give up when he corrects you. For the LORD disciplines those he loves, and he punishes each one he accepts as his child."

Hebrews 12:5-6

At times, God must discipline you to help you grow. This is similar to the way loving parents discipline, or train, their children. The discipline is not enjoyable for either the parents or the children, but it is essential so that the children learn right from wrong. Hebrews 12:11 says, "No discipline is enjoyable while it is happening—it's painful! But afterward there will be a peaceful harvest of right living for those who are trained in this way."

When you feel God's hand of correction, accept it as proof of his love. God is urging you to stay on his paths instead of stubbornly going your own way.

GOD'S PROMISE

Our earthly fathers disciplined us for a few years, doing the best they knew how. But God's discipline is always good for us, so that we might share in his holiness. No discipline is enjoyable while it is happening—it's painful! But afterward there will be a peaceful harvest of right living for those who are trained in this way.   HEBREWS 12:10-11

Attitude

Does God care about my attitude as long as I still do what he asks?

God's Response

The Lord of Heaven's Armies says to the priests: "A son honors his father, and a servant respects his master. If I am your father and master, where are the honor and respect I deserve? You have shown contempt for my name! But you ask, 'How have we ever shown contempt for your name?' "You have shown contempt by offering defiled sacrifices on my altar."   *Malachi 1:6-7*

 God's law required that only perfect animals be offered as sacrifices. But the priests in the book of Malachi were allowing the people to offer blind, crippled, and diseased animals to God. God accused them of dishonoring him by offering imperfect sacrifices, and he was greatly displeased.

The New Testament says that our lives should be living sacrifices to God (see Romans 12:1). If you give God only your leftover time, money, and energy, you risk repeating the same sin as these Old Testament worshipers, who were reluctant to give anything of value to God. What you give God reflects your true attitude toward him.

God's Challenge

Learn to know the God of your ancestors intimately. Worship and serve him with your whole heart and a willing mind. For the Lord sees every heart and knows every plan and thought.

1 CHRONICLES 28:9

Wisdom

How can I be more receptive to God's wisdom?

GOD'S RESPONSE

If you need wisdom, ask our generous God, and he will give it to you. He will not rebuke you for asking.   *James 1:5*

Fear of the LORD is the foundation of true wisdom. All who obey his commandments will grow in wisdom.   *Psalm 111:10*

One meaning for the word *wisdom* is "practical discernment." It begins with respect for God and his ways, leads to right living, and results in an increased ability to tell right from wrong. God is willing to give you this wisdom, but you will be unable to receive it if your goals are self-centered instead of God-centered. To learn God's will, you need to read his Word and ask the Holy Spirit to show you how to obey and live out what you have read. Then, do what he tells you.

GOD'S PROMISE

Cry out for insight, and ask for understanding. Search for them as you would for silver; seek them like hidden treasures. Then you will understand what it means to fear the LORD, and you will gain knowledge of God.   PROVERBS 2:3-5

Comparisons

How can I stop comparing myself to others?

GOD'S RESPONSE

All the people gave a great shout, praising the LORD because the foundation of the LORD's Temple had been laid. But many of the older priests, Levites, and other leaders who had seen the first Temple wept aloud when they saw the new Temple's foundation.

Ezra 3:11-12

Believers who are poor have something to boast about, for God has honored them. And those who are rich should boast that God has humbled them. They will fade away like a little flower in the field. The hot sun rises and the grass withers; the little flower droops and falls, and its beauty fades away. In the same way, the rich will fade away with all of their achievements. *James 1:9-11*

Fifty years after its destruction, the Temple was being rebuilt. Some of the older people remembered the grandeur of Solomon's original Temple and wept because the new Temple would never be as glorious as that one. But the beauty of the building was not nearly as important to God as were the attitudes of the builders and worshipers.

God cares more about who we are than what we accomplish. Seek to serve God wholeheartedly. Then you won't be so tempted to compare yourself to others.

GOD'S PROMISE

Pay careful attention to your own work, for then you will get the satisfaction of a job well done, and you won't need to compare yourself to anyone else. GALATIANS 6:4

Suffering

Wouldn't more people turn to God if he kept us from suffering?

God's Response

[Job's wife said,] "Are you still trying to maintain your integrity? Curse God and die." But Job replied, "You talk like a foolish woman. Should we accept only good things from the hand of God and never anything bad?"   *Job 2:9-10*

Just as you cannot understand the path of the wind or the mystery of a tiny baby growing in its mother's womb, so you cannot understand the activity of God, who does all things.   *Ecclesiastes 11:5*

Many people think that believing in God will protect them from trouble, so when calamity comes, they question God's goodness and justice. But the message of Job is not to give up on God because you experience troubles. Faith in God does not guarantee prosperity, and lack of faith does not guarantee troubles in this life. If this were so, people would believe in God simply to get rich.

God is capable of rescuing us from suffering, but he may also allow our suffering to teach us important spiritual lessons, as he did with Job. If we always knew why we were suffering, our faith would never grow.

God's Challenge

Accept the way God does things. . . . Enjoy prosperity while you can, but when hard times strike, realize that both come from God. Remember that nothing is certain in this life.

ECCLESIASTES 7:13-14

Rules

Why does God give us so many rules to follow in order to obey him?

God's Response

You must keep all my decrees and regulations by putting them into practice; otherwise the land to which I am bringing you as your new home will vomit you out. Do not live according to the customs of the people I am driving out before you. It is because they do these shameful things that I detest them.   *Leviticus 20:22-23*

God gave many rules to his people—but not without good reason. He did not withhold good from them; he prohibited only those acts that would bring them to ruin. All of us understand God's physical laws of nature. We know that jumping off a ten-story building will mean death because of the law of gravity. But some of us don't understand how God's spiritual laws work. God forbids us to do certain things because he wants to protect us and keep us from self-destruction.

The next time you are drawn to a forbidden physical or emotional pleasure, remind yourself that its consequences might be suffering and separation from God, who has given good rules for your protection.

God's Promise

This is what [God] told them: "Obey me, and I will be your God, and you will be my people. Do everything as I say, and all will be well!"   JEREMIAH 7:23

Priorities

What is the cost of living with complete integrity?

GOD'S RESPONSE

Better to be poor and honest than to be dishonest and a fool.

Proverbs 19:1

Better to be poor and honest than to be dishonest and rich.

Proverbs 28:6

If you are faithful in little things, you will be faithful in large ones. But if you are dishonest in little things, you won't be honest with greater responsibilities. And if you are untrustworthy about worldly wealth, who will trust you with the true riches of heaven?

Luke 16:10-11

A life of integrity is far more valuable than wealth, but most people don't act as if they believe this. Afraid of not getting everything they want, they will pay any price to increase their wealth—cheat on their taxes, steal from stores or employers, withhold tithes, refuse to give to those in need. But when people know and love God, they realize that a lower standard of living—or even poverty—is a small price to pay for personal integrity.

Do your actions show that you are willing to sacrifice your integrity in order to increase your wealth? What changes do you need to make in order to get your priorities straight?

GOD'S PROMISE

The godly walk with integrity; blessed are their children who follow them.   PROVERBS 20:7

Obedience

When obedience seems to require too much effort, how can I find the energy to do what is right?

God's Response

Work hard to show the results of your salvation, obeying God with deep reverence and fear. For God is working in you, giving you the desire and the power to do what pleases him.   *Philippians 2:12-13*

Sometimes obeying God is just plain hard. It takes discipline, desire, and determination. So what can you do when you don't feel like obeying? God knows that we can't follow him in our own strength. So he has not left you on your own in your struggles to do his will. The Holy Spirit, who lives in you, will come alongside you and help you to *desire* to obey then give you the *power* to do what is necessary. The next time you don't feel like obeying, ask God to give you the desire to do what is pleasing to him.

God's Promise

[The Lord] gives power to the weak and strength to the powerless.

ISAIAH 40:29

Jealousy

Why do I get jealous of the good things in my friends' lives?

GOD'S RESPONSE

As Paul and Barnabas left the synagogue that day, the people begged them to speak about these things again the next week. Many Jews and devout converts to Judaism followed Paul and Barnabas, and the two men urged them to continue to rely on the grace of God. The following week almost the entire city turned out to hear them preach the word of the Lord. But when some of the Jews saw the crowds, they were jealous; so they slandered Paul and argued against whatever he said. *Acts 13:42-45*

The Jewish leaders undoubtedly brought theological arguments against Paul and Barnabas, but Luke tells us that the real reason for their hostility was that "they were jealous." When we see others succeeding where we haven't or receiving the affirmation we crave, it is hard to rejoice with them. Jealousy is our natural reaction. But how tragic it is when our own jealous feelings affect the work of God's Kingdom in a negative way. If we are so busy focusing on what others have that we don't, we won't be focused on working for God or rejoicing in him.

GOD'S PROMISE

Thieves are jealous of each other's loot, but the godly are well rooted and bear their own fruit. PROVERBS 12:12

Prayer

Am I really supposed to pray at all times? How is that possible?

GOD'S RESPONSE

Pray in the Spirit at all times and on every occasion. Stay alert and be persistent in your prayers for all believers everywhere.

Ephesians 6:18

Devote yourselves to prayer with an alert mind and a thankful heart.   *Colossians 4:2*

How can anyone pray at all times? One way is to make spontaneous, brief prayer your habitual response to every situation you meet throughout the day. Another way is to order your life around God's desires and teachings so that your very life becomes a prayer. You don't have to isolate yourself from other people and from daily work in order to pray "at all times and on every occasion." You can make prayer your life and your life a prayer while you live in a world that needs God's powerful influence.

GOD'S CHALLENGE

I love the LORD because he hears my voice and my prayer for mercy. Because he bends down to listen, I will pray as long as I have breath!   PSALM 116:1-2

Willing

If God is in control of my life, what does it matter what I do or don't do?

GOD'S RESPONSE

Esther sent this reply to Mordecai: "Go and gather together all the Jews of Susa and fast for me. Do not eat or drink for three days, night or day. My maids and I will do the same. And then, though it is against the law, I will go in to see the king. If I must die, I must die." So Mordecai went away and did everything as Esther had ordered him. On the third day of the fast, Esther put on her royal robes and entered the inner court of the palace.   *Esther 4:15–5:1*

God was indeed in control in the story of Esther, yet God still led Mordecai and Esther to act. We cannot understand how both of these statements can be true at the same time, and yet they are. God chooses to work out his plan through his people. And since he does, we should pray as if everything depends on God and act as if everything depends on us. We should avoid two extremes: doing nothing and feeling that we must do everything.

GOD'S PROMISE

To those who use well what they are given, even more will be given, and they will have an abundance. But from those who do nothing, even what little they have will be taken away.

MATTHEW 25:29

Attitude

My job feels so meaningless—how can I stay motivated?

GOD'S RESPONSE

Boaz asked his foreman, "Who is that young woman over there? Who does she belong to?" And the foreman replied, "She is the young woman from Moab who came back with Naomi. She asked me this morning if she could gather grain behind the harvesters. She has been hard at work ever since, except for a few minutes' rest in the shelter." *Ruth 2:5-7*

Although Ruth's daily task—gleaning grain from harvested fields—was menial, repetitious, backbreaking, tiring, and perhaps degrading, she did it faithfully because she saw her gleaning as God's provision for herself and Naomi.

What is your attitude when the task you have been given doesn't reflect your true potential? The task at hand may be all you can do at the moment, or it may be the work God wants you to do for reasons you can't yet see. Or, as in Ruth's case, it may even be a test of your character that can open up new doors of opportunity.

GOD'S PROMISE

My dear brothers and sisters, be strong and immovable. Always work enthusiastically for the Lord, for you know that nothing you do for the Lord is ever useless.   1 CORINTHIANS 15:58

My Rights

I do so much for other people. Is it wrong to get upset when I don't receive the recognition I deserve?

GOD'S RESPONSE

You must have the same attitude that Christ Jesus had. Though he was God, he did not think of equality with God as something to cling to. Instead, he gave up his divine privileges; he took the humble position of a slave and was born as a human being. When he appeared in human form, he humbled himself in obedience to God and died a criminal's death on a cross.   *Philippians 2:5-8*

Often people excuse selfishness, pride, or other wrong attitudes by claiming their rights. They think, *I can cheat on this test; after all, I deserve to pass this class,* or *I can spend all this money on myself—I worked hard for it.* But as believers, we should have a different attitude, one that enables us to lay aside our "rights" in order to serve others. If we say we follow Christ, we must also live as he lived, having his attitude of humility as we serve, even when we are not likely to get recognition for our efforts. Are you selfishly clinging to your rights, or are you willing to serve without recognition?

GOD'S CHALLENGE

Jesus told [the disciples], "In this world the kings and great men lord it over their people, yet they are called 'friends of the people.' But among you it will be different. Those who are the greatest among you should take the lowest rank, and the leader should be like a servant." LUKE 22:25-26

Kindness

How can I show kindness to others?

GOD'S RESPONSE

The Holy Spirit produces this kind of fruit in our lives: love, joy, peace, patience, kindness, goodness, faithfulness, gentleness, and self-control.   *Galatians 5:22-23*

Do to others whatever you would like them to do to you.
Matthew 7:12

Your love has given me much joy and comfort, my brother, for your kindness has often refreshed the hearts of God's people.
Philemon 1:7

Kindness is included in the fruit produced by the Holy Spirit. You show kindness by being pleasant and gracious, by thinking of ways to serve and help others, and by putting their needs ahead of your own—in other words, by following the example of Jesus. Kindness is not a single act but rather an attitude that leads you to treat others the way you would like them to treat you. When you do that, you bring great refreshment to everyone you meet, and you honor and please the Lord who lives in you.

GOD'S PROMISE

When God our Savior revealed his kindness and love, he saved us, not because of the righteous things we had done, but because of his mercy. He washed away our sins, giving us a new birth and new life through the Holy Spirit.   TITUS 3:4-5

Humility

Does being humble mean giving up success?

GOD'S RESPONSE

The next day John saw Jesus coming toward him and said, "Look! The Lamb of God who takes away the sin of the world! He is the one I was talking about when I said, 'A man is coming after me who is far greater than I am, for he existed long before me.'"

John 1:29-30

True humility and fear of the LORD lead to riches, honor, and long life. *Proverbs 22:4*

Fear of the LORD teaches wisdom; humility precedes honor.

Proverbs 15:33

Although John the Baptist was a well-known preacher who attracted large crowds, he was content to point the way to Jesus and watch him take the higher place. This is true humility, the basis for greatness in preaching, teaching, or any other work you might do for Christ. When you are content to do what God wants you to do and let Jesus Christ be honored for it, God will do great things through you. You may not enjoy "success" the way the world defines it, but your life will be rich, full, and satisfying.

GOD'S PROMISE

Humble yourselves under the mighty power of God, and at the right time he will lift you up in honor. 1 PETER 5:6

Freedom

Why does it sometimes feel as if obeying God restricts my freedom?

GOD'S RESPONSE

The kings of the earth prepare for battle; the rulers plot together against the LORD and against his anointed one. "Let us break their chains," they cry, "and free ourselves from slavery to God."

Psalm 2:2-3

I will say to the prisoners, "Come out in freedom," and to those in darkness, "Come into the light." They will be my sheep, grazing in green pastures and on hills that were previously bare.   *Isaiah 49:9*

Sin is no longer your master, for you no longer live under the requirements of the law. Instead, you live under the freedom of God's grace.   *Romans 6:14*

People often think they will be free if they can just get away from God. Yet everyone serves somebody or something, whether it's a human king, an organization, or even their own selfish desires. Just as a fish is not free when it leaves the water and a tree is not free when it leaves the soil, you are not free when you leave the Lord. You can find the one sure route to freedom by wholeheartedly serving God the Creator. He can set you free to be the person he created you to be.

GOD'S PROMISE

If you look carefully into the perfect law that sets you free, and if you do what it says and don't forget what you heard, then God will bless you for doing it.   JAMES 1:25

Power

Is it okay to have confidence in the power of our country?

GOD'S RESPONSE

Some nations boast of their chariots and horses, but we boast in the name of the LORD our God. Those nations will fall down and collapse, but we will rise up and stand firm.   *Psalm 20:7-8*

Only by your power can we push back our enemies; only in your name can we trample our foes. I do not trust in my bow; I do not count on my sword to save me. You are the one who gives us victory over our enemies; you disgrace those who hate us. O God, we give glory to you all day long and constantly praise your name.

Psalm 44:5-8

As long as there have been armies and weapons, nations have boasted of their power, but such power does not last. Throughout history, empires and kingdoms have risen to great heights only to vanish in the dust. King David, however, knew that the true might of his nation was not in weaponry but in worship, not in firepower but in God's power. Because God alone can preserve a nation or an individual, be sure your confidence is in God, whose power is limitless and whose victory is eternal. In whom do you trust?

GOD'S PROMISE

All the nations you made will come and bow before you, Lord; they will praise your holy name.   PSALM 86:9

Pointing the Way

What is my responsibility in helping others to know and follow Christ?

God's Response

In every nation he accepts those who fear him and do what is right. This is the message of Good News for the people of Israel—that there is peace with God through Jesus Christ, who is Lord of all.

Acts 10:35-36

How can they call on him to save them unless they believe in him? And how can they believe in him if they have never heard about him? And how can they hear about him unless someone tells them?

Romans 10:14

In every nation, across town, and right next door there are hearts that are empty and restless, hearts that need to hear and receive the good news about the love of Jesus. But someone must share that Good News with those who have never heard it. Seeking God in some general way is not enough. People must be introduced to the God of the Bible, and God has given his people the privilege of pointing the way. Is God asking you to show someone the way to him?

God's Challenge

The Scriptures say, "How beautiful are the feet of messengers who bring good news!" ROMANS 10:15

Significance

I'm struggling to see where my life has touched anyone. Will my life count for something?

GOD'S RESPONSE

God's message continued to spread. The number of believers greatly increased in Jerusalem, and many of the Jewish priests were converted, too. *Acts 6:7*

[God] makes the whole body fit together perfectly. As each part does its own special work, it helps the other parts grow, so that the whole body is healthy and growing and full of love. *Ephesians 4:16*

Do not despise these small beginnings, for the LORD rejoices to see the work begin. *Zechariah 4:10*

The Word of God spreads like ripples on a pond where, from a single center, each wave touches the next, spreading wider and farther. The Good News still spreads this way today. You don't have to change the world single-handedly; it is enough just to be part of the wave, touching those around you, who in turn will touch others until all have felt the movement. Don't ever feel that your part is unimportant. No one who is part of God's Kingdom is ever insignificant. You may not see the effect your life is having on others, but God does.

GOD'S PROMISE

God is not unjust. He will not forget how hard you have worked for him and how you have shown your love to him by caring for other believers, as you still do. HEBREWS 6:10

Worth It

If I have to make sacrifices in order to follow God, can I ever really enjoy a relationship with him?

GOD'S RESPONSE

Everything else is worthless when compared with the infinite value of knowing Christ Jesus my Lord. For his sake I have discarded everything else, counting it all as garbage, so that I could gain Christ and become one with him.   *Philippians 3:8-9*

Paul gave up everything—family, friendship, and freedom— in order to know Christ and experience his power. He was beaten, stoned, and imprisoned, and he could still say that everything else in life was worthless compared with the value of knowing Jesus.

You, too, have access to this knowledge and this power, but you may have to make sacrifices to enjoy it fully. What are you willing to give up in order to know Christ: some time in your crowded schedule for prayer and Bible study? your friends' approval? your own personal plans and pleasures? Whatever it is, knowing Christ is more than worth the sacrifice.

GOD'S PROMISE

Joyful are those who listen to me, watching for me daily at my gates, waiting for me outside my home! For whoever finds me finds life and receives favor from the LORD.   PROVERBS 8:34-35

Being Misunderstood

Why is it so hard for my friends to understand why I don't participate in some of the things they do?

God's Response

Bless those who persecute you. Don't curse them; pray that God will bless them. . . . Never pay back evil with more evil. . . . Never take revenge. Leave that to the righteous anger of God. . . . Instead, "If your enemies are hungry, feed them. If they are thirsty, give them something to drink. In doing this, you will heap burning coals of shame on their heads." Don't let evil conquer you, but conquer evil by doing good.   *Romans 12:14-21*

Jesus explained that if you are truly following him, you will at some point be misunderstood, possibly even mocked and persecuted. The message of Christ is countercultural. When you follow it—by praying for your enemies or giving away your money to help others instead of spending it on yourself, for example—it will not make any sense by society's standards. As a result you can expect some ridicule and opposition. But that won't always be the norm. In God's new and future culture of heaven, goodness and righteousness will be the norm.

God's Promise

Everyone will share the story of your wonderful goodness; they will sing with joy about your righteousness.   PSALM 145:7

Compromise

How can I keep from compromising my convictions?

GOD'S RESPONSE

The king assigned them a daily ration of food and wine from his own kitchens. They were to be trained for three years, and then they would enter the royal service. Daniel, Hananiah, Mishael, and Azariah were four of the young men chosen. . . . But Daniel was determined not to defile himself by eating the food and wine given to them by the king. He asked the chief of staff for permission not to eat these unacceptable foods. *Daniel 1:5-6, 8*

Daniel had made up his mind to be devoted to principle, to be committed to a course of action. When Daniel made up his mind not to defile himself, he was being true to a lifelong determination to do what was right and not to give in to the pressures around him.

We, too, are often assaulted by pressure to compromise our standards and live more like the world around us. Merely wanting or preferring God's will and way is not enough to allow us to stand against the onslaught of temptation. Like Daniel, we must resolve in our hearts to obey God.

If someone were watching your behavior, would it be obvious that you've "made up your mind" to obey God?

GOD'S CHALLENGE

Follow only what is good. Remember that those who do good prove that they are God's children, and those who do evil prove that they do not know God. 3 JOHN 1:11

God's Word

What can I do to stay attentive when I read the Bible?

GOD'S RESPONSE

On October 8 Ezra the priest brought the Book of the Law before
the assembly. . . . All the people listened closely to the Book of
the Law. . . . Then Nehemiah the governor, Ezra the priest and
scribe, and the Levites who were interpreting for the people said to
them, "Don't mourn or weep on such a day as this! For today is a
sacred day before the LORD your God." For the people had all been
weeping as they listened to the words of the Law. . . . So the people
went away to eat and drink at a festive meal, to share gifts of food,
and to celebrate with great joy because they had heard God's words
and understood them.   *Nehemiah 8:2-3, 9, 12*

The people listened attentively to Ezra as he read God's Word,
and their lives and hearts underwent a change. They wept because
of the power of the words they heard being read.

Because we hear the Bible so often, we can become numb to the
power of its words and apathetic to its teachings. Instead, as we
listen closely to every verse, we should ask the Holy Spirit to help us
understand what we hear and then answer the question, *How does
this apply to my life?*

GOD'S PROMISE

My child, pay attention to what I say. Listen carefully to my
words. Don't lose sight of them. Let them penetrate deep into
your heart, for they bring life to those who find them, and healing
to their whole body.   PROVERBS 4:20-22

Action

How do I know when to take action and when to wait for God's timing?

Mordecai sent this reply to Esther: "Don't think for a moment that because you're in the palace you will escape when all other Jews are killed. If you keep quiet at a time like this, deliverance and relief for the Jews will arise from some other place, but you and your relatives will die. Who knows if perhaps you were made queen for just such a time as this?"   *Esther 4:13-14*

After King Xerxes had issued the decree to kill the Jews, Mordecai and Esther could have despaired, decided to save only themselves, or just waited for God's intervention. Instead, they saw that God had placed them in their positions for his time and his purpose, so they seized the moment and acted.

When you are in a position to help, don't withdraw, don't behave selfishly, don't wallow in despair, and don't wait for God to fix everything. Instead, ask God for his direction—and then act! God may have placed you where you are "for just such a time as this."

Trust in the LORD and do good. Then you will live safely in the land and prosper.   PSALM 37:3

God's Light

Why do my friends try to bring me over to "the dark side" by sinning?

GOD'S RESPONSE

God's light came into the world, but people loved the darkness more than the light, for their actions were evil. All who do evil hate the light and refuse to go near it for fear their sins will be exposed. But those who do what is right come to the light so others can see that they are doing what God wants.   *John 3:19-21*

Satan, who is the god of this world, has blinded the minds of those who don't believe. They are unable to see the glorious light of the Good News.   *2 Corinthians 4:4*

Many people don't want their lives exposed to God's light because they are afraid of what it will reveal about them. So don't be surprised when these same people are threatened by your desire to obey God and do what is right. They are afraid that the light in you may expose some of the darkness in their own lives. The solution is for you to stay in the light and pray that your friends will see how much better it is to live in light than in darkness.

GOD'S PROMISE

Jesus spoke to the people once more and said, "I am the light of the world. If you follow me, you won't have to walk in darkness, because you will have the light that leads to life."   JOHN 8:12

Jealousy

Is it wrong to feel jealous that evil people are allowed to turn to God, even after all they've done?

GOD'S RESPONSE

When God saw what they had done and how they had put a stop to their evil ways, he changed his mind and did not carry out the destruction he had threatened. This change of plans greatly upset Jonah, and he became very angry. So he complained to the LORD about it: "Didn't I say before I left home that you would do this, LORD? That is why I ran away to Tarshish! I knew that you are a merciful and compassionate God, slow to get angry and filled with unfailing love. You are eager to turn back from destroying people. Just kill me now, LORD! I'd rather be dead than alive if what I predicted will not happen." *Jonah 3:10-4:3*

Jonah revealed the reason for his reluctance to go to Nineveh. He didn't want the Ninevites forgiven; he wanted them destroyed. Jonah did not understand that the God of Israel was also the God of the whole world. Does it upset you when some unlikely person turns to God? If so, you need to remember that no one—including you—deserves God's forgiveness. You have the privilege of spreading the news of this wonderful gift to all the world. As you do this, you will be able to rejoice when others come to Christ.

GOD'S PROMISE

We have an advocate who pleads our case before the Father. He is Jesus Christ, the one who is truly righteous. He himself is the sacrifice that atones for our sins—and not only our sins but the sins of all the world. 1 JOHN 2:1-2

Shortcuts

What's wrong with taking the easy way out?

GOD'S RESPONSE

There is a path before each person that seems right, but it ends in death.   *Proverbs 14:12*

Good planning and hard work lead to prosperity, but hasty shortcuts lead to poverty.   *Proverbs 21:5*

The "path before each person that seems right" may offer many options and require few sacrifices. Easy choices, however, should make you take a second look. Is this solution attractive because it allows you to be lazy? because it doesn't ask you to change your life-style? because it requires no moral restraints? The right choice often requires hard work and self-sacrifice. Don't be enticed by apparent shortcuts that seem right but end in regret. Instead, look for solutions that will help develop your character and will lead to greater wisdom later on.

GOD'S PROMISE

When you were slaves to sin, you were free from the obligation to do right. And what was the result? You are now ashamed of the things you used to do, things that end in eternal doom. But now you are free from the power of sin and have become slaves of God. Now you do those things that lead to holiness and result in eternal life. For the wages of sin is death, but the free gift of God is eternal life through Christ Jesus our Lord.   ROMANS 6:20-23

Follow

How does God expect me to follow him if he leads me away from what I know and love?

GOD'S RESPONSE

As for Philip, an angel of the Lord said to him, "Go south down the desert road that runs from Jerusalem to Gaza." So he started out, and he met the treasurer of Ethiopia, a eunuch of great authority under the Kandake, the queen of Ethiopia. . . . Philip ran over and heard the man reading from the prophet Isaiah. Philip asked, "Do you understand what you are reading?" The man replied, "How can I, unless someone instructs me?" And he urged Philip to come up into the carriage and sit with him. . . . So beginning with this same Scripture, Philip told him the Good News about Jesus.   *Acts 8:26-27, 30-31, 35*

Philip had been having a successful ministry preaching to great crowds in Samaria (see Acts 8:5-8), but he obediently left that ministry to travel on a desert road. Because Philip went where God sent him, the Good News was introduced to Ethiopia.

Follow God's leading, even if doing so feels like a demotion. At first you may not understand God's reasons or plans, but if you love him and continue to follow him, he will be there to guide you into what is best for you.

GOD'S PROMISE

This is what the LORD says—your Redeemer, the Holy One of Israel: "I am the LORD your God, who teaches you what is good for you and leads you along the paths you should follow."

ISAIAH 48:17

Complaining

Does it anger God when I complain about my circumstances?

GOD'S RESPONSE

Moses heard all the families standing in the doorways of their tents whining, and the LORD became extremely angry. Moses was also very aggravated. And Moses said to the LORD, "Why are you treating me, your servant, so harshly? Have mercy on me! What did I do to deserve the burden of all these people?" . . . Then the LORD said to Moses, "Gather before me seventy men who are recognized as elders and leaders of Israel. . . . I will take some of the Spirit that is upon you, and I will put the Spirit upon them also. They will bear the burden of the people along with you, so you will not have to carry it alone." *Numbers 11:10-11, 16-17*

First the Israelites complained, and then Moses complained. But God responded positively to Moses and negatively to the rest of the people. What was the difference? The people complained to one another, and nothing was accomplished. Moses took his complaint to God, who could solve any problem.

Many of us are good at complaining to each other. What we need to learn to do is take our problems to the One who can really do something about them.

GOD'S PROMISE

I took my troubles to the LORD; I cried out to him, and he answered my prayer. PSALM 120:1

Excuses

How can I be expected to follow God when I know so little about him?

God's Response

The LORD our God has secrets known to no one. We are not accountable for them, but we and our children are accountable forever for all that he has revealed to us, so that we may obey all the terms of these instructions.   *Deuteronomy 29:29*

We must hold on to the progress we have already made.

Philippians 3:16

 When it comes to following God, it's very easy to make the excuse that you still have too much to learn. But God doesn't expect you to know all about him before you follow him. He does expect you to act on the knowledge and guidance you already have. Even after a lifetime of following God, you will never know all there is to know. The instruction for you is to live up to what God has already told you in his Word and to live out what you already know to be true. God will continue to reveal his truth to you as you follow him. Don't get sidetracked by an unending search for details.

God's Promise

Jesus replied, "But even more blessed are all who hear the word of God and put it into practice."   LUKE 11:28

Daily Praise

How can I maintain my confidence in God's goodness from day to day?

GOD'S RESPONSE

I will praise the LORD at all times. I will constantly speak his praises.

Psalm 34:1

I will exalt you, my God and King, and praise your name forever and ever. I will praise you every day; yes, I will praise you forever. Great is the LORD! He is most worthy of praise! No one can measure his greatness. Your awe-inspiring deeds will be on every tongue; I will proclaim your greatness. Everyone will share the story of your wonderful goodness; they will sing with joy about your righteousness.

Psalm 145:1-3, 6-7

Throughout the Psalms we see David praising God in both the good and the difficult times of his life. Do you find something to praise God for each day? If you're in a difficult place and are having trouble thinking of something to praise God for, remember this: Your circumstances can change from day to day, but God *never* changes. He is and always will be worthy of your praise. When you remember this and choose to praise God in spite of your circumstances, you will find your heart elevated from daily distractions to lasting confidence in your heavenly Father.

GOD'S CHALLENGE

In [the Lord] our hearts rejoice, for we trust in his holy name.

PSALM 33:21

Example

Can I be an example of faith to those around me?

GOD'S RESPONSE

While the Israelites were camped at Acacia Grove, some of the men defiled themselves by having sexual relations with local Moabite women. These women invited them to attend sacrifices to their gods, so the Israelites feasted with them and worshiped the gods of Moab.   *Numbers 25:1-2*

The strength of your faith can often be seen by whether you influence your culture or it influences you. In Numbers 25, the Israelites were easily influenced by some of the sinful practices of the surrounding culture.

What kind of example have you been lately to others? If you are a good role model, you will influence others for good rather than allow yourself to be influenced by evil.

GOD'S CHALLENGE

Remember your leaders who taught you the word of God. Think of all the good that has come from their lives, and follow the example of their faith. Jesus Christ is the same yesterday, today, and forever. So do not be attracted by strange, new ideas. Your strength comes from God's grace.   HEBREWS 13:7-9

Impact

How can I, as a Christian, have the greatest impact on my community?

GOD'S RESPONSE

Owe nothing to anyone—except for your obligation to love one another.   *Romans 13:8*

You must worship Christ as Lord of your life. And if someone asks about your Christian hope, always be ready to explain it. But do this in a gentle and respectful way. Keep your conscience clear. Then if people speak against you, they will be ashamed when they see what a good life you live because you belong to Christ.

1 Peter 3:15-16

God's influence in our lives is often attractive to others. The more you reflect God's character, the more people will be drawn to you and want to be around you—unless they are bent on evil. Those who are determined to do evil will be repelled by your godly living. Nevertheless, although you, like everyone else, will make plenty of mistakes, your goal should be for your neighbors to say, "We can plainly see that God is with you."

Would your neighbors say that about you?

GOD'S PROMISE

[Jesus said,] "You are the light of the world. . . . No one lights a lamp and then puts it under a basket. Instead, a lamp is placed on a stand, where it gives light to everyone in the house. In the same way, let your good deeds shine out for all to see, so that everyone will praise your heavenly Father."   MATTHEW 5:14-16

Faith

What should be the foundation of my faith?

GOD'S RESPONSE

[Jesus said,] "I have come as a light to shine in this dark world, so that all who put their trust in me will no longer remain in the dark."

John 12:46

Faith comes from hearing, that is, hearing the Good News about Christ. *Romans 10:17*

[Jesus said,] "I have told you all this so that you may have peace in me. Here on earth you will have many trials and sorrows. But take heart, because I have overcome the world." *John 16:33*

We live in a fallen world in which good behavior is not always rewarded and bad behavior is not always punished. When we see a notorious criminal prospering or an innocent child in pain, we say, "That's wrong." And it is. Sin has twisted justice and made our world unpredictable and sometimes ugly. That is why faith based on rewards or prosperity is hollow. To be unshakable, faith must be built on the confidence that God's Word is true and that, ultimately, all of his purposes will come to pass.

GOD'S PROMISE

Just as you accepted Christ Jesus as your Lord, you must continue to follow him. Let your roots grow down into him, and let your lives be built on him. Then your faith will grow strong in the truth you were taught, and you will overflow with thankfulness.

COLOSSIANS 2:6-7

Glorious Acts

I hear of God doing great things in other people's lives. Why doesn't he do those things in my life?

GOD'S RESPONSE

Moses said, "This is what the LORD has commanded you to do so that the glory of the LORD may appear to you." *Leviticus 9:6*

Moses and Aaron went into the Tabernacle, and when they came back out, they blessed the people again, and the glory of the LORD appeared to the whole community. *Leviticus 9:22-23*

In Leviticus 9:6, Moses told the people that when they had followed the instructions they had received from the Lord, the glorious presence of the Lord would appear to them. Moses, Aaron, and the people then got to work and followed God's instructions for the Tabernacle. Soon after, the glory of the Lord appeared.

Often we look for God's glorious acts without giving any attention to following his instructions. Do you serve God in the daily routines of life, or do you wait for him to do a mighty act? If you are waiting only for his glorious acts, you may find yourself sidestepping your everyday duty to obey.

GOD'S CHALLENGE

This is what the LORD says: "Be just and fair to all. Do what is right and good, for I am coming soon to rescue you and to display my righteousness among you." ISAIAH 56:1

Feelings of Guilt

If God has forgiven me, why do I still have feelings of guilt?

GOD'S RESPONSE

[Job said, "God] knows where I am going. And when he tests me, I will come out as pure as gold. For I have stayed on God's paths; I have followed his ways and not turned aside." *Job 23:10-11*

Even if we feel guilty, God is greater than our feelings, and he knows everything. *1 John 3:20*

 Job's friend Eliphaz tried to condemn Job by identifying some secret sin that he may have committed. Here Job declares his confidence in his own integrity and in God's justice. We always have sin in our lives, sin we don't even know about, because God's standards are so high and our performance is so imperfect. If we are true believers, however, all our sins—those we know about and those we don't—are forgiven because of what Christ did at the cross on our behalf. The Bible teaches that even if our hearts condemn us, God is greater than our hearts. His forgiveness can overrule our nagging doubts. If we, like Job, are truly seeking God, we can stand up to our own feelings of guilt. If God has forgiven and accepted us, we are forgiven indeed.

GOD'S PROMISE

Since we have been made right in God's sight by faith, we have peace with God because of what Jesus Christ our Lord has done for us. ROMANS 5:1

Truth

How can I be ready to accept truth when I'm confronted by it?

God's Response

The Lord's message spread throughout that region. Then the Jews stirred up the influential religious women and the leaders of the city, and they incited a mob against Paul and Barnabas and ran them out of town.   *Acts 13:49-50*

Come and listen to my counsel. I'll share my heart with you and make you wise.   *Proverbs 1:23*

When the Spirit of truth comes, he will guide you into all truth. He will not speak on his own but will tell you what he has heard. He will tell you about the future.   *John 16:13*

Instead of accepting the truth, the Jewish leaders stirred up opposition among city leaders and influential women and ran Paul and Barnabas out of town. When confronted by a disturbing truth, people often turn away and refuse to listen.

   Ask God to prepare you to hear and accept truth when it comes. Then, when God's Spirit points out needed changes in your life, listen carefully. Don't push the truth away so that over time it no longer affects you.

God's Promise

Let those who are wise understand these things. Let those with discernment listen carefully. The paths of the LORD are true and right, and righteous people live by walking in them.   HOSEA 14:9

God

How can I know what God is like?

GOD'S RESPONSE

Jesus shouted to the crowds, "If you trust me, you are trusting not only me, but also God who sent me. For when you see me, you are seeing the one who sent me." *John 12:44-45*

Christ is the visible image of the invisible God. *Colossians 1:15*

The Son radiates God's own glory and expresses the very character of God, and he sustains everything by the mighty power of his command. *Hebrews 1:3*

It's natural to wonder what God is like. After all, how can we know the Creator when he doesn't make himself visible? Jesus said plainly that those who see him have seen God because he is God.

If you want to know what God is like, study the person and words of Jesus Christ. He is "the visible image of the invisible God."

GOD'S PROMISE

No one has ever seen God. But the unique One, who is himself God, is near to the Father's heart. He has revealed God to us.

JOHN 1:18

Spiritual Apathy

***How can I keep from becoming apathetic to sin
in my life?***

God's Response

David wrote a letter to Joab and gave it to Uriah to deliver. The letter
instructed Joab, "Station Uriah on the front lines where the battle is
fiercest. Then pull back so that he will be killed." . . . The messenger
went to Jerusalem and gave a complete report to David. ". . . Some
of the king's men were killed, including Uriah the Hittite." "Well,
tell Joab not to be discouraged," David said. "The sword devours
this one today and that one tomorrow! Fight harder next time,
and conquer the city!"   *2 Samuel 11:14-15, 22, 24-25*

David's response to Uriah's death seems flippant and insensitive.
While he grieved deeply for Saul and Abner, his rivals, he felt no sorrow at the death of Uriah, a good man with strong spiritual character.
David had become callous to his own sin. The only way he could
cover up his first sin (adultery) was to sin again, and soon he no longer
felt guilty about what he had done. Deliberate, repeated sinning had
dulled David's sensitivity to God's laws and others' rights.

Feelings are not reliable guides for determining right and wrong.
The more you try to cover up sin, the more insensitive you become
toward it. Don't become apathetic about sin, as David did. Confess
your wrongs to God before you forget they are sins.

God's Promise

Blessed are those who fear to do wrong, but the stubborn are
headed for serious trouble.   PROVERBS 28:14

Obedience

I can't predict my future circumstances—how can I be expected to obey God all the time?

God's Response

As the Lord had commanded his servant Moses, so Moses commanded Joshua. And Joshua did as he was told, carefully obeying all the commands that the Lord had given to Moses.

Joshua 11:15

Do not let sin control the way you live.   *Romans 6:12*

Joshua carefully obeyed all the instructions God had given to Moses. This theme of obedience is repeated frequently in the book of Joshua, partly because obedience is one aspect of life the individual believer can control.

You can't always control what happens to you, but you can choose to obey God in whatever circumstances you find yourself. How careful would you say you are in choosing to obey all of God's commands?

God's Challenge

Don't you realize that you become the slave of whatever you choose to obey? You can be a slave to sin, which leads to death, or you can choose to obey God, which leads to righteous living.

ROMANS 6:16

Attitudes

How do my own attitudes affect how I pray for others?

GOD'S RESPONSE

They celebrated the Festival of Unleavened Bread for seven days. There was great joy throughout the land because the LORD had caused the king of Assyria to be favorable to them, so that he helped them to rebuild the Temple of God, the God of Israel.

Ezra 6:22

The king's heart is like a stream of water directed by the LORD; he guides it wherever he pleases.   *Proverbs 21:1*

There are many ways to pray for God's help. Have you ever considered that God can change the attitude of someone or even of a whole group of people? God is infinitely powerful; his insight and wisdom transcend the laws of human nature. The king of Assyria ruled a large and cruel empire. He had conquered the Israelites and taken them away as slaves. And yet when God decided it was time for the Israelites to return home and rebuild the Temple, he made even the king of Assyria favor the idea.

Of course, you must be willing to change your own attitude as a first step, but also remember that no one's attitude is beyond God's power to change it.

GOD'S PROMISE

In every nation [God] accepts those who fear him and do what is right.   ACTS 10:35

Friendship with God

How can I be friends with God?

GOD'S RESPONSE

It happened just as the Scriptures say: "Abraham believed God, and God counted him as righteous because of his faith." He was even called the friend of God. *James 2:23*

Inside the Tent of Meeting, the LORD would speak to Moses face to face, as one speaks to a friend. *Exodus 33:11*

The LORD is a friend to those who fear him. He teaches them his covenant. *Psalm 25:14*

What are the qualities you look for in a friend? Perhaps you would list honesty, loyalty, or availability. God possesses these qualities, and he desires to see these same qualities in you. He wants you to come to him with honesty about your struggles and successes, to remain faithful and loyal to him and his Word, and to make yourself available to him. If you fear separation in your own friendships, how much more should you fear separation from God? Respect him, confide in him, and remain loyal to him, and your friendship with him will be the greatest you have ever known.

GOD'S PROMISE

[Jesus said,] "I no longer call you slaves, because a master doesn't confide in his slaves. Now you are my friends, since I have told you everything the Father told me." JOHN 15:15

Opportunities

***Does God confirm my desires by giving me
opportunities to carry them out?***

GOD'S RESPONSE

Saul soon learned that David was at Keilah. "Good!" he exclaimed.
"We've got him now! God has handed him over to me, for he has
trapped himself in a walled town!" So Saul mobilized his entire army
to march to Keilah and besiege David and his men.   *1 Samuel 23:7*

When you are being tempted, do not say, "God is tempting me."
God is never tempted to do wrong, and he never tempts anyone
else. Temptation comes from our own desires, which entice us and
drag us away.   *James 1:13-14*

When Saul heard that David was trapped in a walled city, he
thought God was putting David at his mercy. Saul wanted to kill
David so badly that he would have interpreted any sign as God's
approval to move ahead with his plan. Had Saul known God better,
he may not have misread the situation.

   Not every opportunity is sent from God. You may want some-
thing so much that you assume that any opportunity to obtain it
is of divine origin. But an opportunity to do something against
God's will can never be from God because God does not tempt you.
When opportunities come your way, double-check your motives.
Make sure you are following God's will, not just your own.

GOD'S PROMISE

The hopes of the godly result in happiness, but the expectations
of the wicked come to nothing.   PROVERBS 10:28

Destiny

Who controls my destiny?

God's Response

In the few days of our meaningless lives, who knows how our days can best be spent? Our lives are like a shadow. Who can tell what will happen on this earth after we are gone? *Ecclesiastes 6:12*

Look here, you who say, "Today or tomorrow we are going to a certain town and will stay there a year. We will do business there and make a profit." How do you know what your life will be like tomorrow? Your life is like the morning fog—it's here a little while, then it's gone. What you ought to say is, "If the Lord wants us to, we will live and do this or that." *James 4:13-15*

[God] will do to me whatever he has planned. He controls my destiny. *Job 23:14*

You cannot predict what the future holds. The only one who knows what will happen is God. Because no human being knows the future, you must live each day so that it will have the value God intends for it. He gives you the freedom to make plans and decisions about your life. Yet ultimately, God's purposes will prevail. As you make plans, don't look just out to the future. Look up to God.

God's Promise

You can make many plans, but the Lord's purpose will prevail.

PROVERBS 19:21

Pleasure

Some people seem to think that pleasure and the Christian life don't mix. Is that true?

GOD'S RESPONSE

I decided there is nothing better than to enjoy food and drink and to find satisfaction in work. Then I realized that these pleasures are from the hand of God.   *Ecclesiastes 2:24*

Oh, how beautiful you are! How pleasing, my love, how full of delights!   *Song of Songs 7:6*

The father of godly children has cause for joy. What a pleasure to have children who are wise.   *Proverbs 23:24*

God created a beautiful world for you to enjoy. He gave you good food and drink and work to do. Perhaps he has given you a family in which to take pleasure, along with friends, eyes to see the beauties of creation, ears to hear glorious music, and innumerable other blessings. In fact, he has abundantly given you all things to enjoy. God is pleased when you enjoy and take pleasure in the gifts he has given you. In this way you show him that you appreciate his generosity and kindness.

GOD'S PROMISE

Since everything God created is good, we should not reject any of it but receive it with thanks. For we know it is made acceptable by the word of God and prayer.   1 TIMOTHY 4:4-5

Peer Pressure

Won't others think I'm a loser for not going along with the crowd?

GOD'S RESPONSE

"Now's your opportunity!" David's men whispered to him. "Today the LORD is telling you, 'I will certainly put your enemy into your power, to do with as you wish.'" So David crept forward and cut off a piece of the hem of Saul's robe. But then David's conscience began bothering him because he had cut Saul's robe. "The LORD knows I shouldn't have done that to my lord the king," he said to his men. "The LORD forbid that I should do this to my lord the king and attack the LORD's anointed one, for the LORD himself has chosen him." So David restrained his men and did not let them kill Saul.

1 Samuel 24:3-7

David already knew that he would one day become king, so when his men urged him to kill Saul, the current king, when he had the chance, it would have been easy for David to go along. His refusal to do so was not evidence of cowardice but of courage—the courage to stand against the crowd and do what he knew was right.

Don't compromise your moral standards by giving in to group pressure or by taking the easy way out.

GOD'S CHALLENGE

Don't try to avoid doing your duty, and don't stand with those who plot evil. . . . Those who are wise will find a time and a way to do what is right, for there is a time and a way for everything, even when a person is in trouble.   ECCLESIASTES 8:3, 5-6

Thoughts

How can I be self-disciplined when I can't control what I think?

GOD'S RESPONSE

Dear brothers and sisters, one final thing. Fix your thoughts on what is true, and honorable, and right, and pure, and lovely, and admirable. Think about things that are excellent and worthy of praise. *Philippians 4:8*

Have you ever heard the expression "Garbage in, garbage out"? What you put into your mind determines what comes out in your words and actions. Paul tells you to fill your mind with thoughts that are true, honorable, right, pure, lovely, admirable, excellent, and worthy of praise. Do you have problems with impure thoughts and daydreams? If so, examine what you are putting into your mind through television, books, conversations, movies, and magazines. Replace harmful input with wholesome material. Above all, fill your mind and heart with God's Word, and ask God to help you focus your mind on what is good and pure. It takes practice, but with the help of the Holy Spirit, you can do it.

GOD'S PROMISE

Those who are dominated by the sinful nature think about sinful things, but those who are controlled by the Holy Spirit think about things that please the Spirit. So letting your sinful nature control your mind leads to death. But letting the Spirit control your mind leads to life and peace.   ROMANS 8:5-6

Devotion

How can I guard my heart against idolatry?

God's Response

[God said,] "Son of man, these leaders have set up idols in their hearts. They have embraced things that will make them fall into sin. Why should I listen to their requests? Tell them, 'This is what the Sovereign LORD says: The people of Israel have set up idols in their hearts and fallen into sin, and then they go to a prophet asking for a message. So I, the LORD, will give them the kind of answer their great idolatry deserves. I will do this to capture the minds and hearts of all my people who have turned from me to worship their detestable idols.'" *Ezekiel 14:3-5*

The Hebrew writers considered the heart to be the core of people's intellects and spirits. Because all people have someone or something that is the object of their hearts' devotion, they have the potential for idolatry within them. But God wants to recapture the hearts of his people.

You must never let anything or anyone captivate your allegiance or imagination in such a way that it weakens or replaces your devotion to God. What would you say are the objects of your heart's devotion?

God's Challenge

Guard your heart above all else, for it determines the course of your life.   PROVERBS 4:23

Emotions

How can I keep my emotions under control?

GOD'S RESPONSE

I cannot keep from speaking. I must express my anguish. My bitter soul must complain.   *Job 7:11*

Morning, noon, and night I cry out in my distress, and the LORD hears my voice.   *Psalm 55:17*

Give all your worries and cares to God, for he cares about you.
1 Peter 5:7

Job felt deep anguish and bitterness, and he was desperate to let out his frustrations at what he didn't understand about the pain he was experiencing. So he spoke honestly to God about his feelings.

If you talk to God about what you are feeling, you can deal with your strong emotions without exploding in harsh words and actions and possibly hurting yourself or others. The next time strong emotions threaten to overwhelm you, express them openly to God in prayer. God will not turn you away for doing so. In fact, he is able to help you gain an eternal perspective on your situation and give you greater ability to deal with it constructively.

GOD'S PROMISE

O my people, trust in him at all times. Pour out your heart to him, for God is our refuge.   PSALM 62:8

Wealth

Why can it be dangerous to long for comfort and wealth?

GOD'S RESPONSE

[Jesus said,] "You say, 'I am rich. I have everything I want. I don't need a thing!' And you don't realize that you are wretched and miserable and poor and blind and naked. So I advise you to buy gold from me—gold that has been purified by fire. Then you will be rich." *Revelation 3:17-18*

The believers in the city of Laodicea assumed that numerous material possessions were a sign of God's spiritual blessing on their lives. Laodicea was a wealthy city, and the church there was also wealthy. But what the Laodiceans could see and obtain had become more valuable to them than what was unseen and eternal.

Wealth, luxury, and ease can make people feel confident, satisfied, and complacent. But no matter what you possess or how much money you make, you have nothing if you don't have a vital relationship with Christ. How does your current level of wealth affect your spiritual desire? Instead of centering your life primarily on comfort and luxury, find your true riches in Christ.

GOD'S CHALLENGE

[Jesus said,] "Don't store up treasures here on earth, where moths eat them and rust destroys them, and where thieves break in and steal. Store your treasures in heaven, where moths and rust cannot destroy, and thieves do not break in and steal. Wherever your treasure is, there the desires of your heart will also be."

MATTHEW 6:19-21

Success

Is it ever possible to gain lasting success?

GOD'S RESPONSE

Be strong and very courageous. Be careful to obey all the instructions Moses gave you. Do not deviate from them, turning either to the right or to the left. Then you will be successful in everything you do. Study this Book of Instruction continually. Meditate on it day and night so you will be sure to obey everything written in it. Only then will you prosper and succeed in all you do.

Joshua 1:7-8

Many people think that prosperity and success come from having power, influence over others, and a relentless desire to get ahead. In contrast, God taught Joshua that in order to succeed, Joshua must (1) be strong and courageous, because the task ahead would not be easy; (2) obey God's law; and (3) constantly read and study God's Word. To be successful, follow God's words to Joshua. You may not succeed by the world's standards, but you will be a success in God's eyes—and his opinion is the one that counts, because it lasts forever.

GOD'S PROMISE

How joyful are those who fear the LORD and delight in obeying his commands. Their children will be successful everywhere; an entire generation of godly people will be blessed. They themselves will be wealthy, and their good deeds will last forever.

PSALM 112:1-3

Possessions

Why does God want to tell me how to use what I own? Isn't it my decision?

GOD'S RESPONSE

[Israel] doesn't realize it was I who gave her everything she has—the grain, the new wine, the olive oil; I even gave her silver and gold. But she gave all my gifts to Baal. *Hosea 2:8*

Remember the LORD your God. He is the one who gives you power to be successful, in order to fulfill the covenant he confirmed to your ancestors with an oath. *Deuteronomy 8:18*

 Material possessions are success symbols in most societies. Israel was a wealthy nation in the time of Hosea, and her people may have accumulated much silver and gold. But the people of Israel didn't recognize God as the giver of all their blessings. Both Hosea's wife, Gomer, who was a prostitute, and the people of Israel used their possessions irresponsibly as they ran after other lovers and other gods.

How do you use your possessions? God wants you to use what he has given you to honor him, the giver of every blessing.

GOD'S CHALLENGE

Here's the lesson: Use your worldly resources to benefit others and make friends. Then, when your earthly possessions are gone, they will welcome you to an eternal home. LUKE 16:9

Helping the Poor

Why should I help those less fortunate than I?

God's Response

"When you put on a luncheon or a banquet," [Jesus] said, " . . . don't invite your friends, brothers, relatives, and rich neighbors. For they will invite you back, and that will be your only reward. Instead, invite the poor, the crippled, the lame, and the blind. Then at the resurrection of the righteous, God will reward you for inviting those who could not repay you."   *Luke 14:12-14*

Why does God put so much emphasis on the way we treat the poor and needy? Because how we treat the poor reflects our true character. When we share with the poor, we know we can expect nothing in return.

Do you, like Christ, give without thought of repayment? You should treat the poor as you would like God to treat you. How can you do this? Begin by asking what you can do to help. Does your church have programs to help feed or house the needy? Could you volunteer with a community group that fights poverty? As one individual, you may not be able to accomplish much, but when you join with similarly motivated people, God can move mountains.

God's Promise

Blessed are those who are generous, because they feed the poor.

PROVERBS 22:9

Opposition

If I'm doing God's will, why do people oppose me?

GOD'S RESPONSE

When I came to the governors of the province west of the Euphrates River, I delivered the king's letters to them. The king, I should add, had sent along army officers and horsemen to protect me. But when Sanballat the Horonite and Tobiah the Ammonite official heard of my arrival, they were very displeased that someone had come to help the people of Israel. . . . When Sanballat, Tobiah, and Geshem the Arab heard of our plan, they scoffed contemptuously. "What are you doing? Are you rebelling against the king?" they asked.

Nehemiah 2:9-10, 19

Don't be surprised, dear brothers and sisters, if the world hates you.

1 John 3:13

 When Nehemiah arrived back in Judah, he was greeted with opposition. In fact, those who had settled in the area when the Jews were taken away as captives had already been opposing the rebuilding of Jerusalem for ninety years.

In every generation there are those who hate God's people and try to block God's purposes. When you attempt to do God's work, some will oppose you; some will hope you fail. If you expect opposition, you will be prepared rather than surprised. Knowing that God is behind your task is the best incentive to move ahead in the face of opposition.

GOD'S PROMISE

My victory and honor come from God alone. He is my refuge, a rock where no enemy can reach me. **PSALM 62:7**

Effort

Sometimes I feel that life requires too much effort and offers too little reward. What's the point of working so hard?

GOD'S RESPONSE

My life is worth nothing to me unless I use it for finishing the work assigned me by the Lord Jesus—the work of telling others the Good News about the wonderful grace of God.   *Acts 20:24*

As for me, my life has already been poured out as an offering to God.   *2 Timothy 4:6*

 Especially in our culture, it's easy to feel as if our lives are failures unless we're getting a lot out of them: recognition, fun, money, success. But Paul considered life worth *nothing* unless he used it for God's work. What he put *into* his life was far more important than what he got out of it.

Which is more important to you—what you get out of life or what you put into it?

GOD'S PROMISE

Either way, Christ's love controls us. Since we believe that Christ died for all, we also believe that we have all died to our old life. He died for everyone so that those who receive his new life will no longer live for themselves. Instead, they will live for Christ, who died and was raised for them.   2 CORINTHIANS 5:14-15

God's Timing

*Why do I feel as if my life is on hold right now?
When will God give me direction?*

GOD'S RESPONSE

When the apostles were with Jesus, they kept asking him, "Lord, has the time come for you to free Israel and restore our kingdom?" He replied, "The Father alone has the authority to set those dates and times, and they are not for you to know." *Acts 1:6-7*

This vision is for a future time. It describes the end, and it will be fulfilled. If it seems slow in coming, wait patiently, for it will surely take place. It will not be delayed. *Habakkuk 2:3*

 Like other Jews, the disciples chafed under their Roman rulers. They wanted Jesus, the Messiah, to free Israel from Rome's political power and then become their king. But Jesus told them that God the Father sets the timetable for all events—worldwide, national, and personal.

If you are waiting for changes in your life but God hasn't yet made those changes a reality, don't become impatient. Instead, trust God's timetable.

GOD'S CHALLENGE

Wait patiently for the LORD. Be brave and courageous. Yes, wait patiently for the LORD. PSALM 27:14

Accomplishments

Why can't I hold on to the good feelings that come with success?

GOD'S RESPONSE

As I looked at everything I had worked so hard to accomplish, it was all so meaningless—like chasing the wind. There was nothing really worthwhile anywhere.   *Ecclesiastes 2:11*

Unfailing love and faithfulness protect the king; his throne is made secure through love.   *Proverbs 20:28*

Teach us to realize the brevity of life, so that we may grow in wisdom.   *Psalm 90:12*

In the book of Ecclesiastes, Solomon describes his many attempts at finding life's meaning as being like "chasing the wind." We feel the wind as it passes, but we can't catch it or keep it. In all our accomplishments, even the big ones, our good feelings are only temporary. Security and self-worth are found not in our accomplishments but far beyond them, in the love of God.

Think about what you consider worthwhile in your life—where you invest your time, energy, and money. Will you one day look back and decide that these, too, were "chasing the wind"?

GOD'S PROMISE

Those who fear the LORD are secure; he will be a refuge for their children.   PROVERBS 14:26

Advice

Where should I look for quality advice?

GOD'S RESPONSE

The words of the godly are like sterling silver; the heart of a fool is worthless. *Proverbs 10:20*

Wise words are more valuable than much gold and many rubies.
Proverbs 20:15

The godly offer good counsel; they teach right from wrong. They have made God's law their own, so they will never slip from his path. *Psalm 37:30-31*

Wounds from a sincere friend are better than many kisses from an enemy. . . . The heartfelt counsel of a friend is as sweet as perfume and incense. *Proverbs 27:6, 9*

An abundance of poor advice is worth far less than a little good advice. We are naturally drawn to people who tell us what we want to hear, but that kind of advice is not helpful. Instead, when we need advice, we need to look to those who will speak the truth, even when it hurts or isn't necessarily what we want to hear. Words from a good person are valuable ("like sterling silver").

Think about the people to whom you go for advice. What do you expect to hear from them?

GOD'S PROMISE

The instruction of the wise is like a life-giving fountain; those who accept it avoid the snares of death. PROVERBS 13:14

Panic

How should I pray in times of panic?

GOD'S RESPONSE

Please, God, rescue me! Come quickly, LORD, and help me. May those who try to kill me be humiliated and put to shame. May those who take delight in my trouble be turned back in disgrace. Let them be horrified by their shame, for they said, "Aha! We've got him now!" But may all who search for you be filled with joy and gladness in you. May those who love your salvation repeatedly shout, "God is great!"   *Psalm 70:1-4*

 Psalm 70 was David's plea for God to come quickly and help him. Yet even in David's moment of desperation, he did not forget praise. Praise is important because it helps us recall who God is and then helps us to remember how great is his power to come to our aid. Often we fill our prayers with requests for ourselves and others, and we forget to thank God for what he has done and to worship him for who he is.

Don't take God—or his help—for granted by treating him merely as a vending machine. Let your praise remind you of his mighty power to help and of his great desire to do so.

GOD'S CHALLENGE

When I am afraid, I will put my trust in you. I praise God for what he has promised.   PSALM 56:3-4

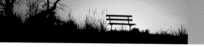

Listening

If God can speak to me, what should I be listening for?

God's Response

On the day of Pentecost all the believers were meeting together in one place. Suddenly, there was a sound from heaven like the roaring of a mighty windstorm, and it filled the house where they were sitting. Then, what looked like flames or tongues of fire appeared and settled on each of them. And everyone present was filled with the Holy Spirit and began speaking in other languages. *Acts 2:1-4*

After the earthquake there was a fire, but the LORD was not in the fire. And after the fire there was the sound of a gentle whisper.

1 Kings 19:12

At Pentecost, God made his presence known to the believers in spectacular ways—sound, fire, and different languages. God may choose to reveal himself to you in a dramatic way, but be wary of forcing your expectations on God. In 1 Kings 19:10-13, Elijah also needed a message from God. There was a great wind, then an earthquake, and finally a fire. But God's message came in "the sound of a gentle whisper." God may use dramatic methods to communicate—or he may speak in gentle whispers. If you expect God to communicate in various ways, you'll be less likely to miss what he's trying to tell you.

God's Promise

Your word is a lamp to guide my feet and a light for my path.

PSALM 119:105

Unfinished

I feel as if I've hit a plateau on my spiritual journey. Has God given up on me?

GOD'S RESPONSE

I am certain that God, who began the good work within you, will continue his work until it is finally finished on the day when Christ Jesus returns.   *Philippians 1:6*

Do you sometimes feel as if you aren't making any progress in your spiritual life? Philippians 1:6 reminds you that when God starts a project, he completes it! As God did for the believers at Philippi, he will help you grow in grace until he has completed his work in your life. When you are discouraged, remember that God won't give up on you. He promises to finish the work he has begun. When you feel incomplete, unfinished, or distressed by your short-comings, remember God's promise and provision. Don't let your present condition rob you of the joy of knowing Christ or keep you from growing closer to him.

GOD'S PROMISE

Now you have every spiritual gift you need as you eagerly wait for the return of our Lord Jesus Christ. He will keep you strong to the end so that you will be free from all blame on the day when our Lord Jesus Christ returns. God will do this, for he is faithful to do what he says.   1 CORINTHIANS 1:7-9

Attitudes

What is the secret to maintaining a positive attitude?

GOD'S RESPONSE

For the despondent, every day brings trouble; for the happy heart, life is a continual feast.   *Proverbs 15:15*

Now, dear brothers and sisters, one final thing. Fix your thoughts on what is true, and honorable, and right, and pure, and lovely, and admirable. Think about things that are excellent and worthy of praise.   *Philippians 4:8*

 Our attitudes color the whole of our personalities—what we think about, what we say, what we do. We cannot always choose what happens to us, but we *can* choose our attitudes toward each situation. The secret to a positive attitude is filling our minds with thoughts that are true, pure, and lovely and that focus on the good things in life. This was Paul's secret—even in a dark prison cell—and it can be ours, too, as we face the struggles of daily living.

Look at your attitude, and then examine what you allow to enter your mind and what you choose to focus on. Where does your thought life need some changes?

GOD'S PROMISE

You will keep in perfect peace all who trust in you, all whose thoughts are fixed on you!   ISAIAH 26:3

Holiness

What does God see when he looks at me?

God's Response

I have kept the ways of the LORD; I have not turned from my God to follow evil. I have followed all his regulations; I have never abandoned his decrees. I am blameless before God; I have kept myself from sin.   *2 Samuel 22:22-24*

Purify me from my sins, and I will be clean; wash me, and I will be whiter than snow. . . . Create in me a clean heart, O God. Renew a loyal spirit within me.   *Psalm 51:7, 10*

Now [God] has reconciled you to himself through the death of Christ. . . . As a result, he has brought you into his own presence, and you are holy and blameless as you stand before him without a single fault.   *Colossians 1:22*

 In the above verses from 2 Samuel, David was not denying that he had ever sinned. Psalm 51 shows his tremendous anguish over his sin against Uriah and Bathsheba. But David had experienced God's forgiveness, and he knew that God had made him clean again— "whiter than snow"—and had the power to give him "a clean heart."

Through Jesus Christ in his death and resurrection, we also are made clean and holy when we ask him to forgive our sins. God replaces our sin with his purity, and he no longer sees our sin.

God's Promise

By that one offering [Christ, our High Priest,] forever made perfect those who are being made holy.   HEBREWS 10:14

Pride

How can I tell if pride is taking root in my heart?

GOD'S RESPONSE

Jonathan attacked and defeated the garrison of Philistines at Geba. The news spread quickly among the Philistines. So Saul blew the ram's horn throughout the land, saying, "Hebrews, hear this! Rise up in revolt!" All Israel heard the news that Saul had destroyed the Philistine garrison at Geba and that the Philistines now hated the Israelites more than ever.   *1 Samuel 13:3-4*

 Saul's son Jonathan had attacked and destroyed the Philistine outpost, but Saul took all the credit. Although this was normal in that culture, it didn't make his action right. Saul's prideful attitude started out small—he took credit for a battle that was won by his son. Left unchecked, Saul's pride grew into an obsession; thus, it destroyed him, tore his family apart, and threatened the well-being of the nation.

Taking credit for the accomplishments of others is one indicator that pride is taking root in your life. If you notice this in yourself or if others point it out to you, take immediate steps to put it in check by giving credit to those who deserve it. Do you know someone who could use a little more credit or who has been ignored but doesn't deserve to be? Give credit where credit is due.

GOD'S PROMISE

Those who exalt themselves will be humbled, and those who humble themselves will be exalted.   MATTHEW 23:12

Confession

Is there a right way to confess my sins to God?

GOD'S RESPONSE

Confess your sin to the LORD, the God of your ancestors, and do what he demands. Separate yourselves from the people of the land and from these pagan women.   *Ezra 10:11*

I confessed all my sins to you and stopped trying to hide my guilt. I said to myself, "I will confess my rebellion to the LORD." And you forgave me! All my guilt is gone.   *Psalm 32:5*

 Confession is more than merely accepting Christ's forgiveness for what we have done. Confession is talking with God about what we have done wrong and agreeing with him that those things, whether thoughts, words, or actions, really are wrong and contrary to his will. It is telling God that we are sorry and renouncing those acts of disobedience. Finally it is receiving his forgiveness and recommitting ourselves to obeying his will instead of our own.

GOD'S PROMISE

People who conceal their sins will not prosper, but if they confess and turn from them, they will receive mercy.   PROVERBS 28:13

Decisions

How can I know if I'm making the right decisions?

GOD'S RESPONSE

Saul said, "Let's chase the Philistines all night and plunder them until sunrise. Let's destroy every last one of them." His men replied, "We'll do whatever you think is best." But the priest said, "Let's ask God first."   *1 Samuel 14:36*

I will bless the LORD who guides me; even at night my heart instructs me. I know the LORD is always with me. I will not be shaken, for he is right beside me.   *Psalm 16:7-8*

We understand these things, for we have the mind of Christ.
1 Corinthians 2:16

 It is human nature to first make our own plans and *then* ask God to bless them. But the right way to make decisions is to first ask God what plans we *should* make. By constantly consulting with God through prayer and Bible reading, you will gain insights that will help you know "the mind of Christ" and allow you to make better decisions and live the way God desires. When you consistently communicate with God and ask him for wisdom, he will counsel you so that you will have the wisdom to make the best decisions.

GOD'S PROMISE

The commands of the LORD are clear, giving insight for living.
PSALM 19:8

Faithfulness

Is God's rescue of us dependent on our faithfulness to him?

GOD'S RESPONSE

Shadrach, Meshach, and Abednego replied, "O Nebuchadnezzar, we do not need to defend ourselves before you. If we are thrown into the blazing furnace, the God whom we serve is able to save us. He will rescue us from your power, Your Majesty. But even if he doesn't, we want to make it clear to you, Your Majesty, that we will never serve your gods or worship the gold statue you have set up."   *Daniel 3:16-18*

 Shadrach, Meshach, and Abednego were pressured to deny God, but they chose to be faithful to him no matter what happened! They trusted that God was able to deliver them, but they were more determined to be faithful regardless of the consequences. If God always rescued those who were true to him, Christians would not need faith. Their religion would be a great insurance policy, and there would be lines of selfish people ready to sign up.

We should be faithful to God whether he intervenes on our behalf or not. Our eternal reward and rescue from God's judgment are worth any suffering we may have to endure first.

GOD'S PROMISE

If we are faithful to the end, trusting God just as firmly as when we first believed, we will share in all that belongs to Christ.

HEBREWS 3:14

God's Love

Does God's love for me have any limits?

GOD'S RESPONSE

[God said,] "At that time I will plant a crop of Israelites and raise them for myself. I will show love to those I called 'Not loved.' And to those I called 'Not my people,' I will say, 'Now you are my people.' And they will reply, 'You are our God!'"   *Hosea 2:23*

May you have the power to understand, as all God's people should, how wide, how long, how high, and how deep his love is.

Ephesians 3:18

When your will is weak, your thinking confused, and your conscience burdened with a load of guilt, you must remember that God cares for you continuously; his compassion never fails. When friends and family desert you, coworkers don't understand you, and you are tired of being good, God's love never fails. When you can't see the way or seem to hear God's voice, and when you lack the courage to go on, God's love never fails. When your short-comings and your awareness of your sins overcome you, God's love never fails. God's amazing, unconditional, never-ending love has no limits.

GOD'S PROMISE

Sing for joy, O heavens! Rejoice, O earth! Burst into song, O mountains! For the LORD has comforted his people and will have compassion on them in their suffering.   ISAIAH 49:13

Faithfulness

Can my faithfulness to God really have an impact on someone else's life?

GOD'S RESPONSE

King Darius sent this message to the people of every race and nation and language throughout the world: "Peace and prosperity to you! I decree that everyone throughout my kingdom should tremble with fear before the God of Daniel. For he is the living God, and he will endure forever. His kingdom will never be destroyed, and his rule will never end. He rescues and saves his people; he performs miraculous signs and wonders in the heavens and on earth. He has rescued Daniel from the power of the lions."   *Daniel 6:25-27*

King Darius was convinced of God's power because Daniel was faithful both in his private life and in his public life. Because of Daniel's faithfulness, God chose to rescue him from the lions' den in order to make an impact on the king. Although Daniel was a captive in a foreign land, his devotion to God was a testimony to the powerful rulers there. God doesn't always rescue us even when we are faithful, but if we aren't faithful, why would he even want to?

Whatever your current situation, be faithful to God. Then, in good times or bad, let him decide how he will use you to make an impact on others.

GOD'S PROMISE

May [God] give you the power to accomplish all the good things your faith prompts you to do. Then the name of our Lord Jesus will be honored because of the way you live.

2 THESSALONIANS 1:11-12

Accomplishments

Is it wrong to feel good when I accomplish something significant?

God's Response

God made all sorts of wild animals, livestock, and small animals, each able to produce offspring of the same kind. And God saw that it was good.   *Genesis 1:25*

People should eat and drink and enjoy the fruits of their labor, for these are gifts from God.   *Ecclesiastes 3:13*

People sometimes feel guilty for enjoying the fruits of their labors or for feeling good about an accomplishment. This need not be so. Just as God was pleased with the good that resulted from his work, we can be pleased when good things result from our efforts. We should enjoy our work—or anything else we can do to God's glory—as a gift from God because it is good. Just be careful not to let the good of your accomplishments trick you into thinking it came about all because of you and what you did. That's the beginning of pride, which will lead to a fall. But appreciating the good work God does through you is humbling and awesome. Enjoy it.

God's Promise

How joyful are those who fear the Lord—all who follow his ways! You will enjoy the fruit of your labor. How joyful and prosperous you will be!   PSALM 128:1-2

Giving

Why must I give back to God?

God's Response

"You have cheated me! But you ask, 'What do you mean? When did we ever cheat you?' You have cheated me of the tithes and offerings due to me. . . . Bring all the tithes into the storehouse so there will be enough food in my Temple. If you do," says the LORD of Heaven's Armies, "I will open the windows of heaven for you. I will pour out a blessing so great you won't have enough room to take it in! Try it! Put me to the test!"   *Malachi 3:8, 10*

The people had ignored God's command to give a tithe of their income to his Temple. They may have feared losing what they had worked so hard to get, but in this they misjudged God. "Give, and you will receive," Jesus says in Luke 6:38.

God wants you to participate in the cycle of giving in order to bless others. Your gifts may be God's provision to someone else, and someone else's gifts might one day bless you. When you give, remember that the blessings God promises are not always material and that you may not experience those fully here on earth, but you will certainly receive them in your future life with him.

God's Promise

Give, and you will receive. Your gift will return to you in full—pressed down, shaken together to make room for more, running over, and poured into your lap. The amount you give will determine the amount you get back.   LUKE 6:38

Encouragement

How can I be an encouragement to someone who has just decided to follow God?

GOD'S RESPONSE

When Saul arrived in Jerusalem, he tried to meet with the believers, but they were all afraid of him. They did not believe he had truly become a believer! Then Barnabas brought him to the apostles and told them how Saul had seen the Lord on the way to Damascus and how the Lord had spoken to Saul. He also told them that Saul had preached boldly in the name of Jesus in Damascus. *Acts 9:26-27*

It is difficult to change your reputation, especially when it was bad to begin with, and Saul (later known as Paul) had a terrible reputation with the Christians because of his zealous persecution of them. But Barnabas became the bridge between Saul and the apostles and told them about Saul's powerful conversion and his bold preaching in Damascus.

New Christians, especially those with tarnished reputations, need sponsors, people who will come alongside them to encourage them, teach them, and introduce them to other believers. Do you know people who need a Barnabas in their lives? If you are willing, God may give you that privilege.

GOD'S CHALLENGE

We who are strong must be considerate of those who are sensitive about things like this. We must not just please ourselves. We should help others do what is right and build them up in the Lord.

ROMANS 15:1-2

Follow-Up

I've helped a friend come to know God. Is there more I can do?

GOD'S RESPONSE

Barnabas went on to Tarsus to look for Saul. When he found him, he brought him back to Antioch. Both of them stayed there with the church for a full year, teaching large crowds of people.

Acts 11:25-26

Brothers and sisters, we urge you to warn those who are lazy. Encourage those who are timid. Take tender care of those who are weak. Be patient with everyone.   *1 Thessalonians 5:14*

In a sense, helping someone come to faith in Christ is only the beginning. Barnabas and Saul stayed at Antioch for a full year, teaching the new believers. They could have left for other cities, but they saw the importance of follow-up and training and helping the new believers become grounded in their newfound faith.

Have you helped someone believe in God? Spend time teaching, encouraging, and praying for that person.

GOD'S PROMISE

Care for the flock that God has entrusted to you. Watch over it willingly, not grudgingly—not for what you will get out of it, but because you are eager to serve God. Don't lord it over the people assigned to your care, but lead them by your own good example. And when the Great Shepherd appears, you will receive a crown of never-ending glory and honor.   1 PETER 5:2-4

Solid Rock

What are the benefits of trusting God?

God's Response

The Lord is my shepherd; I have all that I need. He lets me rest in green meadows; he leads me beside peaceful streams. He renews my strength. He guides me along right paths, bringing honor to his name. Even when I walk through the darkest valley, I will not be afraid, for you are close beside me. Your rod and your staff protect and comfort me.   *Psalm 23:1-4*

The Lord is my rock, my fortress, and my savior; my God is my rock, in whom I find protection. He is my shield, the power that saves me, and my place of safety.   *Psalm 18:2*

[God] alone is my rock and my salvation, my fortress where I will not be shaken.   *Psalm 62:6*

 When you trust in God, you will find permanence and stability. You may lose a great deal—family, jobs, material possessions—but you cannot be shaken from God's favor. He will be your rock-solid foundation, your shepherd, and your protector. He will never leave or desert you. When you trust your life to the eternal God, you can remain steady in your faith through shifting circumstances.

God's Promise

He will not let you stumble; the one who watches over you will not slumber.   PSALM 121:3

Repentance

How can I change the direction of my life?

GOD'S RESPONSE

A very large crowd of people from Israel—men, women, and children—gathered and wept bitterly. Then Shecaniah . . . said to Ezra, "We have been unfaithful to our God, for we have married these pagan women of the land. . . . We will follow the advice given by you and by the others who respect the commands of our God." . . . Then Ezra the priest stood and said to them: ". . . Confess your sin to the LORD, the God of your ancestors, and do what he demands." *Ezra 10:1-3, 10-11*

The people confessed their sin to God. They acknowledged their wrongdoings. Then they asked Ezra for advice about restoring their relationship with God. True repentance does not end with an acknowledgment of sin—that would be mere lip service. Repentance involves turning away from the wrong actions and turning toward God and what is pleasing to him. It leads to changed attitudes and behavior.

When you sin and are truly sorry, confess your sin to God, ask his forgiveness, and accept his mercy. Then, as an act of thankfulness for your forgiveness, make the needed course corrections to stay on the path of right living with God.

GOD'S PROMISE

Samuel said to all the people of Israel, "If you are really serious about wanting to return to the LORD . . . determine to obey only the LORD; then he will rescue you." 1 SAMUEL 7:3

Struggles

Can my struggles really bring me closer to God?

GOD'S RESPONSE

What joy for those whose strength comes from the LORD, who have set their minds on a pilgrimage to Jerusalem. When they walk through the Valley of Weeping, it will become a place of refreshing springs. The autumn rains will clothe it with blessings. They will continue to grow stronger, and each of them will appear before God in Jerusalem.   *Psalm 84:5-7*

In the days when this psalm was written, the annual pilgrimage to the Temple passed through the barren Valley of Weeping. No specific valley has been identified, and the "weeping" may have been a symbolic reference to the times of struggles and tears through which people must pass on their way to meet God.

The process of growing stronger in your relationship with Christ is often preceded by a journey through difficult, barren places in your life. If you love to spend time with God, you will see your adversity as an opportunity to reexperience God's faithfulness. If you are walking through your own Valley of Weeping today, be sure your pilgrimage leads toward God, to where you can experience his presence, not away from him.

GOD'S PROMISE

You have sorrow now, but I will see you again; then you will rejoice, and no one can rob you of that joy.   JOHN 16:22

Fountain of Life

What does the Bible mean when it says that God's wisdom brings life?

GOD'S RESPONSE

Discretion is a life-giving fountain to those who possess it, but discipline is wasted on fools.   *Proverbs 16:22*

Fear of the LORD is a life-giving fountain; it offers escape from the snares of death.   *Proverbs 14:27*

When God our Savior revealed his kindness and love, he saved us, not because of the righteous things we had done, but because of his mercy. He washed away our sins, giving us a new birth and new life through the Holy Spirit. He generously poured out the Spirit upon us through Jesus Christ our Savior.   *Titus 3:4-6*

For centuries people have searched for a fountain of youth, a spring of water that legend says brings eternal life and vitality. No one has ever found it. But there is a way to experience peace and happiness now and eternal life forever.

When you discover the life-giving principles of God's Word, you see how God washes away the deadly effects of sin. This gives you the assurance of eternal life in a perfect place called heaven. But it also gives you a joyful perspective on your present life because you know your future is secure. The fountain of youth is only a dream, but God's life-giving fountain described in the Bible is a reality.

GOD'S PROMISE

You are the fountain of life, the light by which we see.

PSALM 36:9

Vision

How do I obtain good spiritual vision?

GOD'S RESPONSE

The people's minds were hardened, and to this day whenever the old covenant is being read, the same veil covers their minds so they cannot understand the truth. And this veil can be removed only by believing in Christ.   *2 Corinthians 3:14*

Elisha prayed, "O LORD, open his eyes and let him see!" The LORD opened the young man's eyes, and when he looked up, he saw that the hillside around Elisha was filled with horses and chariots of fire.
2 Kings 6:17

It seems ironic that the only way for some of us to see better is to cover our eyes with glasses or contact lenses. But the same is true when it comes to spiritual vision. We need the lens of faith—the ability to believe that there is much more happening than we can see.

When you face difficulties that seem insurmountable, remember that spiritual armies that you cannot see are fighting battles on your behalf. Open your spiritual eyes to view God's power.

GOD'S PROMISE

Jesus responded, "Didn't I tell you that you would see God's glory if you believe?"   JOHN 11:40

Circumstances

How can people maintain their trust in God in the midst of terrible circumstances?

GOD'S RESPONSE

Who can teach a lesson to God, since he judges even the most powerful?   *Job 21:22*

If [God] chooses to remain quiet, who can criticize him?

Job 34:29

The LORD of Heaven's Armies has spoken—who can change his plans? When his hand is raised, who can stop him?   *Isaiah 14:27*

Although baffled by the reasons for his suffering, Job affirmed God's superior understanding by asking, "Who can teach a lesson to God?" The way you react to your personal struggles shows your attitude toward God. Instead of becoming angry with God, continue to trust him, whatever your circumstances are. Although it may be difficult to see at the time, God is still in control. Commit yourself wholeheartedly to him so that you will not resent his timing.

How do you react when you find yourself in less-than-ideal circumstances?

GOD'S CHALLENGE

I keep praying to you, LORD, hoping this time you will show me favor. In your unfailing love, O God, answer my prayer with your sure salvation.   PSALM 69:13

Problems

How should I talk to God about my problems?
What kind of help can I expect from him?

GOD'S RESPONSE

The council threatened [Peter and John] further, but they finally
let them go because they didn't know how to punish them without
starting a riot. . . . When they heard the report, all the believers
lifted their voices together in prayer to God: "O Sovereign Lord,
Creator of heaven and earth, the sea, and everything in them. . . .
O Lord, hear their threats, and give us, your servants, great boldness
in preaching your word. Stretch out your hand with healing power;
may miraculous signs and wonders be done through the name of
your holy servant Jesus."   *Acts 4:21, 24, 29-30*

Notice how the believers prayed. First, they praised God; then
they told God their specific problem and asked for his help. They
did not ask God to remove the problem but rather to help them
meet it with courage and boldness.

This is a model for us to follow when we pray. We may ask God
to remove our problems, and he may choose to do so. But we must
also recognize that often God will leave the problem but give us the
strength and courage to deal with it. And if he chooses to leave the
problem with us, it is because he will bring greater good from our
learning to deal with it than would come if he took it away.

GOD'S PROMISE

I can do everything through Christ, who gives me strength.

PHILIPPIANS 4:13

Slow Down

How can I avoid ignoring God when life gets so busy?

GOD'S RESPONSE

Joshua told the Israelites, "Come and listen to what the LORD your God says. Today you will know that the living God is among you."

Joshua 3:9-10

My children, listen to me, for all who follow my ways are joyful.

Proverbs 8:32

I listen carefully to what God the LORD is saying, for he speaks peace to his faithful people. But let them not return to their foolish ways. *Psalm 85:8*

Just before crossing over into the Promised Land, Joshua gathered the people to hear the words of the Lord. Their excitement was high. No doubt they wanted to rush right in, but Joshua made them take time to stop and listen before proceeding.

We live in a fast-paced age where everyone rushes just to keep up. It's easy to get caught up in our many tasks and become too busy for what God says is most important—listening to his words. Before you make your schedule, take time to focus on what God wants from all your activities. Knowing what God has said before you rush into your day may help you to avoid foolish mistakes.

GOD'S CHALLENGE

We must listen very carefully to the truth we have heard, or we may drift away from it. HEBREWS 2:1

Renewal

How can I overcome the weariness of burnout?

GOD'S RESPONSE

Celebrate the Festival of Trumpets each year on the first day of the
appointed month in early autumn. You must call an official day for
holy assembly, and you may do no ordinary work.   *Numbers 29:1*

I long to obey your commandments! Renew my life with your
goodness.   *Psalm 119:40*

The Festival of Trumpets was one of three great holidays celebrated by the people of Israel. These holidays provided an opportunity for the people to cease normal work and activity, refresh their
minds and bodies, and renew their commitment to God.

If you feel tired or far from God, try taking a "spiritual holiday."
Separate yourself from your daily routine, and concentrate on
renewing your commitment to God. How might you benefit from
taking some time to get away with God?

GOD'S PROMISE

[The Lord] gives power to the weak and strength to the powerless. Even youths will become weak and tired, and young men will
fall in exhaustion. But those who trust in the LORD will find new
strength. They will soar high on wings like eagles. They will run
and not grow weary. They will walk and not faint.

ISAIAH 40:29-31

Procrastination

If God really wants me to do something, won't he confirm it by providing the perfect conditions?

GOD'S RESPONSE

Farmers who wait for perfect weather never plant. If they watch every cloud, they never harvest.   *Ecclesiastes 11:4*

Take a lesson from the ants. . . . Learn from their ways and become wise! Though they have no prince or governor or ruler to make them work, they labor hard all summer, gathering food for the winter.

Proverbs 6:6

Waiting for perfect conditions is the same thing as being inactive. If we wait for the perfect time and place for personal Bible reading, we will never begin. If we wait until we find a perfect church, we will never become members of a church body. If we wait to find the perfect ministry, we will never serve. Take steps now to grow spiritually. Don't wait for conditions that may never exist. What small steps can you take now, despite imperfect conditions?

GOD'S CHALLENGE

Make the most of every opportunity in these evil days.

EPHESIANS 5:16

Crossroads

I'm going through a lot of difficult things right now. Is it wrong to have doubts about who God is?

God's Response

[Job] cursed the day of his birth. He said: ". . . Why wasn't I born dead? Why didn't I die as I came from the womb?"   *Job 3:1-3, 11*

My health may fail, and my spirit may grow weak, but God remains the strength of my heart; he is mine forever.   *Psalm 73:26*

Job was experiencing extreme physical pain as well as grief over the loss of his children and possessions. It's hard to blame him for wishing he could join his family on the other side of the grave. Until tragedy struck, God had provided for Job, protected him, and blessed him with riches. Job's grief placed him at the crossroads of his faith, shattering many of his misconceptions about God and driving Job back to the basics of his faith. He had only two choices: (1) He could curse God and give up, or (2) he could trust God and draw strength from him to continue. There will always be circumstances that challenge your view of who God is. Your doubts at these crossroads are wrong only if you let them cause you to give up and abandon God.

God's Promise

The Sovereign LORD is my strength! He makes me as surefooted as a deer, able to tread upon the heights.   HABAKKUK 3:19

Heroes

Most heroes are those who persevere against hardship. How can I emulate such people?

GOD'S RESPONSE

We give great honor to those who endure under suffering. For instance, you know about Job, a man of great endurance. You can see how the Lord was kind to him at the end, for the Lord is full of tenderness and mercy. *James 5:11*

All these people earned a good reputation because of their faith, yet none of them received all that God had promised. For God had something better in mind for us, so that they would not reach perfection without us. *Hebrews 11:39-40*

God's heroes are those who hold on to their faith in him no matter what happens. The Bible is full of examples of people who never stopped trusting God even though they were mocked, persecuted, or killed for their faith.

God may not ask you to be a martyr for him, but is your faith strong enough to endure even a little ridicule, derision, or scorn? Study the lives of believers who suffered for their faithfulness to Christ, and determine to follow their example and remain faithful to God no matter the cost.

GOD'S PROMISE

The godly people in the land are my true heroes! PSALM 16:3

Helping Others

How can I possibly make a difference when there are so many people in need?

GOD'S RESPONSE

If one of your fellow Israelites falls into poverty and cannot support himself, support him as you would a foreigner or a temporary resident and allow him to live with you.   *Leviticus 25:35*

I don't mean your giving should make life easy for others and hard for yourselves. I only mean that there should be some equality. Right now you have plenty and can help those who are in need. Later, they will have plenty and can share with you when you need it. In this way, things will be equal.   *2 Corinthians 8:13-14*

God said that neglecting the poor is a sin. Permanent poverty was not allowed in Israel. Financially secure families were commanded to help and house those in need. Many times we do nothing, not because we lack compassion, but because we are overwhelmed by the size of the problem and don't know where to begin. God doesn't expect you to eliminate poverty, nor does he expect you to neglect your family while providing for others. But when you do see someone in need, God wants you to give whatever help you can, including hospitality.

GOD'S CHALLENGE

When God's people are in need, be ready to help them. Always be eager to practice hospitality.   ROMANS 12:13

Authenticity

How can I show others that my faith in God is genuine?

GOD'S RESPONSE

Prove by the way you live that you have repented of your sins and turned to God.   *Matthew 3:8*

Faith by itself isn't enough. Unless it produces good deeds, it is dead and useless.   *James 2:17*

We are shown to be right with God by what we do, not by faith alone. . . . Just as the body is dead without breath, so also faith is dead without good works.   *James 2:24, 26*

In Matthew 3:8, John the Baptist called people to more than mere words or ritual; he told them to change their behavior. When he said, "Prove by the way you live that you have repented of your sins," he meant that God looks beyond our words and religious activities to see if our conduct backs up what we say, and he judges our words by the actions that accompany them.

Do your actions match your words? Has your faith become nothing more than ritual? Or does your love for God compel you to live obediently and show God's love to others?

GOD'S CHALLENGE

What is important is faith expressing itself in love.

GALATIANS 5:6

True Words

How do I know if I'm giving a true compliment and not just speaking words of flattery?

GOD'S RESPONSE

Even when you ask, you don't get it because your motives are all wrong—you want only what will give you pleasure. *James 4:3*

May the words of my mouth and the meditation of my heart be pleasing to you, O LORD, my rock and my redeemer. *Psalm 19:14*

In the end, people appreciate honest criticism far more than flattery.
Proverbs 28:23

The difference between a compliment and flattery lies in the motivation behind the words. Sincere compliments are all about the recipients and are designed to build them up. Flattery, on the other hand, is all about you; you say something nice just to get something—even the feeling of self-satisfaction—in return. Never ignore your conscience—it will tell you if you are being sincere.

GOD'S PROMISE

Christ died for us so that, whether we are dead or alive when he returns, we can live with him forever. So encourage each other and build each other up. 1 THESSALONIANS 5:10-11

Culture

Do I have to reject my culture in order to change it?

GOD'S RESPONSE

God gave these four young men an unusual aptitude for understanding every aspect of literature and wisdom. And God gave Daniel the special ability to interpret the meanings of visions and dreams. When the training period ordered by the king was completed, the chief of staff brought all the young men to King Nebuchadnezzar. The king talked with them, and no one impressed him as much as Daniel, Hananiah, Mishael, and Azariah. So they entered the royal service. Whenever the king consulted them in any matter requiring wisdom and balanced judgment, he found them ten times more capable than any of the magicians and enchanters in his entire kingdom. *Daniel 1:17-20*

Daniel and his friends learned all they could about their new culture so that they could do their work with excellence. But while they learned, they also maintained steadfast allegiance to God, and God gave them skill and wisdom.

Culture need not be God's enemy. If it does not violate his commands, it can aid in accomplishing his purposes. We who follow God are free to be competent leaders in our culture, but we are required to pledge our allegiance to God first.

GOD'S PROMISE

[Solomon] prayed, "O LORD, God of Israel, there is no God like you in all of heaven above or on the earth below. You keep your covenant and show unfailing love to all who walk before you in wholehearted devotion." 1 KINGS 8:23

Words

How can I exercise control over my words?

GOD'S RESPONSE

Take control of what I say, O LORD, and guard my lips.

Psalm 141:3

[Jesus said,] "I tell you this, you must give an account on judgment day for every idle word you speak." *Matthew 12:36*

If you claim to be religious but don't control your tongue, you are fooling yourself, and your religion is worthless. *James 1:26*

Exercising self-control over your words includes watching both what you shouldn't say and what you should say. For example, you shouldn't use profanity, complain, lie, or gossip. But you *should* speak up when you see injustice; you *should* encourage those who are down; and you *should* praise God every day.

What comes out of your mouth most often? Ask a friend to make a mental list of your positive and negative words. If you really want to stop negative speech, ask yourself before you speak, *Is it true? Is it kind? Is it necessary?*

GOD'S CHALLENGE

Don't use foul or abusive language. Let everything you say be good and helpful, so that your words will be an encouragement to those who hear them. EPHESIANS 4:29

Faults

When I get annoyed with someone, is it okay to help them see their faults so they will change?

GOD'S RESPONSE

Always be humble and gentle. Be patient with each other, making allowance for each other's faults because of your love.

Ephesians 4:2

Be kind to each other, tenderhearted, forgiving one another, just as God through Christ has forgiven you. *Ephesians 4:32*

No one is ever going to be perfect here on earth, so we must accept and love others in spite of their faults. When we see faults in other people, we should first ask ourselves if those things are simply annoying or if the people are actually doing something wrong. If they are simply annoying, then rather than dwell on others' weakness, pray for them. Then do even more—spend time with those people, and see if you can build relationships with them. Then you will have earned the right to speak to them about it when the opportunity arises.

If people are doing something wrong, you should tell them in order to help them. But always be careful to do it in a spirit of love and patience. People can tell if you really care about them or not, and that makes all the difference in how they will respond to you.

GOD'S PROMISE

Most important of all, continue to show deep love for each other, for love covers a multitude of sins. **1 PETER 4:8**

Forgiveness

How can forgiving others help me to move beyond the hurt they caused?

GOD'S RESPONSE

Daniel (also known as Belteshazzar) was overcome for a time, frightened by the meaning of the dream. Then the king said to him, "Belteshazzar, don't be alarmed by the dream and what it means." Belteshazzar replied, "I wish the events foreshadowed in this dream would happen to your enemies, my lord, and not to you!"

Daniel 4:19

How could Daniel be so deeply grieved at the fate of Nebuchadnezzar—the king who was responsible for the destruction of Daniel's home and nation? Daniel had forgiven Nebuchadnezzar, so God was able to use Daniel.

Often when others have wronged us, we find it difficult to forget the past. We may even be glad when those people suffer. But forgiveness involves putting the past behind us.

Can you love someone who has hurt you? Can you serve someone who has mistreated you? On your own, you can't, but you can ask God to help you forgive, "forget," and love. God may then use you in an extraordinary way in the lives of those who have hurt you in some way.

GOD'S CHALLENGE

Make allowance for each other's faults, and forgive anyone who offends you. Remember, the Lord forgave you, so you must forgive others. **COLOSSIANS 3:13**

Grace

What is grace?

GOD'S RESPONSE

The wages of sin is death, but the free gift of God is eternal life through Christ Jesus our Lord.   *Romans 6:23*

God saved you by his grace when you believed. And you can't take credit for this; it is a gift from God. Salvation is not a reward for the good things we have done, so none of us can boast about it.
Ephesians 2:8-9

Grace is expressed in both a onetime act (God's gift of salvation when you believe in Jesus) and a way of life (God's blessing in continuing to change you and make you more like him). In either case, grace is simply God's special and undeserved favor. Because of God's grace, he gives you many things that you don't deserve and can't take credit for. When you begin to understand God's grace and how freely he gives it, you will want to be a person who extends grace to those around you.

GOD'S PROMISE

All of this is for your benefit. And as God's grace reaches more and more people, there will be great thanksgiving, and God will receive more and more glory.   2 CORINTHIANS 4:15

Discomfort

What can help me make it through life's uncomfortable circumstances?

GOD'S RESPONSE

A great wave of persecution began that day, sweeping over the church in Jerusalem; and all the believers except the apostles were scattered through the regions of Judea and Samaria. . . . But the believers who were scattered preached the Good News about Jesus wherever they went.   *Acts 8:1, 4*

Persecution forced the believers out of their homes in Jerusalem and into other geographical areas, and when they went, they took the Good News with them.

Sometimes you have to become uncomfortable before you'll move. You may not want to experience discomfort—no one does—but God may choose to use it in accomplishing his purpose for us and/or for his Kingdom as a whole, just as he did in the book of Acts. When you are tempted to complain about uncomfortable or painful circumstances, stop and ask whether God might be preparing you for a special task.

GOD'S PROMISE

Jesus turned to his disciples and said, "God blesses you who are poor, for the Kingdom of God is yours. God blesses you who are hungry now, for you will be satisfied. God blesses you who weep now, for in due time you will laugh."   LUKE 6:20-21

Crowded Out

Why do I feel as if my life doesn't have room for God?

GOD'S RESPONSE

[God said,] "You must not have any other god but me."

Exodus 20:3

Jesus replied, "'You must love the LORD your God with all your heart, all your soul, and all your mind.' This is the first and greatest commandment." *Matthew 22:37-38*

The first of the Ten Commandments is "You must not have any other god but me." Jesus said that the greatest commandment of Moses' laws was "You must love the LORD your God with all your heart, all your soul, and all your mind."

God is worthy of your worship and adoration. Your relationship with him must be your top priority, because it affects all you are and all you do. Is *everything* crowding out the *most important thing*—putting God first? Are there just too many people, ideas, goals, and possessions occupying your every waking moment? One of the great lessons of life is that when you make God your top priority, all your other priorities will fall in line and make sense—and you will see more clearly where your time is best spent.

GOD'S PROMISE

The LORD is the only true God. He is the living God and the everlasting King! . . . Say this to those who worship other gods: "Your so-called gods, who did not make the heavens and earth, will vanish from the earth and from under the heavens."

JEREMIAH 10:10-11

In Sync

How can I get my beliefs and my behaviors in sync?

GOD'S RESPONSE

With all these things in mind, dear brothers and sisters, stand firm and keep a strong grip on the teaching we passed on to you both in person and by letter.   *2 Thessalonians 2:15*

Be an example to all believers in what you say, in the way you live, in your love, your faith, and your purity. . . . Keep a close watch on how you live and on your teaching. Stay true to what is right for the sake of your own salvation and the salvation of those who hear you.   *1 Timothy 4:12, 16*

As a Christian, what you do and what you say must be in sync. People will not believe you unless they see you living what you say. If you want others to take your faith seriously and be drawn to Christ, you need to not only talk about your faith passionately but also live out your faith consistently. Do you say you love God? Then be sure that your life expresses that love. Ask yourself, *What actions would convince me that someone is passionate about God?* Then try to model those actions in your own life.

GOD'S PROMISE

You must remain faithful to what you have been taught from the beginning. If you do, you will remain in fellowship with the Son and with the Father.   1 JOHN 2:24

Persecution

What does it mean when I face opposition for living out my faith?

GOD'S RESPONSE

The [religious leaders] called in the apostles and had them flogged. Then they ordered them never again to speak in the name of Jesus, and they let them go. The apostles left the high council rejoicing that God had counted them worthy to suffer disgrace for the name of Jesus. And every day, in the Temple and from house to house, they continued to teach and preach this message: "Jesus is the Messiah."   *Acts 5:40-41*

Have you ever thought of persecution as a blessing, as something to rejoice about? When Peter and John suffered this severe beating, it was the first time any of the apostles had been physically abused because of their faith in Christ. These men knew firsthand how Jesus had suffered, and they praised God for allowing them the privilege of being persecuted and suffering for his sake. If you are mocked or persecuted for your faith, it isn't because you're doing something wrong but because God has counted you "worthy to suffer disgrace for the name of Jesus."

GOD'S PROMISE

Dear friends, don't be surprised at the fiery trials you are going through, as if something strange were happening to you. Instead, be very glad—for these trials make you partners with Christ in his suffering, so that you will have the wonderful joy of seeing his glory when it is revealed to all the world.   1 PETER 4:12-13

Forgiveness

How can I respond to my enemies in a way that will get their attention?

GOD'S RESPONSE

As they stoned him, Stephen prayed, "Lord Jesus, receive my spirit." He fell to his knees, shouting, "Lord, don't charge them with this sin!" And with that, he died.   *Acts 7:59-60*

To you who are willing to listen, I say, love your enemies! Do good to those who hate you. Bless those who curse you. Pray for those who hurt you.   *Luke 6:27-28*

Stephen was ready to suffer like Jesus, even to the point of asking God to forgive those who were responsible for his death by stoning him. Such a response toward those who are our enemies can come only from the power of the Holy Spirit. The Spirit can help you to respond as Stephen did, with love for your enemies. How would you react if someone hurt you because of what you believed?

GOD'S PROMISE

If you forgive those who sin against you, your heavenly Father will forgive you.   MATTHEW 6:14

Desires

How can I increase my desire to be more like Jesus?

GOD'S RESPONSE

You must have the same attitude that Christ Jesus had. Though he was God, he did not think of equality with God as something to cling to. Instead, he gave up his divine privileges; he took the humble position of a slave and was born as a human being. When he appeared in human form, he humbled himself in obedience to God.

Philippians 2:5-8

God is working in you, giving you the desire and the power to do what pleases him. *Philippians 2:13*

If you want to *be* more like Jesus, you must train yourself to *think* more like Jesus. To change our desires to be more like his, we need the power of the indwelling Spirit, the influence of faithful Christians, obedience to God's Word (not just exposure to it), and sacrificial service. Often it is in *doing* God's will that we gain the *desire* to do it. Do what he wants and trust him to change your desires.

GOD'S PROMISE

I will give you a new heart, and I will put a new spirit in you. I will take out your stony, stubborn heart and give you a tender, responsive heart. EZEKIEL 36:26

Invisibility

If God really loves me, why do I often feel as if I'm invisible to others?

GOD'S RESPONSE

O LORD, you have examined my heart and know everything about me. You know when I sit down or stand up. You know my thoughts even when I'm far away. You see me when I travel and when I rest at home. You know everything I do. You know what I am going to say even before I say it, LORD. You go before me and follow me. You place your hand of blessing on my head. *Psalm 139:1-5*

The very hairs on your head are all numbered. *Luke 12:7*

You may feel that you disappear in a crowd, but you are not invisible to God, who knows everything about you—even how many hairs are on your head! He created you for a relationship with him and has a purpose for your life. You were made in God's image, and no one else is exactly like you. That makes you precious to God. As you walk through the crowds today, remember that you are special to God. Get close to him so that you can feel his love and discover what he wants you to do.

GOD'S PROMISE

[Jesus said,] "I am with you always, even to the end of the age."

MATTHEW 28:20

Rituals

How do I know when my religious traditions have become empty rituals?

GOD'S RESPONSE

The people of Israel love their rituals of sacrifice, but to me their sacrifices are all meaningless.   *Hosea 8:13*

Don't act thoughtlessly, but understand what the Lord wants you to do.   *Ephesians 5:17*

Offering a sacrifice on the altar was supposed to have profound spiritual meaning (forgiveness from the punishment sin demands). But for many of the Israelites, the sacrifice had become nothing but an empty ritual. So God refused to grant the benefits that were supposed to come from the sacrifice.

We have traditions and rituals too: attending church, spending time alone with God, celebrating Christian holidays, praying before meals. These traditions can drive God's lessons deep within us. But when we practice them only out of habit, they can become meaningless exercises that we do to gain approval, to avoid the risk of doing something different, to make up for bad behavior, or to "earn" God's favor. We should not reject the traditions of our worship, but we must be careful to think about why we observe them. Then our faith will take on deep meaning and purpose, and our relationship with God will be vital and engaging.

GOD'S PROMISE

These instructions are not empty words—they are your life!
                                    DEUTERONOMY 32:47

Prosperity

Will God bless me if I obey what the Bible says?

GOD'S RESPONSE

[Those who delight in God's law] are like trees planted along the riverbank, bearing fruit each season. Their leaves never wither, and they prosper in all they do.   *Psalm 1:3*

Today I am giving you a choice between life and death, between prosperity and disaster. For I command you this day to love the LORD your God and to keep his commands, decrees, and regulations by walking in his ways.   *Deuteronomy 30:15-16*

When the Bible says, "In all they do, they prosper," it does not mean that those who love and obey God are immune to failure or difficulties. Nor is it a guarantee of health, wealth, and happiness. What the Bible means by prosperity is this: When we apply God's wisdom, the results of our obedience will be good for us and for others and will be blessed by God. Just as a tree soaks up water and bears luscious fruit, we are to soak up God's Word and thus produce actions and attitudes that honor God and bless others. That is the rich, prosperous life the Bible talks about.

GOD'S PROMISE

[Jesus said,] "I am the vine; you are the branches. Those who remain in me, and I in them, will produce much fruit. For apart from me you can do nothing."   JOHN 15:5

Doubt

Is it wrong to question what I believe? Can doubt ever make me stronger?

GOD'S RESPONSE

John the Baptist, who was in prison, heard about all the things the Messiah was doing. So he sent his disciples to ask Jesus, "Are you the Messiah we've been expecting, or should we keep looking for someone else?"   *Matthew 11:2-3*

Peter went over the side of the boat and walked on the water toward Jesus. But when he saw the strong wind and the waves he was terrified and began to sink. . . . Jesus immediately reached out and grabbed [Peter]. "You have so little faith," Jesus said. "Why did you doubt me?"   *Matthew 14:29-31*

John the Baptist, Peter, and many other heroes of the Bible struggled with doubt. Doubt can become sin if it leads you away from God to skepticism, cynicism, and hardheartedness. But God welcomes your questions if they cause you to learn more about him and draw closer to him. Doubt is beneficial when your honest searching keeps you reaching toward God, because this will strengthen your faith. Even the strongest and wisest Christians experience times of uncertainty. The important thing is to see your doubts as the resistance that pushes against you, and thus flexes the muscles of your faith.

GOD'S PROMISE

When doubts filled my mind, your comfort gave me renewed hope and cheer.   PSALM 94:19

Miracles

Can my faith in God really bring about his divine intervention?

GOD'S RESPONSE

Elijah said to her, "Don't be afraid! Go ahead and do just what you've said, but make a little bread for me first. Then use what's left to prepare a meal for yourself and your son. For this is what the LORD, the God of Israel, says: There will always be flour and olive oil left in your containers until the time when the LORD sends rain and the crops grow again!" So she did as Elijah said, and she and Elijah and her family continued to eat for many days. There was always enough flour and olive oil left in the containers, just as the LORD had promised through Elijah.   *1 Kings 17:13-16*

When this widow met Elijah, she thought she was going to be preparing her last meal because she had no more food. But a simple act of faith produced a miracle. She looked at each event in her life as a divine moment from God, so she trusted him and used the last of her food to prepare a meal for Elijah. Faith is the step that comes between promise and assurance. Miracles seem so out of reach for our feeble faith. But every miracle, large or small, begins with an act of obedience. You may not see God work until you take the first step of faith.

GOD'S PROMISE

[Jesus said,] "Anything is possible if a person believes."

MARK 9:23

Restlessness

Sometimes I get the feeling that life is meaningless. Why am I so unsatisfied?

GOD'S RESPONSE

Everything is wearisome beyond description. No matter how much we see, we are never satisfied. No matter how much we hear, we are not content. History merely repeats itself. It has all been done before. Nothing under the sun is truly new. Sometimes people say, "Here is something new!" But actually it is old; nothing is ever truly new. We don't remember what happened in the past, and in future generations, no one will remember what we are doing now.

Ecclesiastes 1:8-11

Many people feel restless and dissatisfied. They wonder, *If I am really living in line with God's will, why am I so tired and unfulfilled? At the end of my life, will I be happy with what I accomplished? Will trying something new and different take away my restlessness?*

When these kinds of questions arise, they often test your faith, challenging you to search for true and lasting meaning. As you look at the restlessness in your own life, you will discover that all the options for meaning and real satisfaction lead back to God. Perhaps God is prompting you to take a hard look at what brings true purpose and satisfaction to life because he's confident that you will discover him in the process.

GOD'S CHALLENGE

Everything else is worthless when compared with the infinite value of knowing Christ Jesus my Lord.   PHILIPPIANS 3:8

Discouragement

I'm experiencing a major letdown in my spiritual life. Where has God gone?

God's Response

Elijah was afraid and fled for his life. He went to Beersheba, a town in Judah, and he left his servant there. Then he went on alone into the wilderness, traveling all day. He sat down under a solitary broom tree and prayed that he might die. "I have had enough, Lord," he said. "Take my life, for I am no better than my ancestors who have already died."   *1 Kings 19:3-4*

Elijah experienced the depths of fatigue and discouragement just after two great spiritual victories: the defeat of the prophets of Baal and the answered prayer for rain. Often discouragement sets in after great spiritual experiences, especially those requiring great physical effort or involving intense emotion. To lead Elijah out of his depression, God first let Elijah do nothing but rest and eat. Only after Elijah had time to recover physically did God confront him with the need to return to his mission—to speak God's words in Israel. Elijah's battles were not over; he still had work to do.

When you feel let down and discouraged after a great spiritual experience, take time to rest and be restored physically; then remember that God still has work for you to do.

God's Promise

The Lord is close to the brokenhearted; he rescues those whose spirits are crushed.   PSALM 34:18

Protection

In what ways does God protect me?

GOD'S RESPONSE

Guard me as you would guard your own eyes. Hide me in the shadow of your wings.   *Psalm 17:8*

The LORD says, "I will rescue those who love me. I will protect those who trust in my name. When they call on me, I will answer; I will be with them in trouble."   *Psalm 91:14-15*

Sight is so precious that we will go to almost any length to protect the pupils ("apples") of our eyes. That is how precious we are to God, and that is the way God will protect us. We must not conclude, however, that God is failing to protect us if we experience troubles. God's protection has far greater purposes than helping us avoid pain; it is to make us better servants for him. God protects us not only by sometimes helping us escape painful circumstances but also by guiding us through them.

GOD'S PROMISE

With your unfailing love you lead the people you have redeemed. In your might, you guide them to your sacred home.

EXODUS 15:13

Obedience

I'm under so much pressure! Does it really matter how I do the job as long as I get it done?

God's Response

Saul stayed at Gilgal, and his men were trembling with fear. Saul waited . . . seven days for Samuel, as Samuel had instructed him earlier, but Samuel still didn't come. Saul realized that his troops were rapidly slipping away. So he demanded, "Bring me the burnt offering and the peace offerings!" And Saul sacrificed the burnt offering himself. *1 Samuel 13:7-9*

I have acted with integrity; I have trusted in the Lord without wavering. Put me on trial, Lord, and cross-examine me. Test my motives and my heart. *Psalm 26:1-2*

Rather than wait for a priest who was authorized to perform a sacrifice, Saul became impatient and offered the sacrifice himself. This was against God's laws and against the specific instructions Samuel had given Saul. Under pressure from the approaching enemy, Saul took matters into his own hands and disobeyed God. Offering a sacrifice to God before a crucial moment was a good thing, but Saul did it in the wrong way. Our true spiritual character is revealed under pressure. The methods we use to accomplish our goals are as important as the attainment of those goals.

God's Promise

Obedience is better than sacrifice. *1 SAMUEL 15:22*

Reputation

What is the key to having a good reputation?

GOD'S RESPONSE

Ruth fell at [Boaz's] his feet and thanked him warmly. "What have I done to deserve such kindness?" she asked. "I am only a foreigner."

"Yes, I know," Boaz replied. "But I also know about everything you have done for your mother-in-law since the death of your husband. I have heard how you left your father and mother and your own land to live here among complete strangers. May the LORD, the God of Israel, under whose wings you have come to take refuge, reward you fully for what you have done."

Ruth 2:10-12

Ruth's life exhibited many admirable qualities. She was hard-working, loving, kind, loyal, faithful, and brave. These qualities gained for her a good reputation, but only because she displayed them *consistently* in all areas of her life. Wherever Ruth went or whatever she did, her character remained the same.

Your reputation is built over time as people watch you at school, at your workplace, in your community, at home, in your church. A good reputation is the result of *consistently* living out the qualities you believe in—no matter who you're with or where you are.

GOD'S PROMISE

Choose a good reputation over great riches; being held in high esteem is better than silver or gold.   PROVERBS 22:1

Conscience

Is my conscience a good measure of my obedience to God?

GOD'S RESPONSE

[Jonah] went down to the port of Joppa, where he found a ship leaving for Tarshish. He bought a ticket and went on board, hoping to escape from the LORD by sailing to Tarshish. But the LORD hurled a powerful wind over the sea, causing a violent storm that threatened to break the ship apart. Fearing for their lives, the desperate sailors shouted to their gods for help and threw the cargo overboard to lighten the ship. But all this time Jonah was sound asleep down in the hold. *Jonah 1:3-5*

My conscience is clear, but that doesn't prove I'm right. It is the Lord himself who will examine me and decide. *1 Corinthians 4:4*

While the storm raged, Jonah was sound asleep belowdecks. Even as Jonah ran from God, his actions apparently didn't bother his conscience. But the absence of guilty feelings isn't always a good measure of whether what we are doing is right. Because we can easily deceive ourselves and live in denial about what is true, we cannot evaluate our obedience or disobedience on the basis of our feelings. Instead, we must compare what we do with God's standards and his commands. How closely does your conscience fall in line with the standards of God's Word?

GOD'S CHALLENGE

Come back to your God. Act with love and justice, and always depend on him. HOSEA 12:6

Feelings

Can I trust my feelings?

GOD'S RESPONSE

O LORD, God of my salvation, I cry out to you by day. I come to you at night. Now hear my prayer; listen to my cry. For my life is full of troubles, and death draws near. I am as good as dead, like a strong man with no strength left. They have left me among the dead, and I lie like a corpse in a grave. I am forgotten, cut off from your care.   *Psalm 88:1-5*

Our feelings may be as obvious and painful as those expressed by the psalmist, but they are never the complete picture. In fact, our feelings can be very unstable. When we bring our unedited feelings to God, we allow him to point out where they are incomplete. We are in trouble whenever we give our feelings divine authority or assume that God can't handle what we feel. Praying the words of the psalms teaches us to bring all of our feelings to God and trains us to experience his presence even when our feelings tell us he's far away.

GOD'S PROMISE

Don't worry about anything; instead, pray about everything. Tell God what you need, and thank him for all he has done. Then you will experience God's peace, which exceeds anything we can understand. His peace will guard your hearts and minds as you live in Christ Jesus.   PHILIPPIANS 4:6-7

Advice

What should I do when people offer their advice when I haven't asked for it?

God's Response

One day Naomi said to Ruth, "My daughter, it's time that I found a permanent home for you, so that you will be provided for. Boaz is a close relative of ours, and he's been very kind. . . . Now do as I tell you—take a bath and put on perfume and dress in your nicest clothes. Then go to the threshing floor, but don't let Boaz see you until he has finished eating and drinking. Be sure to notice where he lies down; then go and uncover his feet and lie down there. He will tell you what to do."

"I will do everything you say," Ruth replied.   *Ruth 3:1-5*

As a foreigner, Ruth may have thought that Naomi's advice was odd. But Ruth followed the advice because she knew Naomi was kind, trustworthy, and filled with moral integrity. Each of us knows parents, older friends, or relatives who are always looking out for our best interests. Be willing to listen to the advice of those who are older and wiser than you are. The experience and knowledge of such people can be invaluable. You need not always follow their advice, but if you at least take the time to listen to it, you will have more information on which to base choices that are wise and good for you.

God's Promise

Get all the advice and instruction you can, so you will be wise the rest of your life.   PROVERBS 19:20

Dissatisfaction

How can I fight feelings of dissatisfaction with my life?

GOD'S RESPONSE

The foreign rabble who were traveling with the Israelites began to crave the good things of Egypt. And the people of Israel also began to complain. "Oh, for some meat!" they exclaimed. "We remember the fish we used to eat for free in Egypt. And we had all the cucumbers, melons, leeks, onions, and garlic we wanted. But now our appetites are gone. All we ever see is this manna!"   *Numbers 11:4-6*

Let them praise the LORD for his great love and for the wonderful things he has done for them. For he satisfies the thirsty and fills the hungry with good things.   *Psalm 107:8-9*

The people of Israel didn't seem to notice what God was doing for them—freeing them from slavery, making them a nation, giving them a new land—because they were so wrapped up in what God wasn't doing for them.

Before we judge the Israelites too harshly, we need to think about what occupies our attention most of the time. Are we grateful for what God has given us, or are we always thinking about what we would like to have? Let's not allow our unfulfilled desires to cause us to forget the gifts God gives us every day.

GOD'S CHALLENGE

Enjoy what you have rather than desiring what you don't have. Just dreaming about nice things is meaningless—like chasing the wind.   ECCLESIASTES 6:9

Confidence

Is there any hope that I can overcome my temptations and weaknesses?

GOD'S RESPONSE

The LORD said to Joshua, "I have given you Jericho, its king, and all its strong warriors."   *Joshua 6:2*

Despite all these things, overwhelming victory is ours through Christ, who loved us.   *Romans 8:37*

[Jesus said,] "Look, I have given you authority over all the power of the enemy, and you can walk among snakes and scorpions and crush them. Nothing will injure you."   *Luke 10:19*

God told Joshua that Jericho had already been delivered into his hands—the enemy was already defeated! What confidence Joshua must have had as he went into battle! Christians also fight against a defeated enemy. Christ has defeated Satan, the enemy of our souls. So although we still fight *battles* against temptation and weakness every day, we have the assurance that the *war* itself has already been won; the tempter has been defeated. We do not have to be paralyzed by the power of a defeated enemy; we can overcome his temptations through Christ's power.

GOD'S PROMISE

Yes, the LORD is for me; he will help me. I will look in triumph at those who hate me.   PSALM 118:7

Focus

What can I do to maintain my focus as I grow spiritually?

God's Response

I don't mean to say that I have already achieved these things or that I have already reached perfection. But I press on to possess that perfection for which Christ Jesus first possessed me. No, dear brothers and sisters, I have not achieved it, but I focus on this one thing: Forgetting the past and looking forward to what lies ahead, I press on to reach the end of the race and receive the heavenly prize for which God, through Christ Jesus, is calling us.

Philippians 3:12-14

Paul said that his goal was to know Christ, to be like Christ, and to be all Christ had in mind for him to be. Working toward this goal took all of Paul's energies and focus.

This is a helpful example for you to follow. Don't let anything take your eyes off your goal of knowing Christ. With the single-mindedness of an athlete in training, you must lay aside everything harmful and forsake anything that might distract you from being an effective Christian. What is holding you back?

God's Promise

I am certain that God, who began the good work within you, will continue his work until it is finally finished on the day when Christ Jesus returns.   PHILIPPIANS 1:6

Accomplishments

Is it wrong to accept praise for the things I've accomplished?

God's Response

The Israelites said to Gideon, "Be our ruler! You and your son and your grandson will be our rulers, for you have rescued us from Midian." But Gideon replied, "I will not rule over you, nor will my son. The Lord will rule over you! However, I do have one request—that each of you give me an earring from the plunder you collected from your fallen enemies." *Judges 8:22-24*

The Israelites praised Gideon for rescuing them and even asked him to be their ruler. Gideon acknowledged their gratitude by allowing them to give him gifts, which served as income for his work, but he reserved the highest honor for God. It's all right to acknowledge the gratitude or praise of others, but we also need to humbly point others to God, the one who is the source of our accomplishments.

When others praise you, do you accept all the honor for yourself, or do you reserve the greatest praise for God?

God's Challenge

As the Scriptures say, "If you want to boast, boast only about the Lord." When people commend themselves, it doesn't count for much. The important thing is for the Lord to commend them.

2 CORINTHIANS 10:17-18

Selfishness

If God is so powerful, why does he ask me to do things for him? What's in it for me?

God's Response

You have said, "What's the use of serving God? What have we gained by obeying his commands or by trying to show the Lord of Heaven's Armies that we are sorry for our sins? From now on we will call the arrogant blessed. For those who do evil get rich, and those who dare God to punish them suffer no harm."

Malachi 3:14-15

These verses from Malachi describe an arrogant attitude toward God. When we ask, "What's the use of serving God?" we are really asking, "What does it do for *me*?" Our natural tendency is to be selfish. Our real question should be, "What does it do for *God*?" We must serve God simply because he *is* God and *deserves* to be served.

Although there are certainly personal benefits that come from serving God, the truth is, your service is not about you. It's about expressing your love for God in tangible ways that bless others. Then the world will see what God's love looks like.

God's Challenge

Among you it will be different. Whoever wants to be a leader among you must be your servant, and whoever wants to be first among you must be the slave of everyone else.   MARK 10:43-44

Confession

What's the point of confession? I know I'll probably sin again, and sometimes I still feel guilty.

God's Response

We are lying if we say we have fellowship with God but go on living in spiritual darkness; we are not practicing the truth. But if we are living in the light, as God is in the light, then we have fellowship with each other, and the blood of Jesus, his Son, cleanses us from all sin.   *1 John 1:6-7*

Oh, what joy for those whose disobedience is forgiven, whose sins are put out of sight. Yes, what joy for those whose record the LORD has cleared of sin.   *Romans 4:7*

When we commit to following Jesus, he forgives all the sins we have committed or will ever commit. We don't need to confess the sins of the past all over again, and we don't need to fear that God will reject us if we don't keep our slate perfectly clean. But God wants us to confess any new sins we commit because sin damages our desire to communicate with him. Once we have become believers, our relationship with Jesus is secure, but regular confession allows us to enjoy clean hearts and minds and unhindered fellowship with him.

God's Promise

You must remain faithful to what you have been taught from the beginning. If you do, you will remain in fellowship with the Son and with the Father. And in this fellowship we enjoy the eternal life he promised us.   1 JOHN 2:24-25

Repentance

How can I know if I've truly repented?

God's Response

John the Baptist came to the Judean wilderness and began preaching. His message was, "Repent of your sins and turn to God, for the Kingdom of Heaven is near."   *Matthew 3:1-2*

John's message to the people was all about repentance. He was announcing the arrival of the Savior, Jesus, and asking the people to decide whether they would remain loyal to the Pharisees, the religious leaders of the day, or if they would choose to follow Jesus. When John told the people to repent, he meant that they needed to change the direction of their lives, leaving behind the human and sometimes sinful rules and traditions of their religious leaders and following the path of Jesus, the Son of the living God.

You face the same decision today: whether to continue living by your own rules or to daily proclaim loyalty to Jesus and living his way, which is what God created us to do. For whom are you living?

God's Challenge

The grace of God has been revealed, bringing salvation to all people. And we are instructed to turn from godless living and sinful pleasures. We should live in this evil world with wisdom, righteousness, and devotion to God.   TITUS 2:11-12

Priorities

How can my daily life reflect God's priorities?

GOD'S RESPONSE

Listen, O Israel! The LORD is our God, the LORD alone. And you must love the LORD your God with all your heart, all your soul, and all your strength. And you must commit yourselves wholeheartedly to these commands that I am giving you today.

Deuteronomy 6:4-6

[Jesus said,] "I brought glory to you here on earth by completing the work you gave me to do."   *John 17:4*

How do you find out what is most important to God? Jesus said that the most important commandment is the one in today's verses from Deuteronomy. So begin by loving God with all your heart, soul, and strength. This means listening to what God says in his Word and then setting your heart, mind, and will on doing what he says. When you love God, the Bible becomes a shining light that guides our daily activities and helps us keep our priorities straight.

GOD'S PROMISE

We can be sure that we know him if we obey his commandments.

1 JOHN 2:3

Obedience

Will God ever ask me to do something that causes me pain?

GOD'S RESPONSE

When the LORD first began speaking to Israel through Hosea, he said to him, "Go and marry a prostitute, so that some of her children will be conceived in prostitution. This will illustrate how Israel has acted like a prostitute by turning against the LORD and worshiping other gods." So Hosea married Gomer, the daughter of Diblaim, and she became pregnant and gave Hosea a son. *Hosea 1:2-3*

It is difficult to imagine Hosea's feelings when God told him to marry a woman who was a prostitute and therefore would be unfaithful to him. Hosea may not have wanted to do what God told him to do, but he obeyed. God often required extraordinary obedience from his prophets who were facing extraordinary times.

God may ask you to do something difficult and extraordinary too. If he does, how will you respond? Will you obey him and trust that he who knows everything has a special purpose in what he is telling you to do? Will you be able to accept the fact that the pain involved in obedience may benefit those you serve and you personally?

GOD'S PROMISE

Who will want to harm you if you are eager to do good? But even if you suffer for doing what is right, God will reward you for it. So don't worry or be afraid of their threats. . . . Remember, it is better to suffer for doing good, if that is what God wants, than to suffer for doing wrong! 1 PETER 3:13-14, 17

Faults

How can I allow God's Word to speak to me?

God's Response

Obviously, the law applies to those to whom it was given, for its purpose is to keep people from having excuses, and to show that the entire world is guilty before God.   *Romans 3:19*

Your job is to obey the law, not to judge whether it applies to you.
James 4:11

Though the laws were written for the people of Israel, they acted as if those laws didn't apply to them. It is easy to listen to a sermon and think of all the other people who need to hear it, or to read the Bible and think of others who should do what it says. The Israelites did this constantly, applying God's laws to others but not to themselves and thus avoiding the changes they themselves needed to make.

As you think of others who need to apply what you are hearing or reading, stop and think about how the truth applies to you. Often our own faults are the first ones we see in others.

God's Challenge

The standard you use in judging is the standard by which you will be judged. And why worry about a speck in your friend's eye when you have a log in your own? How can you think of saying to your friend, "Let me help you get rid of that speck in your eye," when you can't see past the log in your own eye?   MATTHEW 7:2-4

Integrity

How does my willingness to forgive others reflect my integrity?

GOD'S RESPONSE

The men of Gibeon quickly sent messengers to Joshua at his camp in Gilgal. "Don't abandon your servants now!" they pleaded. "Come at once! Save us! Help us! For all the Amorite kings who live in the hill country have joined forces to attack us." So Joshua and his entire army, including his best warriors, left Gilgal and set out for Gibeon. *Joshua 10:6-7*

[Jesus said,] "If another believer sins, rebuke that person; then if there is repentance, forgive. Even if that person wrongs you seven times a day and each time turns again and asks forgiveness, you must forgive." *Luke 17:3-4*

Joshua's response shows his integrity. After having been deceived by the Gibeonites earlier, Joshua and his leaders could have been slow about attempting to rescue them. Instead, they immediately responded to the Gibeonites' call for help.

How willing would you be to help someone who had deceived you? When you make a commitment to someone, is your resolve strong enough to follow through, no matter what that person has done to you?

GOD'S PROMISE

Do not judge others, and you will not be judged. Do not condemn others, or it will all come back against you. Forgive others, and you will be forgiven. LUKE 6:37

Dedication to God

What does it mean to be dedicated to God?

GOD'S RESPONSE

One day as these men were worshiping the Lord and fasting, the Holy Spirit said, "Dedicate Barnabas and Saul for the special work to which I have called them." So after more fasting and prayer, the men laid their hands on them and sent them on their way.

Acts 13:2-3

Anything specially set apart for the LORD—whether a person, an animal, or family property—must never be sold or bought back. Anything devoted in this way has been set apart as holy, and it belongs to the LORD. *Leviticus 27:28*

To dedicate means "to set apart" for a special purpose. The church dedicated Barnabas and Saul to the work God had for them. We, too, should dedicate our pastors, missionaries, and Christian workers for their tasks. We can also dedicate ourselves, our time, our money, and our talents for God's work.

Ask God what he wants you to set apart for his purposes. Anything that is set apart, or dedicated, becomes holy, whether it's a special monetary gift you give to God or the gift of your life in service to God. What part of you would God consider holy?

GOD'S PROMISE

God said: ". . . Come out from among unbelievers, and separate yourselves from them, says the LORD. Don't touch their filthy things, and I will welcome you." 2 CORINTHIANS 6:16-17

Glorifying God

Is it wrong to ask God for honor and success?

GOD'S RESPONSE

Not to us, O LORD, not to us, but to your name goes all the glory for your unfailing love and faithfulness.   *Psalm 115:1*

Honor the LORD for the glory of his name.   *Psalm 29:2*

O nations of the world, recognize the LORD; recognize that the LORD is glorious and strong. Give to the LORD the glory he deserves!
Psalm 96:7-8

The psalmist asked that God's name, not the nations', be glorified. Too often we ask God to glorify his name with ours. We may pray for help to do a good job so that our work will be noticed. Or we may ask that a presentation go well so we will be appreciated. There is nothing wrong with doing our best, looking good, or impressing others; the problem comes when we want to look good for ourselves, no matter what happens to God's reputation in the process. Before you pray, ask yourself, *Who will get the glory if God answers my prayer?*

GOD'S PROMISE

I will rescue you for my sake—yes, for my own sake! I will not let my reputation be tarnished, and I will not share my glory with idols!   ISAIAH 48:11

Decisions

What guidance does the Bible offer for when I face important decisions?

GOD'S RESPONSE

[The apostles] nominated two men: Joseph called Barsabbas (also known as Justus) and Matthias. Then they all prayed, "O Lord, you know every heart. Show us which of these men you have chosen as an apostle to replace Judas in this ministry, for he has deserted us and gone where he belongs." Then they cast lots, and Matthias was selected to become an apostle with the other eleven. *Acts 1:23-26*

The apostles faced a big decision: choosing a replacement for Judas Iscariot, the disciple who had betrayed Jesus. They outlined specific criteria to use in making the choice. When the two "finalists" had been chosen, the apostles prayed and asked God to guide the selection process.

This is a good example of how to proceed when you need to make important decisions. Set up criteria consistent with biblical principles, examine the options in light of those criteria, and ask God for his wisdom and guidance. He will help you to determine the best option—or even reveal an entirely new option you hadn't thought of.

GOD'S PROMISE

When people do not accept divine guidance, they run wild. But whoever obeys the law is joyful. PROVERBS 29:18

Idolatry

The Bible contains so many warnings not to worship other gods. Does that really apply to us today?

God's Response

You must not make for yourself an idol of any kind, or an image of anything in the heavens or on the earth or in the sea. You must not bow down to them or worship them, for I, the LORD your God, am a jealous God who will not tolerate your affection for any other gods.   *Deuteronomy 5:8-9*

Don't be greedy, for a greedy person is an idolater, worshiping the things of this world.   *Colossians 3:5*

God repeatedly warned the people of the Old Testament not to worship idols. We might wonder how they could be so deceived as to worship objects made of wood or stone. Yet God could well give us the same warning, for we are prone to put many things ahead of him. Idolatry is making anything more important than God, and our lives are full of that temptation. Money, cars, family, appearance, success, reputation, security—any of these can easily become idols.

As you look at these false gods that promise everything you want but nothing you need, does idolatry really seem so far removed from your experience?

God's Challenge

Dear children, keep away from anything that might take God's place in your hearts.   1 JOHN 5:21

Lying

Does it really taint my character if I occasionally stretch the truth?

God's Response

The tongue is a small thing that makes grand speeches. But a tiny spark can set a great forest on fire. And the tongue is a flame of fire. It is a whole world of wickedness, corrupting your entire body. It can set your whole life on fire, for it is set on fire by hell itself.   *James 3:5-6*

You may be tempted to believe that it's relatively harmless to tell "little white lies" or to stretch the truth a bit. Doing so may even be useful at times and get you out of a tight spot because it seems to cover up minor character flaws. But if you're not honest with *yourself*, you can deceive yourself into thinking the world revolves around you. If you're not honest with *others*, you destroy the trust that is essential for any relationship to be authentic. Any form of dishonesty originates in the heart and is eventually expressed in your speech, and once you have spoken dishonest words, you can never take them back.

If you find yourself telling even "little" lies, work on changing your heart. And in the meantime, don't say anything at all when you are tempted to say something that just isn't true.

God's Promise

Does anyone want to live a life that is long and prosperous? Then keep your tongue from speaking evil and your lips from telling lies!
PSALM 34:12-13

Pride

Why is pride so destructive?

GOD'S RESPONSE

Pride leads to conflict; those who take advice are wise.

Proverbs 13:10

Don't be selfish; don't try to impress others. Be humble, thinking of others as better than yourselves. Don't look out only for your own interests, but take an interest in others, too.   *Philippians 2:3-4*

I was wrong or *I need advice* are difficult phrases to utter with sincerity because they require humility. But pride is an ingredient in every quarrel. It stirs up conflict and divides people because it refuses to compromise or admit wrongs. In contrast to pride, humility heals because it recognizes it doesn't have all the answers. Guard against pride. If you find yourself frequently arguing with others because you "know you are right," examine your life for further evidence of pride. Be open to the advice of others, ask for help when you need it, and be willing to admit your mistakes. Where do you need to admit, "I was wrong"? When was the last time you said those three words?

GOD'S PROMISE

Haughtiness goes before destruction; humility precedes honor.

PROVERBS 18:12

Priorities

What happens when "things" are a higher priority than God is in my life?

God's Response

The Lord sent this message through the prophet Haggai: "Why are you living in luxurious houses while my house lies in ruins? This is what the Lord of Heaven's Armies says: Look at what's happening to you! You have planted much but harvest little. You eat but are not satisfied. You drink but are still thirsty. You put on clothes but cannot keep warm. Your wages disappear as though you were putting them in pockets filled with holes!"   *Haggai 1:3-6*

God asked his people how they could live in luxury when his house was lying in ruins. The Temple was the focal point of Judah's relationship with God, but it was still in ruins from war. Instead of rebuilding the Temple, the people had put their energies into beautifying their own homes. But the harder the people worked for themselves, the less they had, because they were ignoring their spiritual lives.

The same can happen to you. If you put God first, he will provide for your deepest needs. If you put him in any other place, all your efforts will be futile. If you care only for your own material needs but ignore your relationship with God, you will end up poor, because you will have neglected the most important needs in your life—your spiritual needs—which only God can meet.

God's Promise

Those who love money will never have enough. How meaningless to think that wealth brings true happiness!   ECCLESIASTES 5:10

Obstacles

***How much should I depend on God as I encounter
life's day-to-day obstacles?***

GOD'S RESPONSE

Approximately 3,000 warriors were sent, but they were soundly
defeated. The men of Ai chased the Israelites from the town gate
as far as the quarries. . . . Then Joshua cried out, "Oh, Sovereign
LORD, why did you bring us across the Jordan River if you are
going to let the Amorites kill us?"   *Joshua 7:4-5, 7*

How often do we get involved in a project, only to find it is
much more difficult than we had thought? We could have used
some advice ahead of time. When Joshua first led his troops against
the city of Ai, he thought it would be an easy battle, and he did not
talk to God about it first. Only after Israel was defeated did Joshua
turn to God and ask what had happened.

   Too often we go to God only when obstacles seem great. However, God knows what lies ahead. Talk to him throughout the day,
even if the next steps seem simple. Consulting him even when
a task seems easy may spare you from making grave mistakes or
misjudgments.

GOD'S CHALLENGE

Trust in the LORD with all your heart; do not depend on your own
understanding. Seek his will in all you do, and he will show you
which path to take. Don't be impressed with your own wisdom.
Instead, fear the LORD and turn away from evil.   PROVERBS 3:5-7

Abandonment

How can I reconnect with God when I feel as if he's far away?

GOD'S RESPONSE

The Ark remained in Kiriath-jearim for a long time—twenty years in all. During that time all Israel mourned because it seemed the LORD had abandoned them. Then Samuel said to all the people of Israel, "If you are really serious about wanting to return to the LORD, get rid of your foreign gods and your images of Ashtoreth. Determine to obey only the LORD; then he will rescue you from the Philistines."   *1 Samuel 7:1-3*

Israel mourned, and sorrow gripped the people for twenty years. The Ark was put away, and it seemed as if the Lord had abandoned his people. Samuel roused them to action by saying that if they were truly sorry for their idolatry, they should do something about it.

How easy it is to complain about your problems, even to God, and yet refuse to act, to change, and to do what he requires. Perhaps you haven't even taken the advice he has already given you. If you ever feel as if God has abandoned you, check to see if you have ignored anything he has already told you to do. You may not receive new guidance from God until you have acted on his previous directions.

GOD'S PROMISE

Do not be stubborn, as [your ancestors] were, but submit yourselves to the LORD. . . . For the LORD your God is gracious and merciful. If you return to him, he will not continue to turn his face from you.   2 CHRONICLES 30:8-9

Intimate Prayer

How can I be sure that God will hear me when I pray?

God's Response

The king asked, "Well, how can I help you?" With a prayer to the God of heaven, I replied, "If it please the king, and if you are pleased with me, your servant, send me to Judah to rebuild the city where my ancestors are buried." *Nehemiah 2:4-5*

Having little time to think of a proper response to the king's question, Nehemiah immediately prayed. He knew that God is always present, hears every prayer, and is always in charge. Nehemiah could pray confidently at any time because he had already established an intimate relationship with God during extended times of prayer.

If you want to reach God with your emergency prayers, you need to take time to cultivate a strong relationship with him through times of in-depth prayer.

God's Promise

[The Lord said,] "Make thankfulness your sacrifice to God, and keep the vows you made to the Most High. Then call on me when you are in trouble, and I will rescue you, and you will give me glory." PSALM 50:14-15

Facing Death

How can my relationship with God prepare me for dying one day?

GOD'S RESPONSE

The fighting grew very fierce around Saul, and the Philistine archers caught up with him and wounded him severely. Saul groaned to his armor bearer, "Take your sword and kill me before these pagan Philistines come to run me through and taunt and torture me."

But his armor bearer was afraid and would not do it. So Saul took his own sword and fell on it.   *1 Samuel 31:3-4*

A wise person thinks a lot about death, while a fool thinks only about having a good time.   *Ecclesiastes 7:4*

Saul faced death the same way he faced life: He took matters into his own hands without thinking of God or asking for his guidance. If your life isn't the way you would like it to be now, you can't assume that it will be easier for you to change for the better later on. Nearing death, you will respond to God the same way you have been responding all along. Coming face-to-face with death will show you what you are really like. How do you want to face death? Start facing life that way now.

GOD'S PROMISE

We would rather be away from these earthly bodies, for then we will be at home with the Lord.   2 CORINTHIANS 5:6-10

Fear

How can I overcome my worst fears?

God's Response

The king asked me, "Why are you looking so sad? You don't look sick to me. You must be deeply troubled." Then I was terrified, but I replied, "Long live the king! How can I not be sad? For the city where my ancestors are buried is in ruins, and the gates have been destroyed by fire."   *Nehemiah 2:2-3*

When I am afraid, I will put my trust in you. I praise God for what he has promised. I trust in God, so why should I be afraid? What can mere mortals do to me?   *Psalm 56:3-4*

Nehemiah wasn't ashamed to admit that he was terrified. But having acknowledged his fear, he still refused to allow it to keep him from doing what God had called him to do. So he took a deep breath and proceeded.

When you allow fear to rule you, you give your fear more prominence in your life than you give God. Is there a task God wants you to do, but fear is holding you back? God is greater than all your fears. Recognizing why you are afraid is the first step in committing your fear to God. Then ask God to help you believe that if he has called you to a task, he will give you the strength you need to accomplish it.

God's Promise

What shall we say about such wonderful things as these? If God is for us, who can ever be against us? Since he did not spare even his own Son but gave him up for us all, won't he also give us everything else?   ROMANS 8:31-32

Lukewarmness

I've believed in God for a long time. Will I ever be as excited about him as I was when I first started following him?

GOD'S RESPONSE

I know all the things you do, that you are neither hot nor cold. I wish that you were one or the other! But since you are like lukewarm water, neither hot nor cold, I will spit you out of my mouth! . . . I correct and discipline everyone I love. So be diligent and turn from your indifference.   *Revelation 3:15-16, 19*

Are you lukewarm in your devotion to God? God may discipline you to help you move beyond your uncaring attitude, but he uses only loving discipline because his purpose is not to punish you but to draw you back to him in the kind of relationship you had in the beginning. You can avoid God's discipline by drawing near to him again through confession, service, worship, and studying his Word. Just as the Holy Spirit can rekindle the spark of love in a marriage that has become lukewarm, he can reignite your zeal for God when you ask him to do that work in your heart. That's a prayer he will delight to answer.

GOD'S PROMISE

The LORD corrects those he loves, just as a father corrects a child in whom he delights.   PROVERBS 3:12

God's Power

What's so amazing about God's power?

GOD'S RESPONSE

O LORD, God of Israel, there is no God like you in all of heaven above or on the earth below. . . . Will God really live on earth? Why, even the highest heavens cannot contain you. How much less this Temple I have built!   *1 Kings 8:27*

Don't you realize that your body is the temple of the Holy Spirit, who lives in you and was given to you by God?

1 Corinthians 6:19

In his prayer of dedication at the completion of the Temple, Solomon declared that even the highest heavens cannot contain God. So isn't it amazing that although the heavens can't contain him, he is willing and able, by his Spirit, to live in the hearts of those who love him? The all-powerful God of the universe takes up residence in his people.

GOD'S PROMISE

This is the secret: Christ lives in you. This gives you assurance of sharing his glory.   COLOSSIANS 1:27

God's Power

Why doesn't God do more miraculous things to remind me to trust him?

GOD'S RESPONSE

The LORD said to Moses, "Has my arm lost its power? Now you will see whether or not my word comes true!"   *Numbers 11:23*

God will raise us from the dead by his power, just as he raised our Lord from the dead.   *1 Corinthians 6:14*

How powerful is God? It is easy to trust God when we see his mighty acts (the Israelites saw many), but after a while, in the routine and struggles of daily life, like the Israelites, we forget those mighty acts, and we once again begin to doubt God's power. God never changes, but our view of him often does. The monotony of day-to-day living lulls us into forgetting how powerful God can be.

But God is no less powerful on the days when he does not perform miracles for you to see. One day, he will raise you from the dead, just as he did his Son. When you are tempted to doubt his power, remember that power over death is real power!

GOD'S CHALLENGE

Remember the things I have done in the past. For I alone am God! I am God, and there is none like me.   ISAIAH 46:9

Holy Spirit

How can I tell if the Holy Spirit is really working in my life?

GOD'S RESPONSE

The Holy Spirit produces this kind of fruit in our lives: love, joy, peace, patience, kindness, goodness, faithfulness, gentleness, and self-control. *Galatians 5:22-23*

[Jesus said,] "I am leaving you with a gift—peace of mind and heart. And the peace I give is a gift the world cannot give."

John 14:27

There are many ways to tell that the Holy Spirit is working in your life. The book of Galatians even lists traits that the Spirit produces in the lives of believers. One result of the Holy Spirit's work in your life is deep and lasting peace. Jesus said it is a gift from him. Unlike worldly peace, which is usually defined as the absence of conflict, this peace is confident assurance in any circumstance. With Christ's peace, you have no need to fear the present or the future. If your life is full of stress, ask the Holy Spirit to fill you with the peace of Christ.

GOD'S PROMISE

We have received God's Spirit (not the world's spirit), so we can know the wonderful things God has freely given us.

1 CORINTHIANS 2:12

Insignificance

Why does doing the right thing sometimes seem so insignificant?

GOD'S RESPONSE

Does anyone remember this house—this Temple—in its former splendor? How, in comparison, does it look to you now? It must seem like nothing at all! But now the LORD says: Be strong . . . all you people still left in the land. And now get to work, for I am with you, says the LORD of Heaven's Armies. *Haggai 2:3-4*

Many of the older priests, Levites, and other leaders who had seen the first Temple wept aloud when they saw the new Temple's foundation. *Ezra 3:12*

In the days of Ezra the prophet, many of the older Jews were disheartened when they saw the foundation for this rebuilt Temple and realized that the replacement would not match the size and splendor of the original Temple built during King Solomon's reign. But the fact that something is bigger and more beautiful is no guarantee that it is better.

What you do for God may seem small and insignificant at the time, but God rejoices in what is right and is done for his glory, not necessarily in what is big. Be faithful in the small opportunities God gives you. Begin where you are, and do what you can; then leave the results to God.

GOD'S PROMISE

Do not despise these small beginnings, for the LORD rejoices to see the work begin. ZECHARIAH 4:10

Words

Why is it important to watch what I say?

GOD'S RESPONSE

With their words, the godless destroy their friends.   *Proverbs 11:9*

Upright citizens are good for a city and make it prosper, but the talk of the wicked tears it apart.   *Proverbs 11:11*

An encouraging word cheers a person up.   *Proverbs 12:25*

Kind words are like honey—sweet to the soul and healthy for the body.   *Proverbs 16:24*

The mouth can be used either as a weapon or a tool, hurting relationships or building them up. How sad that it is often easier to destroy relationships than to build them, and most people have received more comments that are destructive than they have those that are constructive. Every person you meet today is either a potential demolition site or a construction opportunity. Your words will make a difference.

GOD'S CHALLENGE

Don't use foul or abusive language. Let everything you say be good and helpful, so that your words will be an encouragement to those who hear them.   EPHESIANS 4:29

Integrity

How do I build a reputation for integrity?

GOD'S RESPONSE

"The LORD bless you, my daughter!" Boaz exclaimed. "You are showing even more family loyalty now than you did before. . . . I will do what is necessary, for everyone in town knows you are a virtuous woman." *Ruth 3:10-11*

Naomi said to [Ruth], "Just be patient, my daughter, until we hear what happens. The man won't rest until he has settled things today." *Ruth 3:18*

The book of Ruth is not only a great love story but also a story of the faithfulness and integrity of both Ruth and Boaz. Ruth's integrity was evident to everyone, and Naomi implied that Boaz would waste no time following through on his promise. He had a reputation for keeping his word and would not rest until he had done so. Such people stand out in any age and culture.

Do others regard you as one who will do what you say? Keeping your word and following through on assignments should be high on everyone's priority list. But if you want to build a reputation for integrity, you will have to do it one action at a time.

GOD'S PROMISE

Be just and fair to all. Do what is right and good, for I am coming soon to rescue you and to display my righteousness among you. Blessed are all those who are careful to do this. ISAIAH 56:1-2

Mistakes

How should I respond when someone reprimands me for doing something wrong?

GOD'S RESPONSE

[Peter replied,] "You can have no part in this, for your heart is not right with God. Repent of your wickedness and pray to the Lord. Perhaps he will forgive your evil thoughts, for I can see that you are full of bitter jealousy and are held captive by sin."

"Pray to the Lord for me," Simon exclaimed, "that these terrible things you've said won't happen to me!" *Acts 8:21-24*

If you stop listening to instruction, my child, you will turn your back on knowledge. *Proverbs 19:27*

The last time a parent, an employer, or a friend confronted you about something you were doing wrong, were you hurt, angry, or defensive? If what you were doing was sinful, learn a lesson from Simon and how he reacted to what Peter told him. He exclaimed, "Pray to the Lord for me."

If someone reprimands you for doing something wrong, it is for your good. Admit your error, and respond with humility by asking that person to pray for you.

GOD'S CHALLENGE

Understand this, my dear brothers and sisters: You must all be quick to listen, slow to speak, and slow to get angry. Human anger does not produce the righteousness God desires. JAMES 1:19-20

Growing Up

I want to become more spiritually mature, so why do I still feel like the same person I was before?

GOD'S RESPONSE

Once you were full of darkness, but now you have light from the Lord. So live as people of light! For this light within you produces only what is good and right and true.   *Ephesians 5:8-9*

Anyone who belongs to Christ has become a new person. The old life is gone; a new life has begun!   *2 Corinthians 5:17*

Living the Christian life and becoming more spiritually mature is a process. It doesn't happen overnight. Although you received a new heart when you came to Christ, don't assume that you will think only good thoughts and express only right attitudes from that time on. If you keep listening to God, you will be changing and growing all the time.

As you look back over the past year, do you see a process of change for the better in your thoughts, attitudes, and actions? The change may be slow, but it will come as you follow Christ and ask him to change you.

GOD'S PROMISE

I am certain that God, who began the good work within you, will continue his work until it is finally finished on the day when Christ Jesus returns.   PHILIPPIANS 1:6

Discipline

How can I help my children grow into responsible adults?

GOD'S RESPONSE

About that time David's son Adonijah, whose mother was Haggith, began boasting, "I will make myself king." So he provided himself with chariots and charioteers and recruited fifty men to run in front of him. Now his father, King David, had never disciplined him at any time, even by asking, "Why are you doing that?" Adonijah had been born next after Absalom, and he was very handsome.   *1 Kings 1:5-6*

Discipline your children while there is hope. Otherwise you will ruin their lives.   *Proverbs 19:18*

Because David had never "interfered" by opposing or even questioning his son, Adonijah did not know what it meant to have limits. He always wanted his own way, regardless of how it affected others. Adonijah did whatever he wanted and paid no respect to God's wishes or anyone else's. Undisciplined young children may look cute to their parents, but they grow into undisciplined adults who destroy themselves and others.

When you set proper limits for your own children, you help them to develop the self-restraint they will need in order to control themselves later. Discipline your children carefully while they are young so that they will grow into self-disciplined adults.

GOD'S PROMISE

Direct your children onto the right path, and when they are older, they will not leave it.   PROVERBS 22:6

Peacemaking

Is there any glory in making peace with others?

GOD'S RESPONSE

I am tired of living among people who hate peace. I search for peace; but when I speak of peace, they want war!   *Psalm 120:6-7*

Those who are peacemakers will plant seeds of peace and reap a harvest of righteousness.   *James 3:18*

Peacemaking is not always popular. Some people prefer to fight for their way. To them, seeking peace is the cowardly way out of a situation. The glory of a battle is in the hope of winning, but when there's a winner, there must also be a loser.

The glory of peacemaking is that it may actually produce two winners. Peacemaking is God's way, and it is more courageous because it seeks the common good rather than just your own good. It is hard work and is sometimes misunderstood, but if you approach it with prayer and courage, Jesus, the Prince of Peace, will help you.

GOD'S PROMISE

God blesses those who work for peace, for they will be called the children of God.   MATTHEW 5:9

Outsiders

How should I respond when I doubt someone is really a Christian?

GOD'S RESPONSE

John said to Jesus, "Teacher, we saw someone using your name to cast out demons, but we told him to stop because he wasn't in our group." "Don't stop him!" Jesus said. "No one who performs a miracle in my name will soon be able to speak evil of me. Anyone who is not against us is for us. If anyone gives you even a cup of water because you belong to the Messiah, I tell you the truth, that person will surely be rewarded."   *Mark 9:38-41*

Jesus had given his disciples some pretty amazing supernatural powers, and in these verses we see the disciples wanting to keep those powers all to themselves. When they saw someone else using these gifts in Jesus' name, they became suspicious. Apparently they thought they were the only ones close enough to Jesus to do miraculous things. Besides, they said, "He wasn't in our group." Jesus quickly condemned the disciples' narrow attitudes.

Beware of putting limits on God or thinking you are the center of his universe. He can and will work through whomever he chooses.

GOD'S PROMISE

Everyone who calls on the name of the LORD will be saved.

ROMANS 10:13

Discernment

Why is the quality of discernment important to my ability to live out my faith?

GOD'S RESPONSE

Give discernment to me, your servant; then I will understand your laws.   *Psalm 119:125*

These proverbs will give insight to the simple, knowledge and discernment to the young.   *Proverbs 1:4*

Faith comes alive when we incorporate the truths of Scripture into our daily tasks and challenges. We need discernment so we can understand how best to live for God. We need it to know how to apply the Bible in the areas where we need help. The Bible is like a salve or ointment: it helps us only when we apply it to the affected areas.

As you read the Bible, ask the Holy Spirit to make you alert to lessons, commands, or examples that you can relate to the areas of your life in which you need wisdom, help, or healing. The more you read the Bible, the more you will be able to discern how and where to apply it.

GOD'S PROMISE

[Jesus said,] "Even more blessed are all who hear the word of God and put it into practice."   LUKE 11:28

Fading Away

***The older I get, the shorter life seems. How can
I make it count?***

GOD'S RESPONSE

People are like the grass. Their beauty fades as quickly as the flowers
in a field. The grass withers and the flowers fade beneath the breath
of the LORD. And so it is with people. The grass withers and the
flowers fade, but the word of our God stands forever.

Isaiah 40:6-8

Your eternal word, O LORD, stands firm in heaven.   *Psalm 119:89*

All athletes are disciplined in their training. They do it to win a
prize that will fade away, but we do it for an eternal prize.

1 Corinthians 9:25

Everything we have in this earthly life—possessions, accomplishments, people—eventually fades away and disappears. Only
God's will, his Word, and the work we do for him will last. That's
why we need to stop grasping for the temporary and begin focusing
our time, money, and energy on what lasts: the Word of God and
our eternal life with Christ.

What are some ways you can refocus your life around his words
and the work of his everlasting Kingdom?

GOD'S PROMISE

You have been born again, but not to a life that will quickly end.
Your new life will last forever because it comes from the eternal,
living word of God.   1 PETER 1:23

God's Accessibility

What must I do to approach God in prayer?

God's Response

The LORD said to Moses, "Warn your brother, Aaron, not to enter the Most Holy Place behind the inner curtain whenever he chooses; if he does, he will die. . . . When Aaron enters the sanctuary area, he must follow these instructions fully. . . . Through this process, he will purify himself and the people, making them right with the LORD."   *Leviticus 16: 2-3, 24*

Aaron had to spend hours preparing himself and following specific instructions before he could meet God, but we can approach God anytime. What a privilege! If we belong to Christ, we have unlimited access to God, something the high priests of the Old Testament never could have imagined! Still, we must never allow ourselves to forget that God is infinitely holy or let the privilege of coming to him in prayer cause us to become careless or casual about the way we approach him. Christ has opened the way to God for us, but ready access does not eliminate our need to prepare our hearts before we draw near in prayer.

God's Promise

Even though Jesus was God's Son, he learned obedience from the things he suffered. In this way, God qualified him as a perfect High Priest, and he became the source of eternal salvation for all those who obey him.   HEBREWS 5:8-9

Giving

Is there a right way and a wrong way to give?

"Animals that are stolen and crippled and sick are being presented as offerings! Should I accept from you such offerings as these?" asks the LORD.   *Malachi 1:13*

A person who promises a gift but doesn't give it is like clouds and wind that bring no rain.   *Proverbs 25:14*

The people sacrificed to God wrongly through (1) expedience—offering sacrifices that cost them as little as possible; (2) neglect—not caring how they offered the sacrifice; and (3) outright disobedience—offering sacrifices in their own way and not in the way God had commanded. Their methods of giving revealed their real attitudes toward God.

How about your attitude? When you give of your time in service or of your financial resources, does expedience, neglect, or disobedience characterize your giving? Right giving—giving that is pleasing and acceptable to God—comes from a generous heart and a desire to give him your very best.

GOD'S CHALLENGE

Generous people plan to do what is generous, and they stand firm in their generosity.   ISAIAH 32:8

Giving

What are the benefits of generous giving?

God's Response

Give freely and become more wealthy; be stingy and lose everything.
Proverbs 11:24

The generous will prosper; those who refresh others will themselves
be refreshed.   *Proverbs 11:25*

These two verses from Proverbs 11 present a paradox: We
become richer by being more generous. The world says to hold
on to as much as possible, but God blesses those who give freely
of their possessions, time, and energy. When we give, God supplies more so that we can give more. In addition, giving helps us
gain a right perspective on our possessions. We realize they were
never really ours to begin with but were given to us by God to be
used to help others. What, then, do we gain by giving? We gain
freedom from enslavement to our possessions, the joy of helping
others, and God's approval.

God's Promise

God is the one who provides seed for the farmer and then bread
to eat. In the same way, he will provide and increase your
resources and then produce a great harvest of generosity in you.
Yes, you will be enriched in every way so that you can always be
generous. And when we take your gifts to those who need them,
they will thank God.   2 CORINTHIANS 9:10-11

Giving

What if I'm not able to give enough to help where it's needed?

God's Response

Andrew, Simon Peter's brother, spoke up. "There's a young boy here with five barley loaves and two fish. But what good is that with this huge crowd?" . . . Then Jesus took the loaves, gave thanks to God, and distributed them to the people. Afterward he did the same with the fish. . . . After everyone was full, Jesus told his disciples, "Now gather the leftovers, so that nothing is wasted." *John 6:8-9, 11-12*

The disciples might have had more resources than the young boy, but they may have thought that since they couldn't solve the entire problem, it would be pointless to give anything. The boy gave what he had, and it made all the difference.

If you offer nothing to God, he will have nothing from you to use. But when you give what you can—even if it's only a little—he has the power to turn it into something great. Whether we offer him our time, our ability, or some other resource, he takes it and multiplies its effectiveness beyond anything we could have imagined. Give what you can to God. He will show you how he can use you when you have a willing heart.

God's Promise

God is the one who provides seed for the farmer and then bread to eat. In the same way, he will provide and increase your resources and then produce a great harvest of generosity in you.

2 CORINTHIANS 9:10

Dependence on God

What does it mean to depend on God?

GOD'S RESPONSE

I said to the LORD, "You are my Master! Every good thing I have comes from you."   *Psalm 16:2*

O our God, we thank you and praise your glorious name! But who am I, and who are my people, that we could give anything to you? Everything we have has come from you, and we give you only what you first gave us!   *1 Chronicles 29:13-14*

When you depend on God, you recognize him as the source of your strength, of your successes, and of all good things in your life. Everything you have comes from his hand of mercy. Because God created you, he knows you inside and out, so you can depend on him to guide you into what is best for you. Dependence on God, who knows you and cares about you, is the secret to living the most fulfilling life possible.

GOD'S PROMISE

Deep in your hearts you know that every promise of the LORD your God has come true. Not a single one has failed!   JOSHUA 23:14

Dependence on God

Why do I need to depend on God? Isn't my life what I choose to make of it?

GOD'S RESPONSE

Christ is the visible image of the invisible God. He existed before anything was created and is supreme over all creation, for through him God created everything in the heavenly realms and on earth. . . . He existed before anything else, and he holds all creation together.   *Colossians 1:15-17*

God is not only the creator of the world but also its sustainer. He holds everything together and keeps all of creation from disintegrating into chaos. Because he is the sustainer of all life, none of us is independent from him. We are his servants, and we must daily trust him to protect us, care for us, and sustain us.

GOD'S PROMISE

The LORD is God, and he created the heavens and earth and put everything in place. He made the world to be lived in, not to be a place of empty chaos. "I am the LORD," he says, "and there is no other."   ISAIAH 45:18

Serious Prayer

How can I learn to pray more sincerely?

God's Response

We fasted and earnestly prayed that our God would take care of us, and he heard our prayer.   *Ezra 8:23*

Ezra knew that God had promised to protect his people, but he didn't take those promises for granted. He also knew that God often chooses to release his blessings as a result of our prayers so that he receives glory and strengthens our faith. Ezra and the people humbled themselves by fasting and praying. Fasting humbled them because going without food was a reminder of their complete dependence on God. It also gave them more time to pray and meditate on God. In response to the people's humble seeking, God answered their prayers.

It's all too easy to fall into praying glibly and superficially. Serious, sincere prayer, in contrast, requires concentration. It puts us in touch with God's will and can really change us. Without serious prayer, we reduce God to nothing more than a drive-through pharmacy with painkillers for our every ailment.

God's Challenge

When you pray, don't babble on and on as people of other religions do. They think their prayers are answered merely by repeating their words again and again. Don't be like them, for your Father knows exactly what you need before you ask him!

MATTHEW 6:7-8

God's Provision

I've asked God so many times to meet my needs. What must I do to get him to answer me?

GOD'S RESPONSE

The very next day [the Israelites] began to eat unleavened bread and roasted grain harvested from the land. No manna appeared on the day they first ate from the crops of the land, and it was never seen again. So from that time on the Israelites ate from the crops of Canaan.   *Joshua 5:11-12*

God had miraculously supplied daily manna to the hungry Israelites during their forty years in the wilderness. In the Promised Land they no longer needed this daily food supply because the land was ready for planting and harvesting. So there, God provided food from the land itself. Prayer is not an alternative to preparation, and faith is not a substitute for hard work. God can and does provide miraculously for his people as needed, but he also expects them to use their God-given talents and resources to provide for themselves. If your prayers have gone unanswered, perhaps what you need is within your reach. Pray instead for the wisdom to see it and the energy and motivation to do what is needed.

GOD'S PROMISE

We will receive from him whatever we ask because we obey him and do the things that please him.   1 JOHN 3:22

Generosity

Is there a way to build a spirit of generosity into my everyday life?

GOD'S RESPONSE

When you harvest the crops of your land, do not harvest the grain along the edges of your fields, and do not pick up what the harvesters drop. It is the same with your grape crop—do not strip every last bunch of grapes from the vines, and do not pick up the grapes that fall to the ground. Leave them for the poor and the foreigners living among you. I am the LORD your God.

Leviticus 19:9-10

It is a sin to belittle one's neighbor; blessed are those who help the poor.   *Proverbs 14:21*

God instructed his people not to keep all of their crops for themselves but to leave some for those in need. He required that they leave the edges of their fields unharvested, thus providing food for travelers and for the poor. It is easy to ignore the poor or forget about those who have less than we do. But God desires that we exhibit generosity to others. In what ways can you "leave the edges of your fields unharvested" to share with those in need?

GOD'S PROMISE

Give freely and become more wealthy; be stingy and lose everything. The generous will prosper; those who refresh others will themselves be refreshed.   PROVERBS 11:24-25

Gratitude

What should I do when God answers my prayers?

GOD'S RESPONSE

That night the secret was revealed to Daniel in a vision. Then Daniel praised the God of heaven. . . . The king said to Daniel (also known as Belteshazzar), "Is this true? Can you tell me what my dream was and what it means?"

Daniel replied, "There are no wise men, enchanters, magicians, or fortune-tellers who can reveal the king's secret. But there is a God in heaven who reveals secrets, and he has shown King Nebuchadnezzar what will happen in the future."   *Daniel 2:26-28*

After Daniel asked God to reveal Nebuchadnezzar's dream to him, he saw a vision of the dream, and he knew that God had answered his prayer. But before Daniel revealed anything to the king, he gave credit to God, explaining that he did not arrive at his knowledge of the dream because of his own wisdom but only because God had revealed it.

How do you feel when God answers your prayers: excited? surprised? relieved? Do you ever pray and, as soon as you get an answer, dash off in your excitement and forget to thank God or give him credit? Match your persistence in prayer with gratitude to God for his answers.

GOD'S PROMISE

Praise the LORD! I will thank the LORD with all my heart as I meet with his godly people. How amazing are the deeds of the LORD! All who delight in him should ponder them.   PSALM 111:1-2

Appreciation

Why is it important to appreciate the "little things" in life?

GOD'S RESPONSE

Every time I think of you, I give thanks to my God. Whenever I pray, I make my requests for all of you with joy.   *Philippians 1:3-4*

Be thankful in all circumstances, for this is God's will for you who belong to Christ Jesus.   *1 Thessalonians 5:18*

One of the best ways to experience God is to notice and appreciate all the so-called little things around you. Often it is when you turn your focus outward that you see many things for which to be thankful. Instead of saying, "I wish," try saying, "I'm thankful." Cultivate an appreciative heart by giving thanks regularly, consistently, and spontaneously. Doing so helps to drive away thoughts of the disappointments that blind you to God's gifts in the here and now. Every moment is an opportunity to see evidence of God's provision and presence.

GOD'S PROMISE

Give thanks to the LORD, for he is good! His faithful love endures forever.   1 CHRONICLES 16:34

Thanksgiving

How can I maintain the spirit of Thanksgiving Day throughout the year?

GOD'S RESPONSE

It is good to give thanks to the LORD, to sing praises to the Most High. It is good to proclaim your unfailing love in the morning, your faithfulness in the evening.   *Psalm 92:1-2*

Since everything God created is good, we should not reject any of it but receive it with thanks.   *1 Timothy 4:4*

Every time I think of you, I give thanks to my God.

Philippians 1:3

During the Thanksgiving holiday, we focus on counting our many blessings and expressing our gratitude to God for them. But those expressions of thanks should be on our lips every day. We can never say thank-you enough to parents, friends, neighbors, leaders, coworkers, and especially to God. When you cultivate an attitude of thanksgiving as an integral part of your life, you will find your attitude toward life and toward God changing. You will become more positive, contented, gracious, loving, and humble.

GOD'S PROMISE

Let your roots grow down into him, and let your lives be built on him. Then your faith will grow strong in the truth you were taught, and you will overflow with thankfulness.   COLOSSIANS 2:7

God's Provision

How will God help me carry out his purposes?

GOD'S RESPONSE

At the usual time for offering the evening sacrifice, Elijah the prophet walked up to the altar and prayed, "O LORD, God of Abraham, Isaac, and Jacob, prove today that you are God in Israel and that I am your servant. Prove that I have done all this at your command. O LORD, answer me! Answer me so these people will know that you, O LORD, are God and that you have brought them back to yourself." Immediately the fire of the LORD flashed down from heaven and burned up the young bull, the wood, the stones, and the dust. It even licked up all the water in the trench!

1 Kings 18:36-38

God flashed fire from heaven in response to Elijah's prayer, and he will help us accomplish what he commands us to do when we work for the glory of his name. The proof may not be as dramatic in our lives as it was in Elijah's, but God will make resources available to us in creative ways to accomplish his purposes. He will give us the wisdom to raise a family, the courage to take a stand for truth, or the means to provide help for someone in need. Like Elijah, we can have faith that when God commands us to do something, he will provide what we need to carry out his command.

GOD'S PROMISE

By his divine power, God has given us everything we need for living a godly life. 2 PETER 1:3

The Poor

What can I do to provide for those in need?

God's Response

When Ruth went back to work again, Boaz ordered his young men, "Let her gather grain right among the sheaves without stopping her. And pull out some heads of barley from the bundles and drop them on purpose for her. Let her pick them up, and don't give her a hard time!"   *Ruth 2:15-16*

If someone has enough money to live well and sees a brother or sister in need but shows no compassion—how can God's love be in that person?   *1 John 3:17*

The characters in the book of Ruth are classic examples of good people in action. Boaz went far beyond the intent of the law regarding gleaners in demonstrating his kindness and generosity. He not only allowed Ruth to glean in his field, but he was aware enough of her need that he also told his workers to purposely let some of the grain fall in Ruth's path. Boaz made it a point to watch for opportunities to help those who were in need, and then he provided out of his own abundance.

What can you do to go beyond the accepted patterns of providing for those who are less fortunate? Are you, like Boaz, doing more than the minimum?

God's Promise

Oh, the joys of those who are kind to the poor! The LORD rescues them when they are in trouble.   PSALM 41:1

Sensitivity

What kinds of things should I be most sensitive to?

GOD'S RESPONSE

God said to Jonah, "Is it right for you to be angry because the plant died?" "Yes," Jonah retorted, "even angry enough to die!" Then the LORD said, "You feel sorry about the plant, though you did nothing to put it there. It came quickly and died quickly. But Nineveh has more than 120,000 people living in spiritual darkness, not to mention all the animals. Shouldn't I feel sorry for such a great city?"

Jonah 4:9-11

Jonah was upset over the fact that the plant had withered, but he apparently felt no sadness over what would have happened to the people of Nineveh if they hadn't heard his message and repented.

You may have cried when a pet died or when an object that had sentimental value for you got broken, but have you cried over the fact that a friend or family member does not know God? It's so easy to be more sensitive to what affects your own interests than to the spiritual needs of the people around you. What causes your heart to break? Are you most upset by your unfulfilled desires or by seeing the enormous needs of those around you?

GOD'S CHALLENGE

My heart is filled with bitter sorrow and unending grief for my people, my Jewish brothers and sisters. I would be willing to be forever cursed—cut off from Christ—if that would save them. ROMANS 9:2-3

Love

How can I learn to love others as God loves me?

GOD'S RESPONSE

God loved the world so much that he gave his one and only Son, so that everyone who believes in him will not perish but have eternal life.   *John 3:16*

Live a life filled with love, following the example of Christ. He loved us and offered himself as a sacrifice for us, a pleasing aroma to God.   *Ephesians 5:2*

The message of the Good News comes to focus in John 3:16. God's love is not static or self-centered; it reaches out and draws others in. Here God sets the pattern of true love, the basis for all love relationships: When you love someone dearly, you are willing to give freely to the point of self-sacrifice. God paid with the life of his Son, the highest price he could pay. Jesus accepted our punishment, paid the price for our sins, and then offered us the new life that he had bought for us. Our love must be like that of Jesus—willingly giving up our own comfort and security so that others might join in receiving God's love.

GOD'S PROMISE

God showed how much he loved us by sending his one and only Son into the world so that we might have eternal life through him.

1 JOHN 4:9

Acceptance

***How should I respond to people who say they are
Christians but don't act as if they are?***

GOD'S RESPONSE

Ananias went and found Saul. He laid his hands on him and said,
"Brother Saul, the Lord Jesus, who appeared to you on the road,
has sent me so that you might regain your sight and be filled with
the Holy Spirit."   *Acts 9:17*

To all who believed [Christ] and accepted him, he gave the right
to become children of God.   *John 1:12*

 Ananias found Saul, as he had been instructed, and greeted
him as "Brother Saul." Ananias feared this meeting because Saul
had come to Damascus to capture the Christians and take them
to Jerusalem as prisoners. But in obedience to the Holy Spirit,
Ananias greeted Saul lovingly, as a member of Christ's family.

It is not always easy to show sincere love to others, especially
when we are afraid of them or have doubts about their motives.
Nevertheless, we must follow Ananias's example and lovingly accept
other believers, even when they don't act exactly the way we think
they should. That's the way God treats us.

GOD'S CHALLENGE

Accept each other just as Christ has accepted you so that God will
be given glory.   ROMANS 15:7

Comforting Others

How can I comfort those who are hurting?

GOD'S RESPONSE

When three of Job's friends heard of the tragedy he had suffered, they got together and traveled from their homes to comfort and console him. . . . They sat on the ground with him for seven days and nights. No one said a word to Job, for they saw that his suffering was too great for words.   *Job 2:11-13*

Often the best response to others' suffering is simply to sit with them in silence. Job's friends realized that his pain was too deep for mere words, so they said nothing. It's easy for us to feel we must say something spiritual or insightful to hurting friends, because we want to comfort them or help them in some way. But sometimes the most helpful thing we can offer to show others we care is our presence. Pat answers and trite quotations don't communicate nearly as much as our empathetic silence and loving companionship.

GOD'S PROMISE

God is our merciful Father and the source of all comfort. He comforts us in all our troubles so that we can comfort others. When they are troubled, we will be able to give them the same comfort God has given us.   2 CORINTHIANS 1:3-4

Selflessness

How can I love others selflessly?

God's Response

You were cleansed from your sins when you obeyed the truth, so now you must show sincere love to each other as brothers and sisters. Love each other deeply with all your heart.   *1 Peter 1:22*

[Dorcas] was always doing kind things for others and helping the poor. About this time she became ill and died. . . . But the believers had heard that Peter was nearby at Lydda, so they sent two men to beg him, "Please come as soon as possible!" So Peter returned with them; and as soon as he arrived, they took him to the upstairs room. The room was filled with widows who were weeping and showing him the coats and other clothes Dorcas had made for them.   *Acts 9:36-39*

Sincere love involves selfless giving; therefore, a self-centered person can't truly love. God's love and forgiveness free you to take your eyes off yourself and to meet others' needs. The believer Tabitha (Dorcas) used her resources to provide for the poor, making coats and other garments to clothe those who could not provide for themselves. She saw a need and did what she could to meet it.

Christ sacrificed his life to show that he loves you. Now you can love others by giving of yourself sacrificially.

God's Challenge

Don't use your freedom to satisfy your sinful nature. Instead, use your freedom to serve one another in love.   GALATIANS 5:13

Sharing

What is the key to wanting to share more with others?

God's Response

All the believers were united in heart and mind. And they felt that what they owned was not their own, so they shared everything they had.   *Acts 4:32*

[Job] said, "I came naked from my mother's womb, and I will be naked when I leave. The Lord gave me what I had, and the Lord has taken it away. Praise the name of the Lord!"   *Job 1:21*

Tell [those who are rich] to use their money to do good. They should be rich in good works and generous to those in need, always being ready to share with others.   *1 Timothy 6:18*

The key to wanting to share more is to see your possessions and resources not as your own but as God's. He gives these gifts to you, hoping that you will use them responsibly and in serving others. When you don't have a sense of ownership over something, it is much easier to let it go freely into the hands of someone who may really need it.

How do you feel about your possessions? When you adopt the attitude that everything you have belongs to God and you are only sharing what is already his, you will find yourself looking for ways to share with others what God has made available to you.

God's Challenge

Don't forget to do good and to share with those in need. These are the sacrifices that please God.   HEBREWS 13:16

Planting

What should I do when people aren't interested in hearing about Christ?

GOD'S RESPONSE

I planted the seed in your hearts, and Apollos watered it, but it was God who made it grow.   *1 Corinthians 3:6*

When [the members of the council in Athens] heard Paul speak about the resurrection of the dead, some laughed in contempt, but others said, "We want to hear more about this later." That ended Paul's discussion with them, but some joined him and became believers.   *Acts 17:32-34*

 Sometimes your role is simply to plant a seed. You can't make people believe; only the Holy Spirit can soften their hearts and make them ready. Your job is simply to tell them the Good News and let God do the rest. So don't try to do God's work today—just use the opportunities God gives you to plant seeds of kindness, encouragement, and service and to tell your own story of how Jesus has changed you. Then enjoy watching God make the seed grow.

GOD'S CHALLENGE

The Scriptures say, "How beautiful are the feet of messengers who bring good news!"   ROMANS 10:15

Effective Servants

*I struggle with telling people about my faith,
especially those who seem so opposed to it. How
can I be more bold and effective?*

GOD'S RESPONSE

We asked the leaders, "Who gave you permission to rebuild this
Temple and restore this structure?" And we demanded their names
so that we could tell you who the leaders were. This was their
answer: "We are the servants of the God of heaven and earth, and
we are rebuilding the Temple that was built here many years ago
by a great king of Israel." *Ezra 5:9-11*

It is not always easy to speak up for your faith in an unbelieving world, but that is what God has called his people to do. When
you face pressure and intimidation, one thing that helps is to
remember that you are a worker for God. Your primary allegiance
is to him.

When you contemplate the possible reactions and criticisms
of those hostile to your faith, you can become paralyzed with fear.
If you try to offend no one or to please everyone, you won't be
effective. God is your leader, and his mission is the most important
one. So don't be intimidated, and don't be afraid to let others know
by your words and actions about the one you really serve.

GOD'S PROMISE

God has not given us a spirit of fear and timidity, but of power,
love, and self-discipline.   2 TIMOTHY 1:7

Hiding

I believe in God, but do I really have to tell others about my faith?

GOD'S RESPONSE

Joseph of Arimathea, who had been a secret disciple of Jesus (because he feared the Jewish leaders), asked Pilate for permission to take down Jesus' body. When Pilate gave permission, Joseph came and took the body away. With him came Nicodemus, the man who had come to Jesus at night. *John 19:38-39*

Joseph of Arimathea and Nicodemus were secret followers of Jesus. They were afraid to make their allegiance known because of their positions in the Jewish community. Yet after Jesus had died, they risked their reputations to provide for Jesus' burial because they had become convinced that Jesus really was the Son of God, their Messiah.

Are you a secret believer? Do you hide your faith from your friends and fellow workers? Is Jesus asking you to do something that might bring your faith out into the light? This might be an appropriate time to step out of hiding and let others know about the one you follow.

GOD'S PROMISE

[Jesus said,] "You are the light of the world—like a city on a hilltop that cannot be hidden. No one lights a lamp and then puts it under a basket. Instead, a lamp is placed on a stand, where it gives light to everyone in the house. In the same way, let your good deeds shine out for all to see, so that everyone will praise your heavenly Father." MATTHEW 5:14-16

Discouragement

How can I fight discouragement as I'm trying to do God's work?

GOD'S RESPONSE

When we arrived in Macedonia, there was no rest for us. We faced conflict from every direction, with battles on the outside and fear on the inside. But God, who encourages those who are discouraged, encouraged us by the arrival of Titus. His presence was a joy, but so was the news he brought of the encouragement he received from you.   *2 Corinthians 7:5-7*

We have been greatly encouraged in the midst of our troubles and suffering, dear brothers and sisters, because you have remained strong in your faith. It gives us new life to know that you are standing firm in the Lord.   *1 Thessalonians 3:7-8*

Discouragement and fear are two of the greatest obstacles to completing God's work. Most often they come when we least expect them. Discouragement eats away at our motivation, and fear paralyzes us so that we don't act at all. When facing these common challenges, it helps to remember that God's people in every age have faced them too and with God's help have overcome them. By standing together with other believers, you can overcome fear and discouragement and complete whatever God has asked you to do.

GOD'S PROMISE

Because the Sovereign LORD helps me, I will not be disgraced. Therefore, I have set my face like a stone, determined to do his will. And I know that I will not be put to shame.   ISAIAH 50:7

Despair

I'm so discouraged. What can I do to keep from falling into complete despair?

God's Response

"Don't call me Naomi," she responded. "Instead, call me Mara, for the Almighty has made life very bitter for me. I went away full, but the LORD has brought me home empty. Why call me Naomi when the LORD has caused me to suffer and the Almighty has sent such tragedy upon me?" . . . Ruth told her mother-in-law about the man in whose field she had worked. She said, "The man I worked with today is named Boaz." "May the LORD bless him!" Naomi told her daughter-in-law. "He is showing his kindness to us as well as to your dead husband. That man is one of our closest relatives, one of our family redeemers." *Ruth 1:20-21; 2:19-20*

Naomi harbored feelings of bitterness, but her faith in God was still alive, and she praised God for Boaz's kindness to Ruth. In spite of her many sorrows, she still trusted God and acknowledged his goodness.

You may feel bitter about a situation that didn't turn out as you had hoped, but don't despair. Each day is a new opportunity for you to experience God's care for you. Don't miss those opportunities because your bitterness had blinded your eyes to the good things God may be bringing into your life even now.

God's Promise

[God] lifted me out of the pit of despair, out of the mud and the mire. He set my feet on solid ground and steadied me as I walked along. PSALM 40:2

Good Times, Bad Times

How should I respond to both the good times and the bad times of life?

GOD'S RESPONSE

Enjoy prosperity while you can, but when hard times strike, realize that both come from God. Remember that nothing is certain in this life. *Ecclesiastes 7:14*

We have depended on God's grace, not on our own human wisdom.
2 Corinthians 1:12

God allows everyone to experience both good times and bad. They are blended into our lives in such a way that we can't predict the future, nor can we always count on human wisdom and power to fix things. When the good times come, we tend to take the credit. In bad times, we tend to blame God without even thanking him for the good that he will bring out of our pain.

When life appears calm and under control, don't let self-satisfaction or complacency make you too comfortable, or God may allow bad times to drive you back to him. When life seems uncertain and out of control, don't despair. God is in control and will bring good results out of tough times.

GOD'S PROMISE

I create the light and make the darkness. I send good times and bad times. I, the LORD, am the one who does these things.

ISAIAH 45:7

Perspective

Where can I get the best perspective on my problems?

GOD'S RESPONSE

O LORD, how long will you forget me? Forever? How long will you look the other way? How long must I struggle with anguish in my soul, with sorrow in my heart every day? How long will my enemy have the upper hand? . . . But I trust in your unfailing love. I will rejoice because you have rescued me. I will sing to the LORD because he is good to me.   *Psalm 13:1-2, 5-6*

Sometimes all we need to do is talk over a problem with a friend to help put it in perspective. In this psalm, the phrase "how long" occurs four times in the first two verses, which indicates the depth of David's distress. But David acknowledged his feelings to God and found strength. By the end of his prayer, he was able to express hope and trust in God.

Through prayer we can express our feelings and talk out our problems with God. He helps us regain the right perspective, and from this we gain his peace.

GOD'S PROMISE

Don't worry about anything; instead, pray about everything. Tell God what you need, and thank him for all he has done. Then you will experience God's peace, which exceeds anything we can understand. His peace will guard your hearts and minds as you live in Christ Jesus.   PHILIPPIANS 4:6-7

Contentment

What is the key to contentment in life?

GOD'S RESPONSE

[Paul said,] "I have never coveted anyone's silver or gold or fine clothes. You know that these hands of mine have worked to supply my own needs and even the needs of those who were with me."

Acts 20:33-35

I have learned how to be content with whatever I have. I know how to live on almost nothing or with everything. I have learned the secret of living in every situation, whether it is with a full stomach or empty, with plenty or little. For I can do everything through Christ, who gives me strength.   *Philippians 4:11-13*

No matter what Paul's circumstances were, he was content wherever he was with whatever he had, as long as he could do God's work. Examine your own attitudes toward wealth and comfort. If you focus more on what you don't have than on what you have, it's time to rethink your priorities and put God's work back in first place. You may find that your attitudes toward wealth and comfort are keeping you from the real and lasting contentment that come from serving Christ.

GOD'S PROMISE

Don't love money; be satisfied with what you have. For God has said, "I will never fail you. I will never abandon you."

HEBREWS 13:5

Prayer

Is there one best time to pray to God?

GOD'S RESPONSE

Listen to my voice in the morning, LORD. Each morning I bring my requests to you and wait expectantly.   *Psalm 5:3*

It is good to give thanks to the LORD, to sing praises to the Most High. It is good to proclaim your unfailing love in the morning, your faithfulness in the evening.   *Psalm 92:1-2*

I rise early, before the sun is up; I cry out for help and put my hope in your words.   *Psalm 119:147*

Let me hear of your unfailing love each morning, for I am trusting you. Show me where to walk, for I give myself to you.

Psalm 143:8

One key to enjoying a close relationship with God is to pray regularly and consistently. The Bible has many references to praying in the morning. Although there is no specific command to pray in the morning, many people find that their minds are less burdened by problems and they still have the opportunity to commit the whole day to God. Regular communication benefits any friendship and is certainly necessary for a strong relationship with God.

Do you have a regular time to pray and read God's Word? Can you commit to communicating with God each day or—better yet—throughout each day?

GOD'S PROMISE

Come close to God, and God will come close to you.   JAMES 4:8

Problems

With all the problems in my life, how can I possibly be thankful to God?

GOD'S RESPONSE

Give thanks . . . to God the Father in the name of our Lord Jesus Christ.   *Ephesians 5:20*

We know that God causes everything to work together for the good of those who love God and are called according to his purpose for them.   *Romans 8:28*

When you feel down, you may find it difficult to give thanks. But take heart, because God works out everything for your good if you love him. One of the ways God combats evil is to bring good results from bad circumstances. Look for ways he has done that in your life, and thank him for it. Expressing your thanks to God takes the focus off yourself and places it on him, helping you to be aware of where and how he might be working to turn your problems into spiritual triumphs.

GOD'S CHALLENGE

Always be joyful. Never stop praying. Be thankful in all circumstances, for this is God's will for you who belong to Christ Jesus.   1 THESSALONIANS 5:16-18

A Better Gift

How does God respond when I ask him for help with my problems?

God's Response

As [Peter and John] approached the Temple, a man lame from birth was being carried in. Each day he was put beside the Temple gate . . . so he could beg from the people going into the Temple. When he saw Peter and John about to enter, he asked them for some money. . . . Peter said, "I don't have any silver or gold for you. But I'll give you what I have. In the name of Jesus Christ the Nazarene, get up and walk!"   *Acts 3:2-3, 6*

The lame man asked for money, but Peter gave him something much better—the use of his legs. We often ask God to solve a small problem, but he really wants to give us a whole new life *and* help for all our problems. When we ask God for help, he may say, "No, I have something for you that is much better." You may ask God for what you want, but don't be surprised when he gives you what you really *need*.

God's Promise

Your Father knows exactly what you need even before you ask him!   MATTHEW 6:8

The Lights of Christmas

What's one way I can focus on the birth of Christ during the Christmas season?

God's Response

The people who walk in darkness will see a great light. For those who live in a land of deep darkness, a light will shine.   *Isaiah 9:2*

A child is born to us, a son is given to us. The government will rest on his shoulders. And he will be called: Wonderful Counselor, Mighty God, Everlasting Father, Prince of Peace.   *Isaiah 9:6*

The one who is the true light, who gives light to everyone, was coming into the world.   *John 1:9*

In a time of great darkness, God promised to send a light that would shine on everyone living in the shadow of death. That light is both the "Wonderful Counselor" and "Mighty God." This message of hope from the Old Testament prophet Isaiah was fulfilled in the birth of Jesus Christ and the establishment of his eternal Kingdom. He came to deliver people from their slavery to sin. The apostle John referred to Jesus as the "true light." Jesus referred to himself as "the light of the world."

Whenever you see the lights of Christmas, let them remind you that they are symbols of Christ, the true light.

God's Promise

Jesus spoke to the people once more and said, "I am the light of the world. If you follow me, you won't have to walk in darkness, because you will have the light that leads to life."   JOHN 8:12

Contentment

How can I find contentment regardless of life's circumstances?

God's Response

Teach those who are rich in this world not to be proud and not to trust in their money, which is so unreliable. Their trust should be in God, who richly gives us all we need for our enjoyment. . . . They should be rich in good works and generous to those in need, always being ready to share with others. By doing this they will be storing up their treasure as a good foundation for the future so that they may experience true life. *1 Timothy 6:17-19*

The Bible repeatedly teaches that our deepest contentment and joy do not come from the pursuit of happiness, pleasure, or material wealth but from an intimate relationship with God. Why? Because God is good. In fact, he is the source of goodness, so what God says is good brings contentment. One thing God says is always good is serving others, because it demonstrates his love. And it is always good when someone else experiences God's love through you. The harder you focus on pleasing yourself, the more you will miss real contentment because you will be missing out on what is really good. The less you focus on yourself, the more content you will be and the more good you will do for others.

God's Promise

You will keep in perfect peace all who trust in you, all whose thoughts are fixed on you! ISAIAH 26:3

God's Power

Can I really trust in God's power?

GOD'S RESPONSE

It is not by force nor by strength, but by my Spirit, says the LORD of Heaven's Armies.   *Zechariah 4:6*

I will show love to the people of Judah. I will free them from their enemies—not with weapons and armies or horses and charioteers, but by my power as the LORD their God.   *Hosea 1:7*

Many people believe that to survive in this world they must be tough, strong, unbending, and harsh. But God says, "Not by force nor strength, but by my Spirit." The key words are "by my Spirit." It is only through the power of God's Spirit that anything of lasting value is accomplished. The returned exiles in the book of Zechariah were indeed weak—harassed by their enemies, tired, discouraged, and poor. But they had God on their side!

As you live for God, determine not to trust in your own strength or abilities. Instead, depend on God's Spirit! Then you will experience true power.

GOD'S PROMISE

I pray that from his glorious, unlimited resources he will empower you with inner strength through his Spirit. . . . Now all glory to God, who is able, through his mighty power at work within us, to accomplish infinitely more than we might ask or think.

EPHESIANS 3:16, 20

Rest

My life is so busy. How can I find the time to rest?

GOD'S RESPONSE

The creation of the heavens and the earth and everything in them was completed. On the seventh day God had finished his work of creation, so he rested from all his work.   *Genesis 2:1-2*

Jesus said, "Let's go off by ourselves to a quiet place and rest awhile."
Mark 6:31

We live in a fast-paced, action-oriented world! There always seems to be something else to do and little if any time to rest. Yet from the very beginning, God demonstrated that rest is appropriate and right. If God, who never grows tired, rested from his work, then it should not surprise us that we who are finite need to take time to rest. Jesus demonstrated this principle when he and his disciples left in a boat to get away from the crowds.

Like Jesus, you must be proactive and set aside moments in which you can rest. Those times of rest will refresh you and restore your strength for times of service. Are you getting enough rest?

GOD'S PROMISE

I lay down and slept, yet I woke up in safety, for the LORD was watching over me.   PSALM 3:5

Praise

What produces a genuine desire to worship God?

GOD'S RESPONSE

With every bone in my body I will praise him: "LORD, who can compare with you? Who else rescues the helpless from the strong? Who else protects the helpless and poor from those who rob them?" *Psalm 35:10*

[Jesus replied,] "If [the people] kept quiet, the stones along the road would burst into cheers!" *Luke 19:40*

 Praise is creation's natural response to the greatness of the Creator. It is not unusual for people to burst into spontaneous applause or cheers when a head of state or a celebrity enters a room, and your natural response when you enter God's presence through worship or prayer should be praise. The Bible teaches that God created the universe and provides for your needs; he alone is worthy of your highest praise.

When you consider who God is and what he has done for you, praise is the only possible response. Jesus said that if people didn't lift their voices in praise, the very rocks and stones would cry out!

GOD'S PROMISE

Happy are those who hear the joyful call to worship, for they will walk in the light of your presence, LORD. They rejoice all day long in your wonderful reputation. They exult in your righteousness.

PSALM 89:15-16

Generosity

*I want to be a more generous giver, but how do
I start?*

GOD'S RESPONSE

When they arrived at the Temple of the LORD in Jerusalem,
some of the family leaders made voluntary offerings toward the
rebuilding of God's Temple on its original site, and each leader
gave as much as he could.   *Ezra 2:68-69*

Whatever you give is acceptable if you give it eagerly. And give
according to what you have, not what you don't have.
2 Corinthians 8:12

As the Temple reconstruction progressed, everyone contrib-
uted freewill offerings according to his or her ability. Some were
able to give huge gifts and did so. The rebuilding required everyone's effort and cooperation, and the people gave as much as they
could.

   Often we limit our giving to a tithe, or 10 percent, of our
income. The Bible, however, emphasizes that we should give from
the heart *all* that we are able. Let God's call to give generously—
not the amount you have left over—determine the size of your gift.

GOD'S PROMISE

You must each decide in your heart how much to give. And don't
give reluctantly or in response to pressure. "For God loves a
person who gives cheerfully." And God will generously provide
all you need.   2 CORINTHIANS 9:7-8

First Harvest

What can I give God that will please him?

GOD'S RESPONSE

The LORD said to Moses, "Give the following instructions to the people of Israel. When you enter the land I am giving you and you harvest its first crops, bring the priest a bundle of grain from the first cutting of your grain harvest." *Leviticus 23:9-10*

As you harvest your crops, bring the very best of the first harvest to the house of the LORD your God. *Exodus 34:26*

 The Festival of First Harvest was an annual spiritual celebration at the beginning of the harvest. It required that the very first crops harvested be given as an offering to God. The Israelites could not eat food from their harvest until they had given the first of the harvest to God.

Today God still expects us to set aside his portion first. Giving leftovers to God is no way to express our gratitude to the one who has given us everything we have in the first place.

GOD'S PROMISE

Giving thanks is a sacrifice that truly honors me. If you keep to my path, I will reveal to you the salvation of God. PSALM 50:23

Holidays

How can I maintain my spiritual focus during the holidays?

GOD'S RESPONSE

Sing praises to God, our strength. Sing to the God of Jacob. Sing! Beat the tambourine. Play the sweet lyre and the harp. Blow the ram's horn at new moon, and again at full moon to call a festival!   *Psalm 81:1-3*

This festival will be a happy time of celebrating with your sons and daughters. . . . You must celebrate this festival to honor the LORD your God at the place he chooses, for it is he who blesses you with bountiful harvests and gives you success in all your work. This festival will be a time of great joy for all.   *Deuteronomy 16:14-15*

Israel's holidays reminded the people of God's great miracles. They were times of rejoicing, praising God, and renewing their strength for life's daily struggles.

At Christmas, do your thoughts revolve mostly around presents? Is Easter only a warm anticipation of spring and Thanksgiving only a good meal and an afternoon of football? Remember the spiritual origins of these special days, and use them as opportunities to honor God for his goodness to you, your family, and your nation.

GOD'S CHALLENGE

Nehemiah continued, "Go and celebrate with a feast of rich foods and sweet drinks, and share gifts of food with people who have nothing prepared. This is a sacred day before our LORD."

NEHEMIAH 8:10

Jesus

What should my response be to Jesus?

GOD'S RESPONSE

[The wise men] entered the house and saw the child with his mother, Mary, and they bowed down and worshiped him.

Matthew 2:11

We praise God for the glorious grace he has poured out on us who belong to his dear Son.   *Ephesians 1:6*

"My Lord and my God!" Thomas exclaimed.   *John 20:28*

The wise men had traveled thousands of miles to see the newborn King of the Jews. When they finally found him, they responded with joy and bowed down, worshiped Jesus, and presented wonderful gifts to honor him.

How different from the approach we often take today! We expect God to come looking for us, explain himself, prove who he is, and give us gifts. Those who are wise still seek Jesus, because he is unlike any other person ever born and he was sent for a special purpose. Do you really know who he is? What gift can you give to Jesus, who gave his life for you?

GOD'S PROMISE

[Jesus said,] "Look! I stand at the door and knock. If you hear my voice and open the door, I will come in, and we will share a meal together as friends."   REVELATION 3:20

Immanuel

How can I experience God's presence?

GOD'S RESPONSE

The Lord himself will give you the sign. Look! The virgin will conceive a child! She will give birth to a son and will call him Immanuel (which means "God is with us"). *Isaiah 7:14*

[Jesus said,] "I will send the Holy Spirit, just as my Father promised."

Luke 24:49

More than seven hundred years before Jesus was born, Isaiah prophesied the coming of Messiah. He foretold many things about Jesus' birth, including the fact that the child would be called Immanuel, which means "God is with us." Jesus was God in the flesh; thus, God was literally among us, or "with us."

Through the Holy Spirit, Christ is present today in the life of every believer. Perhaps not even Isaiah understood how far-reaching the meaning of the name *Immanuel* would be. The Christmas story isn't just a nice tradition. It is our reminder that the God of the universe is truly here "with us."

GOD'S PROMISE

Those who obey God's commandments remain in fellowship with him, and he with them. And we know he lives in us because the Spirit he gave us lives in us. 1 JOHN 3:24

Afraid

Why am I afraid of how my life will change if I give myself completely to God?

GOD'S RESPONSE

After the wise men were gone, an angel of the Lord appeared to Joseph in a dream. "Get up! Flee to Egypt with the child and his mother," the angel said. "Stay there until I tell you to return, because Herod is going to search for the child to kill him." . . . Herod was furious when he realized that the wise men had out-witted him. He sent soldiers to kill all the boys in and around Bethlehem who were two years old and under, based on the wise men's report of the star's first appearance.   *Matthew 2:13, 16*

 Herod was afraid that this newborn King would one day take his throne. He completely misunderstood the reason for Christ's coming. Jesus didn't want Herod's throne; he wanted to show Herod the Kingdom of Heaven. Jesus wanted to give Herod abundant life, not take away his present life.

Today people are often afraid that Christ wants to take things away when, in reality, he wants to give them real freedom, peace, and joy. Don't fear the changes Christ brings about. When he is on the throne of your life, you have nothing to be afraid of.

GOD'S PROMISE

The thief's purpose is to steal and kill and destroy. My purpose is to give them a rich and satisfying life.   JOHN 10:10

Legacy

Can I provide a spiritual legacy for my children and friends?

GOD'S RESPONSE

Joshua, who was now very old, called together all the elders, leaders, judges, and officers of Israel. He said to them, "I am now a very old man. . . . "Be very careful to follow everything Moses wrote in the Book of Instruction. Do not deviate from it, turning either to the right or to the left. . . . Rather, cling tightly to the LORD your God as you have done until now." *Joshua 23:1-2, 6-8*

Joshua was dying, so he called together all the leaders of Israel together to give them his final words of encouragement and instruction. His whole message can be summarized the words of Joshua 23:8: "Cling tightly to the LORD your God." Joshua had been a living example of those words, and he wanted that to be his legacy.

For what do you want to be remembered? What do you want to pass on to your children and associates? You can leave them nothing better than the admonition to hold on to God and to the memory of a person who did.

GOD'S PROMISE

Those who are righteous will be long remembered.   PSALM 112:6

Legacy

Will my life story be told one day?

God's Response

Boaz took Ruth into his home, and she became his wife. When he slept with her, the LORD enabled her to become pregnant, and she gave birth to a son. . . . The neighbor women said, "Now at last Naomi has a son again!" And they named him Obed. He became the father of Jesse and the grandfather of David.   *Ruth 4:13, 17*

 To some, the book of Ruth may be just a nice story about a girl who was fortunate to be in the right place at the right time. But in reality, the events recorded in the book of Ruth were part of God's preparation for the births of King David and of Jesus, the promised Messiah. Just as Ruth was unaware of this larger purpose in her life, we will not know the full purpose and importance of our lives until we are able to look back from the perspective of eternity.

To have your life count, you must make daily choices with God's eternal values in mind. Because of Ruth's faithful and consistent obedience, her life and legacy were significant, even though she couldn't see all the results. Live in faithful obedience to God, knowing that the significance of your life will extend beyond your lifetime. The rewards will outweigh any sacrifice you have made.

God's Promise

The love of the LORD remains forever with those who fear him. His salvation extends to the children's children of those who are faithful to his covenant, of those who obey his commandments!

PSALM 103:17-18

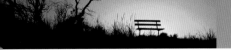

Planning

If God really controls the outcome of my life, why should I plan for the future?

GOD'S RESPONSE

We can make our own plans, but the LORD gives the right answer.
Proverbs 16:1

The LORD will work out his plans for my life—for your faithful love, O LORD, endures forever.   *Psalm 138:8*

In doing God's will, there must be a partnership between our own efforts and God's sovereign control. He wants us to use our minds, to seek the advice of others, to make plans, to work hard—and to trust him for the outcome. Yes, the results are up to him, but planning and praying help us act according to God's direction.

As you make plans for the coming year, ask God to guide you, and then act on your plans as you trust in him. In this way, you can be confident that whatever the results are, they are God's perfect will for you.

GOD'S PROMISE

Commit your actions to the LORD, and your plans will succeed.
PROVERBS 16:3

New Direction

How can I make sure that I'm going in God's direction in the year ahead?

God's Response

[The wise men] entered the house and saw the child with his mother, Mary, and they bowed down and worshiped him. Then they opened their treasure chests and gave him gifts of gold, frankincense, and myrrh. When it was time to leave, they returned to their own country by another route, for God had warned them in a dream not to return to Herod.   *Matthew 2:11-12*

After finding Jesus and worshiping him, the wise men were warned by God not to return to their home country through Jerusalem as they had intended.

Finding Jesus may mean that your life takes a different direction, one that is responsive and obedient to God's Word. Will you commit to reading enough of the Bible in the coming year that you will hear God speak to you through it? Then, once you know his Word and know what he wants you to do, are you willing to be led a different way?

God's Promise

Seek his will in all you do, and [God] will show you which path to take.   PROVERBS 3:6

Alpha and Omega

*How can I make sure that I please God as I end this
year and look forward to the next one?*

GOD'S RESPONSE

This is what the LORD says—Israel's King and Redeemer, the LORD
of Heaven's Armies: "I am the First and the Last; there is no other
God."   *Isaiah 44:6*

"I am the Alpha and the Omega—the beginning and the end," says
the Lord God. "I am the one who is, who always was, and who is
still to come—the Almighty One."   *Revelation 1:8*

Alpha and omega are the first and last letters of the Greek
alphabet, the language in which the New Testament of the Bible
was originally written. The Lord God is the beginning and the end.
He is the eternal Lord and ruler of the past, the present, and the
future. Without him, you have nothing that is eternal, nothing that
can change your life, nothing that can save you from sin.

Is the Lord your reason for living, "the Alpha and Omega" of
your life? Honor the one who is the beginning and the end of all
existence, wisdom, and power. Then you will please God no matter
what day of the year it is.

GOD'S PROMISE

"Be still, and know that I am God! I will be honored by every
nation. I will be honored throughout the world." The LORD of
Heaven's Armies is here among us; the God of Israel is our
fortress.   PSALM 46:10-11

Index